The Great AMERICAN Shopping Experience

THE HISTORY OF AMERICAN RETAIL FROM MAIN STREET TO THE MALL

Stephen H. Provost

CRAVEN STREET

B O O K S

Fresno, California

The Great American Shopping Experience: The History of American Retail from Main Street to the Mall
Copyright © 2021 by Stephen H. Provost. All rights reserved.

All photos by author unless otherwise noted.

Book design by Andrea Reider

Published by Craven Street Books
An imprint of Linden Publishing
2006 South Mary Street, Fresno, California 93721
(559) 233-6633 / (800) 345-4447
CravenStreetBooks.com

Craven Street Books and Colophon are trademarks of
Linden Publishing, Inc.

ISBN 978-1-61035-991-7

135798642

Printed in the United States of America
on acid-free paper.

Library of Congress Cataloging-in-Publication Data on file.

ACKNOWLEDGMENTS

Scott Adams, Bettina Bradbury, Paul Gilmore, Pam Globman, Barry Greene, Connie Hansen, Ruth Kehler, Linda J. King, Bruce Kopytek, Brenda Lowe, Marilyn Madrid, Melanie Marquis, Terri Martin, Joe Moore, Laura Serna-Maytorena, Lora Simpson Nordgeeen, Christine Quinn, Mark Rainey, Karen Redding, Kathe Tanner.

CONTENTS

INTRODUCTION: SANTA'S STOREFRONT

Christmas is coming, and you know what that means: colored lights and manger scenes, carolers and evergreens, hot chocolate and cold winter nights. Some of us will go out skating on a frozen pond surrounded by barren trees beneath a slate-gray sky, breathing in the winter chill and exhaling those billowy clouds of warm winter mist that make us feel a bit like snow dragons. Others will stay indoors and watch football or take in a holiday movie. Maybe we'll watch George Bailey find redemption in *It's a Wonderful Life* or learn to believe in Kris Kringle once again thanks to *Miracle on 34th Street*.

It's there that we'll find another Christmastime tradition: the Great American Department Store. One such store, Gimbels, went out of business more than thirty years ago, and millennials might not have even heard of it if it weren't for *Miracle*, which still hits the airwaves like clockwork every holiday season. It's the story of a certain Mr. Kringle who takes a job as Macy's seasonal Santa—and promptly spreads Christmas cheer by suggesting one customer might find what she's looking for at the store's bitter rival, Gimbels.

Children look through a store window at toys on display during the Christmas season in this undated photo. Bain Collection, Library of Congress.

Gimbels shows up again in a more recent Christmas film, *Elf*. Will Ferrell stars as an adopted elf who's mistaken for an employee in the Gimbels toy department. There was just one problem: By the time the movie was filmed in 2003, Gimbels had been out of business for sixteen years. So, the filmmaker had to work some digital magic to transform another department store into

Gimbels. That store, ironically, was none other than the Macy's on 34th Street in New York City.

Macy's filed for bankruptcy itself in 1992 but survived via a merger with Federated Department Stores of Ohio two years later. It's one of the few that has. The shifting economy, driven in discount stores and the era of internet shopping, has gutted many once-busy indoor malls, forcing scores of department stores to close up shop. Most recently, Sears filed for bankruptcy protection. Once the most famous and successful department store in America, it tried to stay afloat by merging with discount retailer Kmart in 2004, but fourteen years later, it couldn't come up with the money to make a scheduled debt payment despite having downsized from 3,500 locations to around 700. As of this writing, more than 140 others were targeted for closure.

Whether Sears could emerge from bankruptcy and continue to operate was unclear. Many of its former competitors have tried and failed. The brick-and-mortar scrap heap is littered with the skeletons of once-flourishing chains that failed to survive into the new age of retail: vacant echo chambers at either end of the local shopping mall, their once-vibrant neon lettering stripped away and replaced by wooden For Lease signs. Names long embedded in the public consciousness are now etched on tombstones in a growing department store graveyard. Names like Bullock's, Gemco, Globman's, Gottschalks, I. Magnin, Kress, Liberty House, Marshall Field's, May Co., Mervyn's, Montgomery Ward, Robinson's, White Front, F.W. Woolworth, and Zody's. The list goes on. Some have been absorbed by Macy's; many others simply closed up shop.

A few survivors carry on: Belk, Dillard's, J.C. Penney, Kohl's, Saks, and Neiman Marcus among them. But the heyday of the department store is long past, having lasted about a century before crumbling under its own weight at the end of the last millennium. Just as lumbering dinosaurs gave way to smaller, more adaptable creatures millions of years ago, the retail giants of the twentieth century have been supplanted by leaner, more efficient retailers. Online sites such as Amazon and eBay. Discount stores like Walmart and Dollar General, inspired not by the lavish retail palaces of the postwar boom but by the more modest (and modestly priced) five-and-dimes of an earlier era.

Globman's lasted for 76 years. Daly's in Eureka, California, closed in 1995 after exactly 100 years in business. Gimbels lasted a full century as well. Gottschalks, born in Fresno, hung around slightly longer, closing its doors after 105 years in business. Their passing leaves a void that hard to fill by clicking "buy" on the two-dimensional image of a shopping cart at the upper right-hand corner of our computer screen.

We still drink hot chocolate at Christmastime; we still sing carols and smile at the twinkling lights; maybe some of us even still skate on frozen ponds. But although we cursed the crowds and the traffic and the lines at the cashier, we can't help but feel there's something missing at the holidays without a trip to the local department store. So, we watch *Miracle on 34th Street* and read books like this to remember how it used to be, how many of us wish it still could be again. That would be a real Christmas miracle.

1

HUMBLE BEGINNINGS

If you want to know the origins of the department store, you need look no further than the general store, the one-stop-shop for rural America during the nineteenth century. Back then, most of America *was* rural, so there were a lot of general stores. Most towns had one, just the way most towns had a newspaper. There weren't enough people in a country town to support a row of specialty retailers, but there were enough who needed the basics: food on the table, tools for the woodshed, dinnerware for the table, coats for the winter, and stationery for writing letters to relatives back east.

Before the age of the motorcar, it simply wasn't practical to take a trip to "the city" (whether it be New York, Boston, Richmond, or Chicago) to procure these items.

Autumn leaves have drifted onto the inset entryway to the old Globman's flagship store on Church Street in Martinsville, Virginia. The building now houses a furniture outlet. Stephen H. Provost, 2019.

The food would spoil by the time you got it back home, and the bumpy, dusty cart paths might leave you with broken dishes and ripped or dirty clothing by the time you made it back.

The general store filled a much-needed niche by collecting all the necessities under a single roof (along with a few minor luxuries), and it naturally became a gathering place for the townsfolk and those in the surrounding area. General stores might even give you a stool to sit on and serve you a sandwich or an "elixir," and they became even more indispensable with the advent of the telephone. It's hard to imagine in an era when hand-held smartphones are the rule rather than the exception, but there was a time when most people didn't even have a landline in their homes. They had to travel down the road to the general store to place or receive phone calls, because it had the only phone for miles around.

These general stores, immortalized (at least for my generation) in TV shows like *The Waltons* and *Petticoat Junction*, were the forerunners of two distinct but related retail phenomena: the department store and the five-and-dime. Insofar as there was any specialization, it occurred in larger cities, where grocers and hardware stores were often separate from so-called dry-goods establishments that carried clothing, textiles, cosmetics, and personal hygiene products.

The dry-goods industry gave rise to a number of department stores, many of which were founded by immigrants seeking to make a living in their new home. In 1890, a Jewish immigrant from Germany named Emil Gottschalk moved from Sacramento to Fresno, California, then a city of about 15,000 people. He got a job at a dry-goods store and worked his way up to become manager there, only to quit when the owner reneged on a promise to give him a share of the business after ten years.

That setback, however, turned out to be temporary. On a visit to the barbershop one day, Gottschalk overheard a local developer say he was looking for a tenant to occupy the ground floor of a four-story project he was building downtown. Gottschalk approached the developer and secured a lease for 30,000 square feet, where he would launch E. Gottschalk & Co. in 1904.

Seven years later, a Russian Jew named Abe Globman arrived in Philadelphia. At first, Globman (born Abo Gleibman) earned what he could by selling shoelaces and handkerchiefs from a cart, but he soon abandoned that enterprise and went to work at a dry-good stores for $3 a week.

Globman moved to Virginia in 1913, where he earned a better salary ($5 a week) working for a friend and managed to pull together $400—enough to pay for merchandise to stock a new store, along with the first month's rent on a 2,000-square-foot building in downtown Martinsville. The town in south-central Virginia wasn't as big as Fresno (fewer than 3,000 people lived there at the time), but there was plenty of opportunity for an entrepreneur like Globman—if he could get his new store off the ground. He hit a snag, however, almost immediately. After paying rent for the building and buying the merchandise to stock it, he had just $12 left. Unfortunately, that was $28 short of the freight charge to ship the merchandise from Philly to Martinsville.

"They told me I needed an endorser, and I knew no one in this town," Globman told his grandson, Barry Greene, who would later lead the company. "I had just gotten off the train myself, so I went back to the store, sat on a box of shoes, and cried."

Those shoes turned out to be his salvation: "In walked a local farmer with thirteen children in tow, all in need of—that's right—shoes. I sold him anything I could to get that $28, and when he left, I was in business."

Globman married Mamie "Masha" Zimmerman in 1915, and the pair took just one day for a honeymoon before they got to work, spending twelve to sixteen hours in the store every day but Sunday.

FROM PEDDLERS TO PRINCES

Being from Philadelphia, Globman may have been inspired by John Wanamaker's Grand Depot, an old railroad station he transformed into the city's first true department store in 1876. The palatial building was the successor to Wanamaker's Oak Hall, a men's clothing store he had founded in 1861.

Along with A.T. Stewart's six-story Iron Palace in New York (built in 1862), Wanamaker's represented the dawn of the modern department store age, and men like Globman and Gottschalk built upon the foundations laid by these early entrepreneurs.

John Wanamaker's Grand Depot, seen here in an 1876 illustration, was housed in an old train station. Wanamaker later moved the business into an even more elaborate building. Public domain.

As these early endeavors demonstrated, the evolution from general store to department store was far from linear. It naturally occurred faster in big cities than it did in the countryside. Places like Philadelphia and New York City were large enough to support such retail "palaces" long before they appeared in towns like Fresno and Martinsville. But even though that evolution progressed at different speeds in urban and rural America, the process itself was remarkably similar: As populations grew, so did the demand for a variety of goods—and the number of entrepreneurs willing to meet that demand.

The profile of these entrepreneurs was also similar. Stewart and Wanamaker were exceptions. The Irish-born Stewart had turned to retail after abandoning plans to be a minister, eventually amassing a fortune surpassed only by the fortunes of the Vanderbilt and Astor families among New York's elite. Wanamaker, the son of Swiss-born parents and a devout Christian, had been born in Philadelphia.

But most of the pioneers in this burgeoning new retail industry were men like Gottschalk and Globman, Jewish immigrants from Eastern Europe who had come to America to seek their fortunes. Many of them, like

Adam Gimbel, started off as peddlers—carrying goods such as textiles and watches from one place to another, foreshadowing the door-to-door sales techniques used to hawk encyclopedias, Avon cosmetics, and Fuller brushes. Such peddlers had been common in Europe, not only in Jewish but also in Roma communities, since the Middle Ages, when they camped outside towns in wagons they shared with the goods they sold. In the United States, there were 16,000 peddlers in 1860, according to that year's census, and their names revealed that most of them were Jewish.

Some immigrants got their start in the grocery business, like the Goldblatt brothers in Chicago and, later, Maxwell Kohl to the north in Milwaukee.

Nate and Maurice Goldblatt opened a department store on Chicago's West Side in 1914. Branching out from its origins as a family-owned grocery store and butcher shop, the business eventually became a chain of forty-seven stores operating in Illinois, Indiana, Wisconsin, and Michigan. It thrived during the Depression by offering products at a discount to the Midwest's immigrant communities, people who were barely scraping by. But the Goldblatts themselves lived high on the proverbial hog: Nate Goldblatt owned a mansion in Chicago that featured an indoor pool and décor that included an Egyptian mummy; younger brother Joel owned a 150-foot yacht.

Maxwell Kohl's foray into the department store business came much later, in 1962. By that time, however, he already had thirty-five years of experience in retail. The Polish immigrant had started with a small corner grocery store on Milwaukee's south side in 1927, and nearly two decades later, he built the city's first true supermarket. By the time he opened the first Kohl's department store, he already operated the largest supermarket chain in the

The Gimbel Brothers store in Philadelphia became one of the East Coast's major department store "palaces" during the first decade of the twentieth century. Public domain.

Milwaukee area. (Kohl's would be one of the few department stores to survive the department store meltdown of the 1990s.)

GIMBELS AND MACY'S

Other immigrants, however, got their start in dry goods. Seventeen-year-old Adam Gimbel earned passage to the United States from his native Bavaria in 1835 by working as a ship's hand and began life in his new country as a dock worker in New Orleans. There, he took note of the peddlers who worked the river, carrying large waterproof packs on their backs and offering various goods for sale to rural farmers in the Mississippi Valley.

Intrigued, Gimbel decided to try his hand at the retail game. He purchased some needles, thread, and cloth and produced handbills advertising his goods for sale, which he nailed to trees along the river route. In 1842,

his life as an itinerant peddler came to an end—supposedly thanks to a bout of diarrhea that forced him to stop in Vincennes, Indiana. There, he rented a hotel room where he put his merchandise on display—and sold it all in the span of a week. He restocked and rented a room from a local dentist to establish what he called the Palace of Trade. When the dentist retired, Gimbel took over the entire house.

Gimbels' children (he had fourteen of them) carried on the retail tradition. His seven sons opened the first Gimbel Brothers store in Milwaukee, a four-story shop that featured carpets and dry goods, in 1887. Before a decade had passed, they'd opened another store, this time in Philadelphia. The brothers' famed New York City store opened in 1910 at Herald Square, just a block south of the store that would become their famed rival, Macy's.

Gimbels' biggest rival was, of course, Macy's. The business had been founded by a Massachusetts Quaker named R.H. Macy, who had moved to New York City to set up shop in 1858. He opened four dry-goods stores in the previous twelve years, but they'd all failed to turn a profit, so he set his eyes on the nation's biggest city. Macy had worked on a whaling ship before entering the dry-goods business, and during his time as a seaman, he'd gotten a red star tattooed on his hand. He adopted this as the store's logo, and it remains prominent in the store's iconography in the twenty-first century.

But it wasn't Macy who built the company that bore his name into a true retail powerhouse. That task fell to the sons of a Jewish immigrant named Lazarus Straus, who immigrated to the United States in 1852 and teamed up with a Jewish peddler to open a Georgia dry-goods store. His sons Nathan and Isidor joined him two years later, but the family moved north in 1865 amid rising antisemitism at the end of the Civil War. Instead of founding another dry-goods store, Straus and his sons formed an import business called L. Straus & Co. in New York. This led, in 1874, to a deal with Macy to run his chinaware and glass department.

The department became so successful that the Strauses could afford to buy Macy's outright in 1887, a decade after R.H. Macy's death. They also bought a share of a Brooklyn store called Abraham & Weschler from Joseph Weschler, renaming it Abraham & Straus (or A&S).

In an odd twist of fate, A&S eventually became part of Federated Department Stores, a holding company formed in 1929. Federated flourished to such an extent that it was able to buy Macy's in 1994, two years after the venerable firm filed for bankruptcy. Even though Federated now owned the company, the Macy's name was still better known (thanks in part to those *Miracle on 34th Street* reruns?), so the entire company rebranded itself as Macy's. It also converted all its A&S stores to the Macy's nameplate—including the original A&S in Brooklyn, which continues to operate as a Macy's.

In an odd sort of way, things had come full circle.

While Macy's, Gimbels, and A&S were staking their claims in the New York retail world, the son of another Jewish immigrant family was founding a store of his own across the street from Gimbels. Actually, Andrew Saks got there first: His Saks & Company opened on 34th Street in 1902. Saks died a decade later, and ownership of the store passed to his son Horace. In 1923, Horace sold the company to Gimbels for $8 million, and two years later, the Gimbel brothers opened an uptown branch called Saks Fifth Avenue.

Although Gimbels went out of business in the 1980, Saks continued to operate under different ownership, the Gimbel family having sold both brands in 1973.

TITANIC CONNECTIONS

Two members of prominent New York department store families were aboard the Titanic when it sank in 1912, and the pair suffered very different fates.

Leila Saks Meyer, the daughter of Andrew Saks, embarked on the ill-fated cruise ship just a day or two after her father's death. Meyer made it safely off the Titanic in a lifeboat, but her husband, Edgar, perished after staying behind to help others make it safely off the ship.

"I tried and tried to get Edgar to come into the lifeboat with me and pleaded to be allowed to stay behind and wait until he could leave, he not caring to leave before all the women had been saved," she later recalled. "Mr. Meyer finally persuaded me to leave, reminding me of our 1-year-old child at home. I entered the lifeboat and watched until the Titanic sank, but only for a short time did I see my husband standing beside the rail and assisting other women into boats in which he might have been saved."

Isidor Straus, who with his brother owned Macy's and who had also served one term as a New York congressman (1895–97), suffered the same fate as Edgar Meyer. He and his wife, Ida, were both aboard the Titanic, having reserved a pair of cabins for $351.37—nearly $9,000 when adjusted for inflation. They'd boarded the ship with two of their servants, leaving their daughter behind.

As the ship was sinking, Ida Straus started to step onto Lifeboat No. 8, thinking her husband was right behind her. When she discovered he wasn't, she stepped back out and moved to stand beside her husband. "We have lived together for many years," she told him. "Where you go, I go." Her husband and an officer on board the ship tried to persuade her to board the lifeboat, but she refused, instead handing the fur coat she was wearing to her maid.

"Get in the lifeboat," she said. "You're going to need this more than I will."

The maid survived and eventually returned the coat to the Straus family.

As for the Strauses, they walked together to the opposite end of the ship and were last seen sitting together on deck chairs as the Titanic disappeared beneath the waves.

A crowd of 40,000 people attended their memorial service, which included a eulogy read by Andrew Carnegie.

2

CATALOG HEAVEN

For someone who grew up in the second half of the twentieth century, it was hard to imagine a world without Sears and Montgomery Ward. The two retailers made up two-thirds of what might be called the holy trinity of middle-class department stores, along with J.C. Penney. So, it might come as a surprise that both Sears and Ward were relatively late to the game of brick-and-mortar shopping. Both made their initial impact as catalog houses. They didn't have actual storefronts; they just shipped their goods from mammoth warehouses to customers across the country.

Both companies were based in Chicago, a convenient hub from which to send goods out in all directions across the country. It was already the center of the wholesale dry-goods industry when Aaron Montgomery Ward arrived in 1865.

Although the Sears catalog became all but synonymous with mail-order shopping, it was Ward who was first to the table. His idea was simple: Keep prices low by stocking up in bulk and selling directly to the customer, eliminating the middleman. It was a fantastic business plan, but Ward faced a few obstacles, one immediate and the others longer-term. The first was the Chicago fire of October 1871, which destroyed his entire inventory and forced him to start from scratch.

The other two problems were deeper rooted. One was access: At the time, the postal service didn't deliver parcels to rural America; it lacked the resources to do so. If a package was mailed to you, either you had to head into town and pick it up at the post office or you had to pay someone extra to deliver it. Farmers, of course, didn't have the time or money to do this; if they were going into town, they might as well visit the general store and pick out something they could see for themselves. Catalog houses, meanwhile, didn't like anything that discouraged people from using their services.

This was of particular concern at the turn of the twentieth century, when six in ten residents lived in rural America. Catalogs, in consequence, carried a variety of items tailored for the rural customer: plows, forges, tools, cream separators, windmills . . . the list went on.

So, it's no surprise that both farmers and catalog houses began arguing for something called rural free delivery. (If you were alive in the sixties, you might remember the Andy Griffith spinoff show called Mayberry RFD. That's what the RFD in the title stood for.) RFD service called for mail to be delivered directly to farmers and other families in rural areas.

But RFD had powerful opponents as well. Among them were the people already getting paid extra to deliver those packages. More significant, however, was opposition from local merchants, owners of various general stores who were already worried about being undercut by big catalog houses. Their rationale was simple: Ward wanted to eliminate the middleman, and they *were* that middleman. They didn't have access to the breadth of merchandise available via catalog, and they had to charge a little more to simply stay afloat. The ledger just didn't add up: They couldn't compete.

Fortunately for RFD proponents, they had an important advocate in none other than John Wanamaker, owner of Philadelphia's first and largest department store and also, from 1889 to 1893, postmaster general of the United States.

In his annual report from 1891, Wanamaker reported that a limited experiment in rural free delivery that year had been a rousing success. Forty-six small towns received the service between February and September, at a cost of $10,000. Wanamaker wrote that the encouraging results raised hopes that RFD would do away with the necessity for "long, disagreeable trips to the post-office without result." It would supplant a system under which "users of the mails carried their letters to a single point, there to lie until the beneficiaries of the mail should call for them."

Wanamaker added: "Why should the cities have fancy mail service and the old colonial system still prevail in the country districts?" He argued that "the country is always tributary to the city; it makes the city. The extension of the postal facilities will make the businessman more prosperous and enterprising."

Customers order from a Sears catalog in 1940. Both Sears and Montgomery Ward began as catalog businesses before adding brick-and-mortar department stores in the early twentieth century. Library of Congress.

That's what people like Ward were counting on. It took a while for Wanamaker's vision to reach fruition. It wasn't until his final year as postmaster general that Congress passed legislation to mandate the practice, and even then, it was slow to spread.

"Imagine what it must have been like," Thomas Owens Jr. said in a 1996 interview with *Postal Life*. "A lean rider galloping on horseback from farm to farm, placing a letter or newspaper in a cigar box, lard pail or other creative receptacle at the end of a long lane. The roads, worn with wagon-wheel ruts and mud from a summer rain, or nearly blocked by thigh-high snowdrifts, challenge man and horse as they deliver the day's correspondence."

Owens was a retired postmaster of Charles Town, West Virginia, where RFD service had been launched a century earlier in 1896. Why Charles Town? It happened to be the hometown of William L. Wilson, one of Wanamaker's successors as postmaster general. It was one of five routes inaugurated that day.

"Keyes Strider left on horseback from Halltown Post Office, and his cousin Melvin Strider delivered mail from the Uvilla Post Office," Owens said. "Melvin Strider was only 15 years old. He couldn't even collect a paycheck until he turned sixteen, and he rode his bicycle. Mind you, these routes were all around 20 miles long."

Sixteen years later, in 1912, Congress approved something called parcel post. Before that, the postal service wouldn't deliver anything heavier than four pounds, leaving residents to rely on private delivery services. Under the Parcel Post Act, the postal service was required to "embrace all other matter, including farm and factory products . . . not exceeding eleven pounds in weight, nor greater in size than seventy-two inches in length and girth combined."

The advent of rural free delivery helped pave the way for a new age of catalog shopping, and parcel post threw open the floodgates. Mail-order companies started to make a killing: 300 million packages were mailed during the first six months of parcel post service, which allowed companies like Butler Brothers, Montgomery Ward, and Sears, Roebuck (all centrally located in Chicago) to thrive.

THE SEARS REVOLUTION

Ward had already been joined in the fray by Richard Sears, who started a mail-order watch company in 1886 and partnered with watch repairman Alvah Roebuck the following year. It was an instant success. Sears's first catalog, offering watches and jewelry, did so well he was able to sell the company for $100,000 in 1889. Three years later, he and Roebuck were back at it, having founded a new mail-order business called Sears, Roebuck & Co. They started out selling watches and jewelry again, but by 1894 they had expanded their catalog to 322 pages of merchandise ranging from sewing machines to sporting goods. Sears called it the *Book of Bargains*, a title that later gave way to *The Great Price Maker*.

Sears shipped his catalogs across the country: "This book will be sent free to any address," it proclaimed on the cover of Catalogue No. 117. "Write us a letter or postal card and say, 'Send me your large Catalogue' and we will send it FREE." (Don't try that today: The offer expired on December 31, 1908.)

The items described inside ran the gamut. There was a cylindrical "washing machine" mounted on three wooden legs that appeared to operate using a hand crank on the side. A "talking machine"—also with a crank on the side, in the form of a stylized key—used cylinders rather than a vinyl records to play back sounds. The cylinders came in cans, and the contraption was described as "a thoroughly well-made machine, and not to be compared in any way with the cheap machines that have been so extensively advertised recently." In other words, phonographs.

You could buy an early recliner, which occupied an evolutionary way station somewhere between a barber chair and a La-Z-Boy. Prices started at just $6.25 for velour, but you could get a fancy brocaded plush model for just twenty cents more or a "fabricoid leather" model

**In the 1890s, rural free delivery brought catalogs directly to the door of farmers and other small-town residents who had previously needed to drive into town to pick up their mail. This delivery truck made the rounds about 1910.
Public domain.**

for $7.15. Before you rush to the dictionary to look up "fabricoid," it means what you might suspect: artificial.

Also available: an "emigrant covered wagon" in various sizes ranging from $3.68 to $8.65 and a pair of basketball hoops. Yes, they had basketball in 1908, but the netting was sewn together at the bottom. Only later did players figure out it was easier to retrieve the ball if they left an opening. Still, the price was reasonable at $2.74 per pair. This was back in the days when a penny was actually worth enough to make a difference.

There were teddy bears for sale—they were "all the rage," the catalog crowed. There was a stereoscope (ancestor of the View-Master) for just 60 cents, an ice-block refrigerator, an early camera, and even a granite monument for your grave that was one of the more expensive items in the catalog at "only $72.00."

You could even buy a do-it-yourself kit with everything you needed to "build, paint, and complete" your own house. The plans were included free of charge, and the kits eventually proved so popular they eventually warranted a catalog all their own. Mail-order homes might sound odd today, but they were a catalog staple, offered through the Sears Modern Homes program all the way up through 1940. And there wasn't just one model. The 1918 catalog offered a dozen floor plans of "machine made houses, already cut to fit," ranging in price from $669 to $1,153. You could put one together in ninety days.

In just over three decades, Sears sold 75,000 prefab houses. And that wasn't all: If you lived in the country, you could "build your own modern farm buildings" out of cypress, "material that will last you a lifetime." A separate Book of Barns was available with 1,200 models for everything from barns to toolsheds, granaries to hog houses.

Even with all this building going on, Sears didn't open its first brick-and-mortar store until 1925, more than three decades after the company started. A year later, Wards opened its first retail outlet, in Plymouth, Indiana. It had more than 530 stores by 1929, while Sears operated more than 300. Sears actually made an offer to buy Wards but was rebuffed, and both companies made it through the Depression thanks to their relatively low prices and emphasis on value—the number of Sears outlets, in fact, had almost doubled by the time the economy finally improved.

The third member of the middle-tier department store trio, J.C. Penney, didn't start as a catalog company but as a Main Street retailer. It was founded by a man whose very name seemed to herald success for the enterprise: James Cash Penney. He opened his first store in 1902, and the business was so successful he had 500 a year before Sears even opened its first. That total doubled in the space of just four years, to 1,000 in 1928.

Penney finally issued its first catalog in 1963, but by that time, rural areas had become far more accessible with the advent of the interstate highway system, and many of them were far less rural, with big brick-and-mortar stores all their own that carried a wide selection of products that made catalogs redundant. Many shoppers used them to preview and identify products they might want to focus on during their next trip to the store.

For a short time, a hybrid called a "catalog showroom" became popular. Customers could go in and look at samples of various items, but there weren't shelves stocked full of them. Instead, if you liked the item in question, you could order it out of a catalog on the premises. Best Products, founded in 1957, was perhaps the most well known. It had 180 locations by the time it went out of business four decades later. Others included Ardan, Whitmark, Consumers, Brendle's, Ellman's, and K's. The trend had run its course by the end of the twentieth century, and most such showrooms are now out of business.

3

WELCOME TO THE PALACE

While department stores like Sears, Penney's, and Wards catered to the middle class, others targeted a more well-to-do clientele. They didn't just stock winter overcoats, they carried furs. And their jewelry was *fine* jewelry, not the discount rings and necklaces you'd find under glass at discount stores (more on them later).

Early businesses shied away from calling themselves "department stores," a term that didn't appear until the late 1880s, and "dry goods" remained the preferred term among many retailers well into the twentieth century. Although they catered to women, they were run almost exclusively by men, and although women's apparel would become their bread and butter from the twenties onward, that wasn't always the case. Dry-goods shops didn't sell a lot of women's clothing: Ready-to-wear, off-the-rack apparel was scarce, because most women served as their own seamstresses. Singer had produced its first sewing machine back in 1851, and the device soon became standard equipment for the well-off American home-maker. The selection at early dry-goods stores reflected this reality. It more closely resembled what you'd find in a modern fabric shop than a mid-twentieth-century department store: Textiles, ribbons, needles, and thread were typical offerings, as they had been for the itinerant peddlers who founded many of the stores. It was only as the economy improved following World War I and the twenties started to roar that department stores shifted their focus from fabric to fashions.

The first dry-goods businesses weren't any bigger than modern specialty shops: 2,000 or 3,000 square feet in two- or three-story row buildings clustered around a city's downtown core. The most successful of these quickly outgrew such modest quarters and built bigger, grander "palaces" five, ten, or even twenty stories high, with arched windows, decorative cornices in white stonework, and eye-catching clocks beside or above their street-corner entrances.

John Wanamaker helped set the standard early on. In 1878, his Grand Depot became the first store to have electric lighting, and a year later, it was the first one with a telephone. It also became the first to use pneumatic tubes to transport cash and documents, in 1880—a technology that stood the test of time. They were still being used in department stores a century later.

"I remember the pneumatic tubes that sent change back to the cashier!" recalled Santa Monica native Bettina Bradbury when asked what she remembered about the department stores of yesteryear.

So do I.

The "whoosh" of the containers as they disappeared from view and the "clunk" as they arrived from another part of the building are sounds that anyone who dealt with them will recall. At the newspaper where I worked in Fresno, California, they were still used near the end of the twentieth century to convey page proofs from the newsroom to the prepress department and back again.

Three years after it opened, Wanamaker's had a whopping forty-nine departments, selling everything from furniture and pianos to books and bicycles. Wanamaker replaced his Grand Depot with a new store on Broadway in 1910 that was even more elaborate than its predecessor. Its dedication was deemed such an important

The central court at Wanamaker's in Philadelphia was the centerpiece of perhaps the most lavish store interior of its time. The world's largest pipe organ, top center, looked down over customers on the ground floor. Today, the store is a Macy's. Carol M. Highsmith, 2007, Library of Congress.

event that President William Howard Taft made a point of attending. The new building was twelve floors high and included the world's largest pipe organ, which had been featured at the 1904 World's Fair in St. Louis. It took thirteen rail cars to transport the organ, along with a giant bronze eagle, to the store, but even this massive instrument couldn't produce enough sound to fill the store's central Grand Hall. So, Wanamaker assigned forty employees to the task of expanding it; eventually, the organ featured a total of 25,000 pipes.

Another innovation was the escalator, which Wanamaker's added shortly after the new store opened, in 1912. It wasn't the first store to feature the innovation (New York's Siegel-Cooper had installed one a decade earlier, just a few years after the first working model was built), but it was part of a growing—and necessary— trend. As stores added more floors and attracted more people, elevators simply weren't sufficient to get shoppers where they needed to go. Only so many people could fit on an elevator, and a lot didn't want to be bothered with taking the stairs, but an escalator allowed customers to go from one floor to another in a more-or-less unimpeded flow.

Escalators such as this one at Rich's in Atlanta became fixtures of modern department stores. Siegel-Cooper in New York had one installed just after the turn of the twentieth century, not long after the device was invented. Library of Congress.

It was one of the first stages in a trend away from pampering the customer and toward self-service that would maximize efficiency while putting loyal staffers out of work. The same trend would be seen in other areas of retailing, where such innovations as the shopping cart and self-service gas pump put more and more responsibility in the hands of consumers. Escalators, likewise, left shoppers to their own devices. There wasn't an elevator operator to serve as a guide; you had to time your steps correctly to get on and off the moving contraption without tripping.

Escalators could take some getting used to.

Tennessee artist Connie Hansen recalled growing up in Rochester, where she would visit Sibley's department store with her parents: "When I was quite young, I had a traumatic experience from my winter coat getting caught in the escalator as my dad held my hand. After that, I was afraid I would be sucked down in the part where the stairs disappeared into the floor. It was years before I got over being afraid of escalators."

Christine Quinn of Cambria, California, recalled getting on an escalator when she went shopping with her father at the Laurel Plaza May Co. at the age of eight or nine: "He's wearing a red-and-white medium checked shirt. We get separated, and I see him going up an escalator. I rush to catch up with him and grab his hand to hold for the rest of the ride. Just before the top, I look at him. Not Dad. Confused man who wasn't sure what to do. Then we got Orange Juliuses from the attached mall (my dad, not the confused man)."

Even as they grew more extravagant on the outside, department stores recognized they had to appeal to a broad clientele if they were to succeed. On the one hand, they sought to cultivate a reputation as purveyors of fine goods, but on the other, they needed a way to compete with five-and-dimes that were starting to move from rural areas into metropolitan downtowns by the early 1900s. They found a way to do both by converting dank and musty underground storage areas into bargain centers, where customers looking for "deals" could find them without inconveniencing the upper-crust patrons aboveground.

A number of stores consigned bargain items to their basements (hence, the name "bargain basement"), creating a sort of economic segregation and preserving their image as purveyors of only "fine goods" only to those who remained on the main floors. In Lowell, Massachusetts, a store called The Bon Marché—unrelated to the Seattle-based store of the same name—had a large rock outcropping in the basement floor that was simply too massive to be excavated. The owners turned this to their advantage, acclaiming the store's "rock-bottom prices" in the bargain basement.

Filene's in Boston, Marshall Field's in Chicago, and Sibley's in Rochester had bargain basements, too, the most famous of which was Filene's.

Susan Magee remembered she "always got lost" in Filene's basement, and Joni Craft recalled "the smell of the musty basement" at Montgomery Ward in Flint, Michigan. "That's where Mom would get discount school clothes."

As one basement saleswoman at Boston's Jordan Marsh rhymed:

> *Of course, we admire the vast upstairs*
> *With its velvet carpets and easy chairs*
> *But it's nice to be serving the human throng*
> *Down in the basement all day long*

Department stores placed a premium on personal service prior to World War II. When the new Frigidaire refrigerator hit the market in 1941, a sales associate was ready to help customers at Crowley's in Detroit.

SERVICE WITH A SMILE

Department stores in the first half of the twentieth century came equipped with all the bells and whistles. There were scores of departments all under one roof, marble floors, chandeliers, beauty parlors, restaurants, post office branches—the works. But perhaps the biggest perk of shopping at a downtown department store was the service. From the doorman who took your coat at the front entrance to the tailor who took your measurements, these giant "cities within cities" provided staffers to look after your every need. "May I help you" was more than an obligatory greeting; it was backed by genuine sentiment. These stores weren't just selling merchandise; they were offering a complete shopping experience. And that experience wasn't just about selling; it was about cultivating relationships with shoppers.

As big-city stores grew more palatial, their counterparts in smaller markets went upscale, too, adding escalators, marble flooring, gold-plated fixtures, columns, and their names spelled out in tile just outside the main entrance.

It just took a little longer, especially when it came to new technology such as air-conditioning and escalators. The first true air-conditioning system debuted in the mid-twenties at Hudson's in Detroit but only in its basement (because heat rises, floors above the ground were most difficult—and expensive—to cool). The system cost a "cool" quarter of a million dollars. Filene's of Boston followed in 1926 but left its four top floors without air-conditioning for several years; Macy's added air-conditioning at its flagship store in 1929.

In smaller markets, it wasn't until 1937 that Rubenstein's could tout itself as "Shreveport's first air-conditioned department store." That same year, Joseph Horne Co. made a similar claim for Pittsburgh. Escalators, meanwhile, didn't arrive at The Crescent in Spokane until 1948, when the store (named for its location on a crescent-shaped stretch of roadway) became the only department store between Minneapolis and Seattle that could boast of the contraptions.

Saks Fifth Avenue managed to connect with customers—and bolster its reputation as an elite retailer at the same time—when it hired Mrs. Morgan Belmont to oversee its personal shopping bureau. Belmont was the daughter-in-law of August Belmont, a banker and diplomat who also founded the Belmont Stakes horse race. The *New York Daily News* described her as "a leader in the younger social set" who would "attend to the wants of only the crème de crème of the elite." In a sign of how times have changed since then, the *Daily News* referred to this as the second time Mrs. Belmont had sought "real work." (Having previously tried acting, she had grown bored with "the society game.")

Other stores also had female personal assistants to help meet their shoppers' needs. Rich's had Penelope Penn, Burdines featured Jane Gray, and Hess's in Allentown, Pennsylvania, had Sarah Moffett. None of these names belonged to real people, though. They were the Siris and Alexas of their day, minus the electronic tie-in: Employees in the personal services department served as their mouthpiece.

At Rich's, Penelope Penn performed a variety of functions. Of course, she assisted customers with finding just what they wanted at Rich's. But she did much more. She was instrumental in organizing the fourth annual Georgia Peach Festival in 1925, helped customers with the bridal registry, and even "wrote" a Dear Abby–style advice column. Further bolstering her "literary" credentials, she supervised Rich's library, an actual physical location on the sixth floor where customers could sit down in a plush chair (or at a reading table) and enjoy a good book by a fireplace. It was, naturally, right next door to the book department, providing shoppers with incentive to explore the volumes that were for sale. Patrons could check out books for two pennies a day or buy a lifetime library membership for a dollar. The library also kept book-loving shoppers in the store a little longer, just the way the in-store cafeteria did.

Such amenities weren't unusual during a time before cost-cutting and discount stores became the name of the game. They came from a time when service stations still offered, well, *service*: attendants in snappy white uniforms who would check your tires, check the oil, and change your wiper blades if necessary. When all hotels had bellhops, not just rolling carts to help with your bags. When barbers included a straight-edge shave with your haircut, even if they charged more than the proverbial "two bits."

Though gigantic in scale, early department stores weren't yet far enough removed from the old general store to have forgotten their roots. Shopping assistants like Penelope Penn were one way of at least retaining the illusion of personalized service at stores that might serve hundreds or even thousands of customers on a busy weekend.

In smaller communities, the task was easier, and shops often retained some elements of the old general store—at least during the early decades of the twentieth century.

Leon Globman recalled the early days of his parents' store in Martinsville in very much those terms: "There was a pot-bellied stove in the store for heating and cooking. Mother would cook in the store and put my sister and myself on top of the fabrics counter, and we'd sleep there until the store closed."

As department stores grew into large downtown institutions and, later, chains, they remained connected to a time when the shopkeeper knew every customer by face and by name. That was becoming a greater challenge as the population grew, but it was still a challenge that store owners strived to meet. It was good business, and more than that, it was good manners.

"All the stories told to me by former shoppers have led to my impression that customer service was Globman's forte," said Pam Globman, wife of company executive vice president Dicky Globman. To illustrate, she told a story she called "Masha and the Hat," involving family matriarch Masha Globman and a regular customer named Ruth Rothrock:

> *Ruth's fiancé was returning from The War, and she planned a train trip to New York City to welcome him home. In those days, all ladies traveled with hat and gloves. Ruth headed to Globman's (of course) to find a hat to go with her travel ensemble. As was often the case, Masha was covering the Ladies' Accessories department while the regular employee took her lunch break. So it was she who assisted Ruth in her search for the perfect hat for the occasion.*

> *They went through the department's extensive inventory, but no hat seemed just right. When they regrouped at the sales counter to consider ordering what she needed, Ruth noticed a hat there. That was the one! It was exactly what she'd been looking for. It. Was. Perfect. Hooray! Masha carefully wrapped and boxed it up and sold it to her.*

> *It was only years later that Masha revealed to Ruth that what she bought had actually been the hat that Masha had worn to work that day, laid aside while she covered the department. Hey, that's no reason to stand in the way of a happy customer! Ruth was not offended in the least by this revelation, by the way. In fact, she seemed to relish the retelling of that encounter.*

4

THE GIANTS

In the early days of the twentieth century, large cities often had more than one big department store—just as they had more than one newspaper. *Miracle on 34th Street* transformed the competition between Gimbels and Macy's into the stuff of legend, but that rivalry was hardly unique. New York City also had a branch of Wanamaker's, along with Lord & Taylor, which opened a ten-story building in 1914.

Lord & Taylor traced its history back to its founding as a dry-goods store in 1826. The shop was named for founder Samuel Lord and partner George Washington Taylor, but the moniker made it *sound* like it catered to the upper crust—the so-called carriage trade. And, in fact, it did. In 1963, it began offering a "Dog Boutique" collection of cashmere, velvet, wool, and even mink-lined winter coats for pets. Earlier, in the 1930s, it had opened a restaurant called the Bird Cage, which featured rolling carts made to resemble Italian race cars. Diners selected sandwiches, salads, and desserts from the cars, and sat in armchairs equipped with attached trays, which initially came with complimentary cigarettes.

Kathe Tanner of Cambria, California, recalled "train rides to New York City and shopping with my mom and grandmother at Lord & Taylor on Fifth Avenue. We dressed up—suits and classy dresses, hats, and white

Macy's towered above Herald Square in New York in 1907. Public domain.

gloves—and had lunch at the famous Bird Cage Restaurant. You took your selections from rolling carts, including the wondrous dessert cart that was so enchanting to a young girl."

Christine Heinrichs remembered shopping at Lord & Taylor in Manhattan in the 1960s.

"Going to Lord & Taylor's was a big treat for me," she said. "It was a way for me, who wasn't in the social class that bought clothes in such fashionable places, to be surrounded by that glittering lifestyle. On the third floor, they had a lunch counter, where the only thing on the menu was Scotch Broth soup. The server wore a white chef's jacket and toque. He sprinkled dried parsley on each cup of soup he served. This was

Siegel-Cooper in New York featured a marble replica of Daniel Chester French's statue *The Republic* on its main floor. The store went all-out, but called it quits in 1917, just two decades after opening for business. Library of Congress.

so glamorous to my teenage self! It was part of the days I spent exploring the city, a warm counter seat where I had a niche in a world that otherwise was closed to me."

Lord & Taylor would become the first major department store to be led by a woman when former comparison shopper Dorothy Shaver was named president in 1945. She had started out with the store in 1924 as a comparison shopper, a sort of retail spy who would visit competitors' stores and report back on how much they were charging for various items. Unlike other women who were promoted to high positions by virtue of connections to their husbands, Shaver rose "exactly as a man would have done—by vote of the mail directors of the Associated Dry Goods Corporation, which controls" the store, *Life* magazine reported. *Time* anointed her "Fifth Avenue's First Lady."

Another store in New York that has largely been forgotten was Siegel-Cooper. There's good reason for that: It's been out of business for nearly a century. The

store traced its roots to Chicago, where it started as a discount store on State Street in a building later occupied by Sears from 1931 to 1986. Just nine years after it opened in 1887, it expanded to New York City, shedding its discount image and joining other department stores of that era in touting those twin drawing cards: luxury and service.

The steel-framed Big Store, completed in 1897 and expanded two years later, was the largest in the world at the time. Siegel-Cooper boasted that it was "a city in itself," offering "everything under the sun" from a photo studio to a bank, a dentist to a theater and a 350-seat restaurant. It invited patrons to "meet me at the fountain," referring to an ornate marble copy of Daniel Chester French's statue The Republic on the main floor. It looked like something straight out of ancient Rome.

But despite all that hoopla and opulence, the store lasted only two decades before closing in 1917. It later became a military hospital and, after that, a warehouse.

THE MID-ATLANTIC

Some fifteen miles west in Newark, another store rose to challenge the New York titans of retail: Bamberger's. "Bam's," as it was affectionately known, was less than two decades old in 1912 when it moved into a massive fourteen-story building that spread out over a full city block. They called it the Great White Store.

A massive sixteen-story addition that also included four basement levels was built in the late 1920s at a cost of $14 million.

How many departments were there at Bam's? One hundred and forty-six in all—and thirty-two elevators to get you there.

At more than 1.2 million (yes, *million*) square feet, Bamberger's boasted goods and services you'd never dream of finding in a modern suburban department store. In addition to what you might consider normal fare, Bam's had a tobacco shop, an optical department, wines and liquors, drugs, and even a greenhouse—and that was just at street level. As you ascended, you could visit a piano salon, a ski shop, and the Fruitador department, where you could purchase Bam's own brand of canned goods.

Three whole floors were dedicated to women's clothing. You could find negligées in the Japanese Room and hats in four French rooms. The Costume Room used theater lighting to showcase evening gowns.

Downstairs was a three-level bargain basement, with a budget beauty salon, a butcher shop, and a deli. Bam's had an in-store post office, a place to get a hunting license, and a public library.

Except for the fact that it had no residential housing, Bamberger's could have been described as a city unto itself. It even had its own electric plant powerful enough to light a city of 65,000, as well as its own radio station. Bamberger Broadcasting Service began broadcasting on WOR radio in 1922, operating out of the department

store's sixth floor; a huge, double-pronged antenna ascended from the rooftop. The station's initial purpose was to help promote the sale of radio receivers. Five years later, it became a charter member of the newly formed CBS Radio Network.

Meanwhile, Bamberger's was prospering. By 1928, it ranked fourth nationally in sales, trailing only Macy's, Marshall Field's, and Hudson's of Detroit. In late June of 1929, however, Louis Bamberger sold the whole kit and kaboodle to Macy's. Less than two months later, the stock market crashed, bringing an emphatic end to the golden age of the downtown department store and ushering in the Great Depression.

Lit Brothers was one of four major department stores competing for customers at Eighth and Market streets in Philadelphia (the others were Gimbels, Wanamaker's and Strawbridge and Clothier). A Ross Dress for Less store later moved into the site. Library of Congress.

Rivalries emerged elsewhere as well. In Philadelphia, Wanamaker's locked horns with no fewer than three major rivals on the corner of Eighth and Market: Gimbels (which had actually started in Milwaukee), Strawbridge & Clothier, and Lit Brothers. A few blocks farther down on Market were two others that completed the so-called

Big Six: Snellenburg's and Frank & Seder. Each of these multistory buildings was impressive in its own right. Frank & Seder extended a dozen stories into the sky. At one time it was the second-tallest store in Philadelphia, behind only Wanamaker's.

Strawbridge & Clothier would become the first major department store to anchor a suburban shopping center in 1930, when it opened a branch in the affluent suburb of Ardmore, and would add a second suburban store a year later in Jenkintown. Both were about ten miles outside Philadelphia.

Washington, DC, was home to Hecht's, Garfinckel's, and Woodward & Lothrop. The two latter stores would be coanchors at Seven Corners, the District's first major shopping center outside downtown, which opened in 1956.

THE MIDWEST

In turn-of-the-century Chicago, Marshall Field was the biggest player. The Windy City's answer to Wanamaker's, it had a Great Hall of its own. And the store itself was even more expansive than its Philadelphia counterpart. The interior featured a magnificent domed ceiling designed by Louis C. Tiffany, design director of the company founded by his father, Tiffany & Co. Featuring 1.6 million pieces of handmade iridescent glass, it was the largest glass mosaic of its kind, a fitting centerpiece for what was, by that time, the biggest store in the world.

Field's doormen met customers at the front entrance, and there was staff to take your umbrella if it was raining and brush the snow off your coat if winter weather had set in. No fewer than thirty-nine marble-floored restrooms

Red Macy's flags now fly along the perimeter of the former Marshall Field building in Chicago, where the iconic corner clock still stands sentinel. Stephen H. Provost, 2019.

were available, each staffed by three maids and stocked with talcum powder, hairpins, and everything necessary to mend a torn dress on the fly: needles, thread, and scissors. There was even a "silence room" for women and children and a children's nursery—complete with nurse.

All this was meant to "give the lady what she wants."

What she wanted was more: more selection, more opulence, more convenience. So, Field gave it to her.

In 1902, Marshall Field's encompassed three buildings and more than 500,000 square feet; a weeklong grand opening celebration attracted half a million people. The store employed 7,000 workers, and it wasn't done yet. The Tiffany dome was part of a 1907 expansion project that replaced the old main building and included the addition of an opulent restaurant called the Walnut Room. By 1914, the store took up an entire city block.

It wouldn't even turn out to be the biggest building in the Field's empire. In 1930, the company opened not the largest department store but the largest building in the world, an Art Deco fortress on the shores of Lake Michigan so big it had its own ZIP code. One of only two locations to have its own stop on Chicago's elevated train system, or the L, the Merchandise Mart wasn't a retail operation but an eighteen-story wholesale showcase with 4 million square feet of floor space and five miles of corridors. By the numbers, it included:

- 29 million bricks
- nearly 4 million cubic yards of concrete
- 200,000 cubic feet of stone
- 4,000 windows
- 380 miles of wiring
- 40 miles of plumbing

This modern castle stretched over not one but two full city blocks, but it was built on the sand of the Great Depression. Begun when the economy was still roaring back in 1928, it didn't open until two years later, the stock market crash occurring in the middle of construction. In this challenging economic climate, Field's jettisoned money hand over fist. The company lost $13 million the first two years it was open and had to reduce its wholesale division from four floors to fewer than two.

The building housed government offices during World War II and was sold in 1945 to Joseph Kennedy, father of the future president. Its biggest single customer was

Schlesinger & Mayer built a $1 million fireproof skyscraper at State and Madison in Chicago, a building later purchased by another major store, Carson's. Today, it's known as the Sullivan Center in honor of the building's designer. Stephen H. Provost, 2019.

probably Hassanal Bolkiah, the sultan of Brunei, who bought 8,000 pieces of furniture in 1983 for his new $350 million palace (at 2 million square feet, it was still only half the size of the Merchandise Mart). The sultan may have been rich from all that oil money, but he knew the value of buying wholesale: He spent $33,000 on two dining room sets, but they would have cost $87,000 retail.

Today, the Merchandise Mart is no longer the largest building in the world—the Pentagon holds that title—but it remains the world's largest commercial building nine decades after workers turned the first shovel of earth to start construction.

Despite all that grandeur, Marshall Field wasn't alone in the Chicago retailing world. It had to contend with several significant rivals, including Schlesinger & Mayer and Carson's.

Schlesinger & Mayer, founded by a pair of German immigrants in 1872, moved to the intersection of State and Madison—which the *Chicago Tribune* would later describe as "the busiest corner in the world"—nine years later. In 1898, the company announced plans to build a $1 million skyscraper with an exterior "wholly of Georgia marble and bronze" on the site, which, interestingly enough, was owned by Marshall Field. The new edifice would be a dozen stories high and fireproof.

In 1902, Leopold Schlesinger sold his half interest in the business, and two years later, Mayer got out of the business as well, citing "the desire for a long vacation." In reality, the company may have overextended itself, and the offer of $5 million for the entire business was too good to refuse. It came from a man named Harry Selfridge, who had been a partner in Marshall Field for fourteen years and wanted to strike out on his own.

Selfridge had played a key role in Field's success and may even have been responsible for coining the phrase "The customer is always right." He announced a grand reopening in July of 1904, then promptly sold the building less than a month later to none other than Marshall Field's rival, Carson's, which occupied the building for more than a century. It's now known as the Sullivan Center, named for the architect who designed it, Louis Sullivan.

(For his part, Selfridge retired, but only briefly, crossing the Atlantic to open a new eponymous department store in London four years later. His London store was designed to make shopping more a pastime than a necessity, offering an array of comforts and conveniences that included American, Colonial, French, and German "retiring rooms," a first-aid room, and an information bureau. He continued to run the store until World War II, eventually becoming a British citizen.)

Detroit was large enough to produce major rivalries as well, with Crowley's and Kern's both competing with Hudson's for customers. Kern's ultimately closed in 1959 and Crowley's downtown store shut its doors in 1977, the rest of the chain folding on the eve of the new millennium.

New England

For decades, Filene's battled archrival Jordan Marsh for shoppers in downtown Boston's retail district. When Filene's opened an eight-floor high-rise there in 1912, a throng of 235,000 shoppers descended on the new store. It seemed "all New England was being poured through the doors," the *Boston Globe* reported, suggesting that "never, perhaps, has a single store in this city had a larger number of patrons on one day."

Filene's cemented its reputation as a purveyor of high fashion when it opened a Paris office in 1910. But its most famous feature was its Automatic Bargain Basement, where shoppers could find closeout luxury apparel for a fraction of the cost—with the original price tags still intact. Filene's bought up discontinued and seasonal goods from fashion leaders for pennies on the dollar, then passed the savings along to its customers. The basement section was called "automatic" because the prices dropped on a set schedule. They were cut by 25 percent after twelve days, another 25 percent after eighteen days, and 25 percent on top of that after twenty-four days. If the goods hadn't sold in a month's time, they went to charity.

The Automatic Bargain Basement opened in 1909 and operated at a loss for the first three years it was open before turning the corner. By the time the Depression came along, it was the engine that drove Filene's: Every other floor reported losses, but the basement was so successful it kept the store afloat during the bleakest years of the thirties. Its popularity endured long after that. When May Department Stores bought the company in 1988, it spun off a separate store called Filene's Basement. (Filene's itself survived until 2006 when, like many other department stores, it was absorbed by Macy's.)

Across the street from Filene's was Jordan Marsh, an even older establishment that covered more than a city block with five separate stores, billing itself as "New England's Largest Store." The Main Store, with its distinctive corner 1880 clock tower, was connected to another section of the store across Avon Street by a marble-lined subway tunnel. You could use the tunnel to avoid navigating the busy street above if you wanted to peruse the home furnishings in the 1898 Annex.

Filene's of Boston was famous for its Automatic Bargain Basement, which opened in 1909 and helped keep the store afloat during the Great Depression. Swampyank, Wikimedia Commons, 2007.

Jordan Marsh expanded again when it purchased the space next door from a rival retailer in 1925, rechristening it the Store for Men. The Bristol Building, another block farther down, housed rugs, housewares, and more furniture. Then there was the New Store, built over the Store for Men and next door to the Main Store between 1947 and 1957. By the time it was done, the whole complex had a footprint of 1.8 million square feet.

For all its size and huge inventory, however, Jordan Marsh was also known for something very small: its blueberry muffins.

Many department stores of the era served food in cafés, tea rooms, and restaurants. Jordan Marsh not only had its own bakery, but it also debuted a Gourmet Center in 1962 to showcase what it made there. The Boston Globe described it as "a haven for the person who wants the best, the off-beat, the foreign or the rarity of food." It carried more than 150 kinds of honey from thirty-one states and thirty other countries, not to mention a hundred varieties of cheese. But at center stage were row upon row of the store's blueberry muffins and éclairs. At Jordan Marsh, "the promise of a sugar-crusted blueberry muffin could make annoying children angelic," the newspaper declared.

The blueberries, one customer recalled, were so fresh it seemed as though they had come just off the branch, and so large she used to cut them in half to share with a roommate. Her boyfriend's mother used to take a trolley ride to buy them and bring them back so he could give them to her. That must have earned him quite a few brownie points (or muffin points), because after a while, she told him not to bother coming on dates with her if he didn't bring those muffins along.

Jordan Marsh ceased to exist in 1991, when its stores were converted to Burdines, but that wasn't the end of the muffins. A baker revived the treats briefly, from 1998 through 2006, and you can still find the recipe. Here it is for those who want to relive those years (or taste what you missed because you never made it to Boston back in the twentieth century):

Ingredients:

- ½ cup softened butter
- 2 cups unsifted flour
- 1–1¼ cups sugar
- 2 large eggs
- ½ cup milk
- 2 teaspoons baking powder
- ½ teaspoon salt
- 2½ cups large fresh blueberries
- 1–1½ teaspoons vanilla extract
- 2 tablespoons sugar (for top of muffins)

Instructions: Preheat your oven to 375 degrees. Cream together sugar and butter in a large mixing bowl until they're light and fluffy, then add one egg at a time, beating after each one's in the bowl. Add the vanilla. Mix all the dry ingredients into a second bowl, and slowly add the contents to the first bowl, alternating with the milk. If you want, use a fork to mash up a half cup of blueberries and stir them in, then add the rest of the whole berries and hand-stir them in.

SpSpray a twelve-muffin baking pan with nonstick spray and fill it with greased cupcake liners, then sprinkle the sugar on top of the muffins and pop them in the oven for twenty-five to thirty minutes. When they're done, allow them to cool at least thirty minutes and store them uncovered.

The South

If you lived in Dixie, you might not have heard of Filene's or Bamberger's, but Rich's in Atlanta and Burdines—"The Florida Store"—would be household names.

Retired Confederate general William Burdine entered the retail business in 1896, a year after his citrus crop was destroyed in a freeze. His first shop was a dry-goods store in Bartow, a Central Florida town of fewer than 2,000 people; two years later, he opened a branch office in Miami and wound up moving there for good. It might have seemed like a lateral move at the time—Miami was just a small fishing village of some 1,200 people in the heart of Seminole country back then. It had just been incorporated as a city and was a stop along a new rail line. Members of the Seminole tribe would line up single file to shop at the store, and their leader would pay for the goods with a wad of money he'd earned selling hides and feathers.

Burdine was "tickled" to make $2,600 during his first year in South Florida, and his decision to move proved prescient, as the area grew to become a winter tourist destination. (Burdines would adopt the tagline "Where Summer Spends the Winter.") By 1930, Miami was a metropolis of more than 100,000 residents, while Bartow remained a sleepy town of a few thousand.

Burdines son Roddey took over after his father died in 1911, earning the title "Merchant Prince of Miami" as the business grew to become the largest volume retailer south of DC and east of New Orleans. The flagship store expanded to six stories, then tacked on a six-story addition to give it more than 200,000 square feet of floor space. It had a radio show hosted by Enid Bur—a fictional character whose name was a rearranged version of Burdine. New stores would open in West Palm Beach, Miami Beach, and Fort Lauderdale, and the chain eventually expanded to more than fifty stores by the turn of the twenty-first century.

Rich's, meanwhile, was prospering one state to the north in Atlanta. Hungarian Jewish immigrant Mauritius Reich founded the dry-goods store in 1867 at the age of twenty, eight years after arriving in America. He called the store M. Rich & Co., using an anglicized version of his name, and converted it into a full-fledged department store shortly after the turn of the century. In 1907, he moved into what the *Atlanta Constitution* called a "magnificent new department store" next door: "With its towering front of white brick and its wide and sweeping windows of bevel plate glass set deep in handsome frames this building attracts universal attention from whatever vantage seen. . . . To enter this magnificent emporium is to enter a shopping mart where everything wanted is found."

If the new building seemed impressive at the time, it lasted less than two decades as Rich's flagship location. Although the 1907 structure remains standing, the store quickly outgrew it and, in 1924, moved into an even bigger site admirers called Rich's Palace of Commerce. With 180,000 square feet of floor space, the multistory structure cost $1.5 million to build and featured a handsome corner entrance topped by a clockface inset into a circular coat of arms. It remained the business' home base from then on.

It was a while before the store expanded beyond Atlanta, opening its first branch in Knoxville, Tennessee, in 1955, an $8 million cube that it described as its "store of tomorrow." Garrett Eckbo was hired to design the outdoor landscaping, including two small parks on either side of the building. Among his innovations was an abstract art piece in a fountain/pool, the same sort of feature Eckbo would use in designing Fresno's Fulton Mall a few years later. Rolling canopies shaded the exterior, which was punctuated with an all-glass section that made the interior staircase visible from the street.

Inside, 200,000 square feet of retail space on four floors beckoned, laid out on square tile floors beneath modern

Atlanta-based Rich's expanded outside Georgia in 1955, opening an $8 million cube-shaped
"store of tomorrow" in Knoxville, Tennessee. The chain, however, sold the building six years later.
It's now the University of Tennessee Conference Center. Stephen H. Provost, 2018.

inset lighting. Furs were sold beneath a sign bearing the image of a stately, prancing fox, and cameras were on sale near the escalator. Lifelike mannequins showcased the latest in apparel, and much of the merchandise was neatly set out in glass cases—even in the toy section, where fancy dolls were on display. There was a beauty salon, a dining room called the Laurel Room (whose chandeliers stood in contrast to the checkerboard floor and cafeteria-style tables), and a snack bar with stools near the appliance section that featured large images of an apple, pear, and bell pepper in cross section over the back wall.

Rich's lasted only six years in Knoxville, selling its store there in early 1961, but it later opened other stores in Georgia as well as branches in Birmingham, Alabama, and two in South Carolina (Columbia and Greenville).

THE WEST

On the West Coast, Bullock's Wilshire stood at the apex of luxury, described by one observer as a veritable "cathedral of commerce." Built in 1929, the Art Deco masterpiece was inspired by a visit to a modern art exhibit in Paris four years earlier. It was designed by John and David Parkinson, a father-son team of architects who also designed the iconic Los Angeles City Hall, Union Station, and Memorial Coliseum. The building featured a 241-foot tower (not unlike the one at City Hall) coated in green copper, with a light that made it visible for miles around at night. It would serve as a branch of the Bullock's downtown LA store, featuring higher-end merchandise and easier access for the discriminating consumer.

To facilitate that access, the five-story building was designed with the front door facing a parking lot rather than the street. Cars would pull up under a carport (porte-cochère), and a valet would do the rest. The carport itself featured a ceiling fresco with a transportation theme, depicting an airplane, a luxury liner, a zeppelin, and the Roman messenger god Mercury.

The shopper then passed through bronze doors into a cosmetics hall described by the *Los Angeles Times* as "more like a marble basilica than a store, with vertical stripes of lights reaching from the pale, rose-colored walls across the ceiling."

More murals greeted customers as they explored the building, including a depiction of Paris that covered an entire wall in the fur salon—which also featured a fireplace. There were chandeliers, wall clocks in various styles, mirrors, and brass palm trees; a series of themed "salons" evoked the atmosphere of everything from the Roaring Twenties to Marie Antoinette's apartments. There was even a saddle shop that featured a plaster horse to assist customers in trying on their breeches.

Clothes weren't displayed on racks but on rosewood stands, in glass cases, or worn by live mannequins, so as to avoid even the hint of clutter.

Established stars shopped there, and future celebrities worked there. William Randolph Hearst bought

Atlanta-based Rich's expanded outside Georgia in 1955, opening an $8 million cube-shaped "store of tomorrow" in Knoxville, Tennessee. The chain, however, sold the building six years later. It's now the University of Tennessee Conference Center. Stephen H. Provost, 2018.

swimsuits for his castle guests at Bullock's Wilshire, Marlene Dietrich bought trousers at the store, and Walt Disney was among the patrons. The penthouse Tea Room, with its cactus-themed décor, drew the likes of Clark Gable, Greta Garbo, Alfred Hitchcock, John Wayne, and Mae West. Angela Lansbury and Richard Nixon's future wife, Pat, worked in the store as salesclerks.

5

CHRISTMASTIME IN THE CITY

Department stores strove to create a modern wonderland, and they were never more successful at achieving this than at Christmastime. At Wanamaker's, 40 percent of the company's revenue rolled in during the Christmas season, and other stores posted similar numbers.

Then, as now, the holidays were make-or-break for retailers, so department stores went all out to attract as many gift-buying patrons as they could. Decorations went up in store windows and on the sales floor, and extra staff was brought in to handle the increased foot traffic.

One of two Santas— each concealed from the other to avoid confusing the kids— works at Macy's during the holiday season in 1942. Library of Congress.

(My mother worked at a local department store one holiday season, gift-wrapping packages for customers—a skill she passed along to me, although I never managed to quite master it.)

At Hess Brothers in Allentown, Pennsylvania, employees all got into the holiday spirit. In 1924, just before closing on Christmas Eve, seventy-five of them gathered in the store's rotunda to sing carols such as Joy to the World and O Holy Night accompanied by piano, harp, trumpet, violin, and cello. No word on whether cookies or cider was served, but the performance did receive favorable reviews from the store's customers.

Macy's launched its annual Thanksgiving Day Parade in 1924. Schuster's in Milwaukee sponsored a yearly Christmas parade beginning in 1927 that was promoted by an elfin character named Billie the Brownie. The parade drew an estimated 200,000 to 250,000 people every year in all kinds of weather until it was discontinued after 1961.

Starting in 1959, Boston's Jordan Marsh cleared out an entire floor in its main store each year to create its Enchanted Village of St. Nicholas. The elaborate display created by German craftsmen was set up around the perimeter of the store's 10,000-square-foot fashion center. At more than 300 feet long, it showcased 250 moving characters: Santa's helpers and their pets. By the numbers, it involved:

- 80,000 pounds of displays
- 45,000 hours to create
- 16,200 mechanical parts
- 4,000 feet of wire
- 240 different-size cartons to transport it via ship to the US
- 160 motors to animate the character.
- 100-plus gallons of paint

Twenty-eight inset displays—with faux building fronts two stories high—were set up for visitors to enjoy (there was one entrance, closest to the displays, for "Good Little Boys and Girls" and another for adults). They were greeted by a mustachioed blacksmith pounding on an anvil, children at the Village

School, chickens in the Village Barn, and Santa getting his beard trimmed by one of his elves. There was a watchmaker, a bakery, a toymaker, a candlemaker, a cobbler, and a post office scene featuring a lovable dog, the figures finely detailed and fully animated. Some of them, like a hurdy-gurdy (complete with monkey) and a giant rotating Christmas tree, were out on the floor itself.

So many people turned out to see the attraction during its first year that the store kept it open an extra week after Christmas to accommodate the crowds. Over the years, new features were added, such as a reindeer stables, a boy with a yo-yo, a chimney sweep, a parrot, and a girl blowing bubbles.

The attraction was discontinued in 1972, "due to the then-waxing big-city singles life that deemphasized shopping as a family experience," the *Boston Globe* later

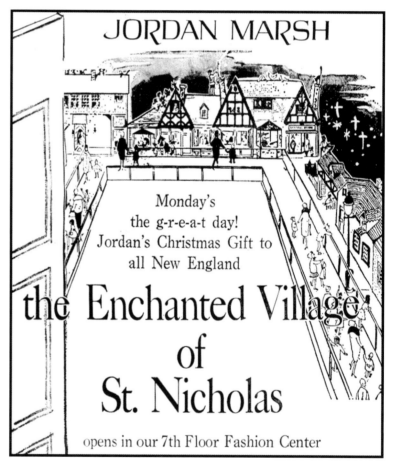

An ad from 1970 announces the mid-November opening of the Enchanted Village of St. Nicholas at Jordan Marsh in Boston.

explained. Jordan Marsh brought it back in 1990 before discontinuing it again in 1998. It was later sold at auction and has more recently been displayed at a furniture store in Avon, Massachusetts.

A similar display graced the second floor of Lit Brothers in Philadelphia each holiday season from 1962 until 1975, two years before it went out of business. The Enchanted Christmas Colonial Village was a "nearly full-scale reproduction of a typical American village of colonial times," with life-size animated figures in fifteen buildings. Like the Jordan Marsh display, it was built in Germany. Visitors could see 200 animated figures going through their daily routines at a blacksmith's shop, a toymaker's shop, and a replica of Ben Franklin's printing press. A group of carolers sang under a lamppost, and there was even a family of animated field mice.

Rich's in Atlanta had a tradition of its own. It installed a monorail called the Snowland Express in the fifties that took kids on a 3½-minute ride onto the store's roof and over the toy department. A few years later, the headlight fell off, so the store's creative minds came up with the idea of replacing it with a pig snout and painting the entire ride pink. They named her Priscilla.

The tradition of the pink pig, however, didn't originate there. In the early 1880s, a resident of Saratoga Springs, New York, began making peppermint candy shaped like a pig. The pig, a Victorian symbol of prosperity, was a natural mascot at Christmastime. The candy caught on, and a tradition soon developed. At Christmas dinner, the head of the household would place the pig in a pouch and smash it with a mallet; others at the table would follow suit, breaking off pieces of the candy and sharing stories of their good fortune and wishes for a prosperous new year.

A Saratoga-based candy company still sells the peppermint pigs. Meanwhile, Macy's—which bought Rich's—continued the train tradition into the twenty-first century at Lenox Square Mall with a new version of

The suburban Sears at Manchester Center in Fresno was brand new in 1956, when it spruced up its plain storefront with holiday trees, "Merry Christmas" lettering, and Santa's sleigh ascending toward the skies. Joe Wolf. Creative Commons 2.0 license: https://creativecommons.org/licenses/by-sa/2.0.

the monorail. It even opened a seasonal Pink Pig store to accompany the attraction, donating part of the ride's proceeds to Children's Healthcare of Atlanta.

Stores across the country decorated their windows with faux firs and their storefronts with Santas, reindeer, candy canes, and stars.

In Philadelphia, Wanamaker's created a dazzling Christmas light show in 1955 that continues to this day (even though the store is now a Macy's). It wasn't just lights. Children would be ushered into the store's Grand Hall every hour to see the Sugar Plum Fairy, Frosty the Snowman, and Rudolph the Red-Nosed Reindeer.

Rudolph may have been made famous by Gene Autry with his 2 million–selling holiday tune in 1949, but the character had actually come to life a decade earlier thanks to another major retailer: Montgomery Ward. That's where thirty-four-year-old copywriter Robert May was employed when the company asked him to create a Christmas story. What May came up with was a variation on The Ugly Duckling for a holiday audience; he considered the names Reginald and Rollo before settling on Rudolph.

May's supervisor initially worried that the red nose might create the impression that our hero had been drinking (W.C. Fields remained a popular movie star in 1939). But May overcame those reservations by taking an employee from the store's art department out to sketch some deer at the zoo. Once the project was approved, May created the booklet, and Wards distributed 2.4 million copies that year alone. The figure was up to 6 million by 1946, when May persuaded Wards to relinquish the copyright. The following year, his brother-in-law, Johnny Marks, created a musical version of the story, complete with melody and lyrics, which Autry recorded, and the rest, like Rudolph, went down in history.

Not so much his Canadian counterpart.

In response to Rudolph, Canada's biggest department store, Eaton's, created its own Santa sidekick in 1948: Punkinhead the Sad Little Bear. The store dubbed him a "truly Canadian teddy bear," and he became ubiquitous. In addition to stuffed bears, his image appeared on watches, coloring books, lamps, gloves, and other items, always with a distinctive shock of orange or yellow hair sticking up out of his head like fronds on a palm tree.

Punkinhead's story closely paralleled Rudolph's, except Punkinhead was teased for his hair rather than his nose. Like Rudolph, he had his own song:

They always call him Punkinhead, he is a sad little bear
And all because they laugh at him and make fun of his hair
It stands straight up and won't lie down no matter what we do
And no one wants to play with him; that's why he feels so blue

Punkinhead, Punkinhead, with a funny looking mop of hair
Punkinhead, Punkinhead, the sad little, cute little bear

Then along came Santa Claus in his sleigh, with a great big "Ho! Ho! Ho!"
With the elves and the clowns in a big parade all dancing through the snow
But one of the clowns got sick one day, no smile was on his face
They tried his hat on every one, but none could take his place

Then up stepped Punkinhead to try, and much to his delight
The mop of hair just held it there; the hat it fit just right!
Now Punkinhead is having fun, he's happy as can be
And so, each year he brings good cheer right to your Christmas tree

Punkinhead, Punkinhead, with a funny looking mop of hair
Punkinhead, Punkinhead, that's a story of a happy little bear

It wasn't particularly original, but as we shall see, Eaton's did create a far more lasting holiday tradition: the Thanksgiving Day parade to usher in the Christmas season.

New Yorkers shop for Christmas on a snowy Sixth Avenue in this photo taken sometime early in the twentieth century. Library of Congress.

VISIONS OF SUGAR PLUMS

Main Street storefronts have been featured in numerous holiday-themed films, one of which produced the modern carol "Silver Bells." That movie, a Bob Hope vehicle called *The Lemon Drop Kid,* has all but vanished into obscurity. But the song's popularity has outlived the era that inspired it, and it's easy to see why. It's hard not to look back fondly on "city sidewalks, busy sidewalks" filled with "children laughing, people passing, meeting smile after smile" as shoppers "rush home with their treasures." Such visions are, increasingly, things of the past, but they're etched in the memories of those who grew up during that era.

Linda J. King certainly recalls them.

"In the 1950s, there was always Foley's Department Store," she said in an interview for this book, referring to the Houston-based chain that spread over six southwestern states. "It was downtown, and Mom would take two of us with her to shop at Christmastime, and I would always sneak off and spend the time on the fourth floor, which they would turn into a fantastic Christmas land filled with toys and trees and—best of all—a Christmas village with electric trains running on tracks set up around a huge center area."

Big cities like New York, Chicago, Philadelphia, and Boston may have been at the epicenter of the developing Christmas tradition, but Main Street celebrations weren't limited to those storied downtowns.

They were everywhere.

Meier & Frank had its own Christmas traditions centered on its sixteen-story flagship store in Portland, Oregon, which opened in 1915.

"My most vivid memory is of Meier & Frank here in Portland at Christmastime," said Shoshana Edwards. "We would come downtown on the trolley—my entire family until I was nine, and then just me and my brother. We would watch the parade the day after Thanksgiving, and then we would go to see the window opening at

M&F. This was in the late forties and early fifties. There was always at least one major animated window. Oh, how I loved that.

"And then, the year I was ten, they added a Christmas floor. The entire tenth floor, which was their primary stock room, became Santa's Workshop. There was a train that wound around through the back stocks, with boxes labeled for shipping to various towns in Oregon, along with trees, snow, and the occasional reindeer."

Rochester had Sibley's, the biggest department store between New York and Chicago. There were other stores in Syracuse, Newark, and elsewhere, but the six-story (plus basement) Rochester site was the flagship.

Rochester site was the flagship.

"At Christmas, my parents would take my sister and me 'downtown' to see the decorations," said Connie Hansen. "There were animated displays in the windows. I clearly remember 'The Night Before Christmas' illustrated with dioramas of moving mechanical dolls. It would take up all the windows as it illustrated different lines of the poem. Another time it was A Christmas Carol.

"The toy department was a child's dream, and of course there was Santa Claus to hear the children's requests. We weren't allowed to believe in Santa (modern parents that didn't want to lie to their children), but we could pretend and go talk to him anyway. Besides having the dioramas in the front windows, they also had a Christmas Tunnel with moving dolls illustrating some Christmas theme. The tunnel ended up in the Toy Shop part of the store. It was magical."

At The Crescent in Spokane, window displays featured such whimsical subjects as fairy ballerinas from *The Nutcracker*; elves roasting marshmallows in a gingerbread house; a beaver chopping down a tree (with an ax!); a scene from Santa's workshop featuring an impressive hot-air balloon; and a woman who looks like a Disney princess riding in an ornate covered carriage, or howdah, on the back of an elephant.

Globman's offered a similar feast for the eyes to those in southern Virginia.

"Globman's in Martinsville *meant* Christmastime," said Mark Rainey, a writer and editor who grew up there and whose mother still lives in the community. "When you went in through the front doors, everything was decked out in extravagant fashion—the owners were Jewish, but they sure knew how to work Christmas. The toy department was downstairs, and as soon as you started down, you could see the end of the toy aisles. Hot Wheels, Creepy Crawlers, Major Matt Mason, G.I. Joe, model kits, board games, bikes, chemistry sets, everything a kid like me needed to be in heaven."

First Lady Eleanor Roosevelt visits with Santa at a Washington, DC, department store in 1934. Library of Congress.

The store's owners gave their employees who celebrated Christmas a special treat, Pam Globman said: "Christmas Eve store hours were covered by the store's [Jewish] family members so that the predominantly Christian employees could celebrate this holiday."

When the big department stores left Main Street and moved to suburban shopping malls, it was never quite the same. And when those malls were replaced by online shopping, a treasured Christmas tradition all but disappeared. Say what you want about the perils of commercialism, the downtown Christmas brought communities together, and with only a few vestiges of that tradition remaining in the form of annual holiday parades and festivities, we're the poorer for it.

An employee arranges a display of stuffed animals for the holiday season at Woolworth's in Washington, DC. John Collier Jr., Library of Congress, 1941.

6

READY, SET, SHOP!

The Air Force Academy band marches at Broadway and 34th Street in New York during the eightieth Macy's Thanksgiving Day Parade. Senior Airman Brian Ferguson, USAF, 2006.

Thanksgiving, of course, ushered in the holiday season, and what better way to do so than with a procession through the heart of downtown?

Holiday parades served as the starting gun of sorts for the holiday shopping season, which began in earnest the day after Thanksgiving. Macy's is by far the most famous, but it wasn't the first. Rival Gimbels actually began its own tradition in Philadelphia four years earlier in 1920, when its employees dressed as clowns and cavorted in the street to kick off the holiday shopping season. In 1924, the year Macy's started its parade in New York, Hudson's did the same thing in Detroit.

But even Gimbels wasn't the first. The tradition started north of the border, where Eaton's department store of

Toronto staged its first Santa Claus Parade on December 2, 1905. It started out as a simple promotion designed to draw attention to the store's indoor holiday display: Santa pulled into Union Station on a train, then rode a wagon through the city to Eaton's five-story downtown shop—which was already promoting itself as "Canada's Greatest Store." Santa played the role of pied piper, leading kids and their parents to the promised land of Eaton's toy shop (where purchases were bound to be made).

Eight live reindeer joined the procession in 1913, and a concert and party were added to the festivities the following year. Floats were included for the first time in 1916—seven of them, each based on a popular fairy tale or nursery rhyme: Cinderella (in a pumpkin coach), Mother Goose, Little Bo Peep, Little Red Riding Hood, Little Boy Blue, Little Miss Muffet, and the Old Woman Who Lived in a Shoe.

That theme would continue as the parade grew, and it carried over when Eaton's established a similar parade at its Winnipeg store. The 1929 edition featured Old King Cole and his Fiddlers Three; the White Rabbit, the Caterpillar, and the Mad Hatter from *Alice's Adventures in Wonderland*; Ali Baba and some of his Forty Thieves. The Edmonton store also had a parade that year, with an ad depicting some of the same characters, along with a group of medieval knights, two of whom shown with a beehive and fish dangling comically from the end of their lances.

The store also had a parade in Montreal.

SPECTACLE, NOT SPIRITUAL

The Eaton parades were all about fun and fancy, not cultural heritage or civic pride. And certainly not religion. Sights and sounds sold products. Appeals to scripture or union labels? Not so much. That's why you didn't see church groups or members of fraternal orders marching down the street. No shepherds or wise men from manger scenes. What you did see were clowns and fairy-tale characters and Santa; what you heard was a cacophony of sound blaring and jangling from noise-makers of all sorts.

"It's tradition . . . that every parader carries something to blow, to jingle, whistle or wave," the company

declared. "Everybody come and wave a mitten—the more the merrier, says Santa."

Did Eaton's parade influence similar holiday festivities in the United States?

It certainly looks that way. Early parades sponsored by Macy's and Hudson's (in Detroit, just four hours away from Toronto) looked a lot like Eaton's spectacles. Hudson's first parade showcased Mother Goose and nine other storybook characters, while Macy's inaugural procession featured Little Red Riding Hood and Robinson Crusoe.

That first New York parade was actually called "Macy's Christmas Parade" and culminated with the "coronation of Santa Claus" at Macy's 75-foot window on 34th Street. There, the store had created a fairy city featuring hundreds of moving marionettes enacting twenty-six different scenes on a continuously moving stage that showcased "romantic castles, hills and lakes" in "an ever-changing panorama," a New Jersey newspaper enthused.

In addition to floats, the parade featured tigers, elephants, and other animals from the Central Park Zoo. But the first balloons didn't soar above the ground until 1927, when Felix the Cat made his debut alongside a 25-foot-long dachshund, turkeys, chickens, ducks, and a 60-foot-long dinosaur—part of an effort to replace real animals with inflated facsimiles. Supposedly, they'd be safer, but that wasn't always the case. Felix made his debut propped up on poles and filled with air, but then parade organizers started using helium and untethering the balloons so they could soar out over the city.

Macy's tried to build enthusiasm for the parade by injecting a little competition. The idea: Let the balloons fly free and see how far they could go, then offer a $100 reward to whoever found and returned them. They were expected to rise up to 3,000 feet and were timed to leak gas slowly and lose altitude gradually over a week to ten days before finally touching down.

A tiger landed first, coming down on the roof of a Long Island residence. It triggered a tug-of-war among motorists who saw it land and then promptly tore it to bits. Another balloon landed in the East River and burst in two, where it was pursued by a pair of tugboats, and a ghost balloon drifted out to sea as a flock of seagulls gave chase.

A photographer sets her sights on Pokémon stalwart Pikachu in the 2013 Macy's Thanksgiving Day Parade. The first balloons had appeared in the annual celebration eighty-six years earlier. Charley Lhasa, 2013. Creative Commons 2.0 license: https://creativecommons.org/licenses/by-sa/2.0.

In 1931, poor Felix was incinerated by a high-tension wire in New Jersey, and a blue hippopotamus disappeared entirely. People called Macy's with bogus reports that the animal had been sighted in Portland, Maine, and miraculously "walking on water" off the Rockaway Peninsula.

The following year, the balloons were unleashed again, and a student pilot reported crossing paths with a 60-foot Tom Cat balloon (evidently not a resurrected Felix but a close cousin). Instead of trying to avoid it, however, she decided to "have a piece of the neck" and dive-bombed the poor helium-filled feline. But the plane got tangled up in the balloon, which wrapped itself around one wing, then cut the engine, sending the plane into a steeper dive. The flight instructor scrambled into the front seat, and when the student tried to change places with him, the cockpit door flew open. Only the fact that one foot became tangled in her seatbelt saved her from falling out. Ultimately, the instructor was able to start the motor again, and the "dead" cat flew loose of the wing, allowing the plane to halt its descent a mere 80 feet above the ground.

Indeed, cats have had their share of problems during the parade. In 1997, a six-story-high Cat in the Hat balloon hit a light pole and snapped off the horizontal piece, which fell on the crowd below. One woman was so badly injured she was in a coma for twenty-four days before recovering. Still, cats have nine lives, and Felix seems to be no exception: He returned to the lineup in 2016, the only original character to appear in that year's parade.

Macy's bought Bamberger's of Newark in 1929, and that store started its own parade two years later. Participants included Santa, a 100-foot dragon,

The Santa Claus Lane Parade in Hollywood kicked off in 1928, and other California retail districts soon
got into the act. Here, Frosty the Snowman hitches a ride through downtown Exeter, California.
Tommy Lee Kreger, 2016. Creative Commons 2.0 license: https://creativecommons.org/licenses/by-sa/2.0.

gunslingers, buccaneers, and, yes, a herd of cats. Two years later, the parade featured "giant men that talk!" and "super bugs that squawk!" according to an ad in the *Hackensack Record*, along with a big, striped balloon cat. But in 1955, the store (which was owned by Macy's) decided to try a different twist, unveiling what it called the "world's first Thanksgiving Eve parade in blacklight." All the streetlamps were switched off, creating a dark backdrop for glowing entries featuring Cinderella, a turkey, and a mountain of ice cream.

The streetlight blackout created an unintended consequence: gridlock on the asphalt. So, the parade moved to a park the following year, only to be discontinued in 1958 as people stopped turning out.

The parade tradition went west in 1928, when Hollywood retailers (who touted Hollywood Boulevard as the "world's largest department store") turned a

mile-long stretch of asphalt between La Brea Avenue and Vine Street into Santa Claus Lane. Parade organizers dug up 100 living fir trees near Big Bear Lake, a resort area east of Los Angeles at an elevation of 6,700 feet, and potted them in wooden planters on either side of the boulevard. With 10,000 bulbs hanging from their branches, they turned the street into what organizers called the nation's most brightly lit thoroughfare.

Actress Mary Pickford helped change street signs that first year to transform Hollywood Boulevard into Santa Claus Lane, and Santa originally rode on a float pulled by a truck before reindeer were recruited in 1931. The short-lived tradition of using live fir trees was discontinued, and 16-foot-tall metal trees were used instead.

The parade was put on hiatus during World War II, but 300,000 spectators turned out to see Jack Benny cut the ribbon and Bob Hope turn on the lights in 1945. That

Once-ubiquitous downtown department stores, with their holiday window displays, have all but vanished, but a few smaller retailers continue the tradition. Among them: Rippe's Apparel on Main Street in downtown Danville, Virginia, which has been in business for more than a century. Stephen H. Provost, 2018.

year's parade also featured George Burns and Gracie Allen, Abbott and Costello, Dinah Shore, and Hoagy Carmichael playing piano on one of the floats. The following year, Gene Autry served as grand marshal and rode on horseback just in front of Mr. Claus, who was greeted with enthusiastic shouts of "Here comes Santa Claus!" from children along the parade route. He used the refrain to craft what would become a classic holiday tune, which he recorded a year later in 1947.

Parade participants over the years included the Marx Brothers, Claudette Colbert, Buster Crabbe, Martha Raye, Joan Caufield, Art Linkletter, Jayne Mansfield, the Three Stooges, and Lassie (with Jon "Timmy" Provost).

Joe E. Brown was the first grand marshal, in 1932, a role that would later be filled by the likes of Ron Howard, William Shatner, Sammy Davis Jr., and Michael Landon.

The Hollywood parade continued, with lesser stars, into the twenty-first century, and the Macy's parade maintained its status as the preeminent holiday procession. But the one that started it all in Toronto? In 1982 it nearly became what company president Fredrik Eaton called a "casualty of the times."

About 500,000 people had lined the streets the previous year, while more than 33 million had watched on television, but Eaton had other priorities: "We don't intend to be specific in dollars and cents," he said, "but at a time when retailers, Eaton's included, have been letting employees go, we don't feel this is a time to continue the parade."

The Montreal and Winnipeg parades had already fallen by the wayside, and it wouldn't be long before Eaton's itself had given up the ghost. The chain filed for bankruptcy in 1997 and went out of business two years later. Still, the parade survived under the supervision of a volunteer group, and other holiday parades inspired by Eaton's continued to be held across North America into the twenty-first century.

When Black Friday comes

Anyone who's lamented seeing Christmas decorations at the local department store before Halloween will be able to tell you: When it comes to retailing, Christmas is part sprint, part marathon. Last-minute shopping is important, but the twelve days of Christmas is a song, not a marketing strategy. Why do all those faux evergreens and Santa figurines start appearing in stores alongside plastic jack-o-lanterns and bags of bite-size candy? Easy: Because the earlier you can get shoppers thinking about what to put under the tree, the better your bottom line will be.

Despite those pre-Thanksgiving teasers that "Christmas is coming," few shoppers get serious about holiday purchases until after the turkey's off the table. How *soon* after it's off the table has changed, though. In the twenty-first century, more retailers have opened *on* Thanksgiving Day, allowing customers to make it through the door that much more quickly.

Until recently, however, the Friday after Thanksgiving served as the traditional starting line for the holiday shopping season.

They call it "Black Friday." Retailers will tell you that's because the surge in sales on that day typically moves their bottom line from the red into the black.

But that's not exactly true.

There's no question that retailers do a lot of business on the day after Thanksgiving. Customers are ready to start buying gifts for their loved ones, and stores fuel the fire by offering huge, limited-time-only deals. Still, Black Friday sounds pretty negative—and that's how it started out. It originally referred to September 24, 1869, the day

the stock market crashed when the Treasury Department announced it was about to flood the market with gold to foil an attempt by a group of investors to drive up the price.

It was also the title of a 1940 science fiction/horror film starring Boris Karloff and Bela Lugosi and was at times used as another name for Friday the 13th. Over time, it came to be used generically anytime something really bad happened on a Friday (such as the assassination of John F. Kennedy).

But there wasn't any reference to the day after Thanksgiving as Black Friday until 1951, and even then, it didn't have anything to do with the Christmas rush. Instead, it came in a magazine called Factory Management and Maintenance, which lamented the tendency of workers to create a four-day weekend for themselves by calling in sick. The magazine referred to chronic absenteeism on Black Friday as a disease "second only to the bubonic plague in its effects."

The first time it was used in reference to holiday shopping was in 1961, when a perfect storm of events stretched Philadelphia police officers to their limit. Like many big cities, the City of Brotherly Love was a magnet for family members coming home for a long holiday weekend. The city's population swelled and, at the same time, throngs of shoppers began to venture forth in response to holiday sales. Meanwhile, one of college football's oldest rivalries, the Army-Navy Game, was scheduled for the following day. Traffic cops, forced to work twelve-hour shifts to deal with all the chaos, weren't too happy about being forced to deal with all this at once, so they started referring to the day as Black Friday.

A public relations newsletter had this to say:

"Santa has brought Philadelphia stores a present in the form of 'one of the biggest shopping weekends in recent history.' For downtown merchants throughout the nation, the biggest shopping days normally are the two following Thanksgiving Day. Resulting traffic jams are an irksome problem to the police and, in Philadelphia, it became customary for officers to refer to the post-Thanksgiving days as Black Friday and Black Saturday. Hardly a stimulus for good business."

With the advent of online shopping and Cyber Monday, malls such as this one in North Carolina aren't as busy
as they used to be on Black Friday—and during the holiday season in general. Stephen H. Provost, 2018.

One solution, the article suggested, would be to start calling the day "Big Friday."

A press release was sent out using that term, but it never caught on.

What *did* work was a later campaign reframing Black Friday as the day that ledgers moved from the red into the black (referring to the old accounting practice of using red ink to record losses and black ink for profits). The idea was that merchants made enough money on the weekend after Thanksgiving to put their business in the black for the remainder of the year. This connection was first made during the eighties.

This sounds reasonable enough, especially in light of the long lines, folding chairs, and even miniature tents that begin appearing outside department stores and big-box retailers before dawn on the morning after Thanksgiving.

DOORBUSTERS

A lot of people buy a lot of things on Black Friday, and when there are more people than there are items for sale at those "doorbuster prices," doors (and other things) can get busted. Literally.

In 2008, a huge mass of shoppers rushed the doors at a Long Island Walmart and trampled a temporary store employee to death in their rush to get inside. The worker, at 6 foot 5 inches and 270 pounds, was "built like an NFL linebacker," according to one report, "but he was no match for an estimated 2,000 people who broke down the doors." Four other people, including a pregnant woman, were injured and taken to the hospital.

What was all the fuss about?

Low prices and limited supplies.

When an item was in high demand, like the Tickle Me Elmo doll, things only got crazier. Mothers across the nation sat up and took notice when Elmo—who giggled and squirmed with delight when his tummy was tickled—appeared on Rosie O'Donnell's popular daytime talk show in 1996. The *Sesame Street* character's "guest appearance" helped put the doll on a list of the fifteen hottest toys that year, as compiled by the trade publication *Toy Book*.

Enthusiasm rose even further when Elmo sat in Bryant Gumbel's lap during a *Today Show* segment on the season's most wanted toys, and the after-Thanksgiving table was set for a Black Friday mob scene. Manufacturer Tyco, which had expected to sell 400,000 of the toys, rushed to make 600,000 more, but it was too little too late for Black Friday shoppers: Most stores had submitted their orders months earlier, and there wasn't enough time to get replacements onto the shelves for the big weekend.

Kay-Bee and Target sold out of all their Elmos in an hour, and one Target store in Nashville ran out in just four minutes. Two women were placed under arrest in Chicago after fighting over one of the dolls, and there were reports of women running after delivery trucks in a desperate attempt to procure an Elmo.

Stores had marked prices down to near cost for Black Friday sales, but afterward, those prices went soaring as scalpers made a killing off moms and dads who hadn't gotten to the store on time. Suddenly, the $30 toy was being advertised for up to $1,000 in classified ads, and

Elmomania continued after Black Friday as more of the toys made it onto store shelves. When a shipment arrived on December 14 at a Walmart in Fredericton, New Brunswick, an unfortunate store clerk happened to be holding one of the dolls. The crowd of 300 caught sight of him and charged like a herd of buffalo. The clerk suffered a broken rib, a concussion, and a pulled hamstring, among other injuries. "I was pulled under, trampled—the crotch was yanked out of my brand-new jeans," he said afterward.

But even in years when the most popular toys weren't so hard to get, post-Thanksgiving sales could get out of hand. According to the Associated Press, Black Friday 2011 was marred by "smash-and-grab looters" and "bloody screams in the shopping aisles." One woman unleashed a blast of pepper spray on twenty other customers at a Walmart in Southern California as she fought her way toward a crate of Xbox game consoles.

"The difference this year is that instead of a nice sweater (to ward off the cold), you need a bulletproof vest and goggles," a shopper in Raleigh, North Carolina, quipped.

It wasn't just stores, but criminals who used the Friday after Thanksgiving as an opportunity to get in the black. In 2007, thieves chose Black Friday to target an armored car, apparently because they knew it would be carrying an unusually large sum of money. They made off with $7.4 million.

As more stores began opening on Thanksgiving itself and more customers began doing their shopping online, Black Friday became a little less crazy. Target and Walmart started opening on Thanksgiving Day in 2012. Then, in 2015, Target announced a plan to offer different deals over a span of ten days, spreading out the opportunities to save—and thinning the crowds in the process. Further defusing the explosive nature of Black Friday, online retailers moved their deals to a new day called Cyber Monday, offering buyers an incentive to wait a couple of extra days to open their wallets.

And they could do it all from the comfort of their own homes.

7

NICKEL AND DIMING

Department stores came into their own at the dawn of the automotive age. As the Model T made cars affordable to the middle class, and roads began to improve, people found it easier to get around. They didn't just leave the house because they *had to*, they started venturing out because they *wanted to*.

Americans probably didn't realize how stir crazy they really were until they had a realistic chance to get out of the house. New prosperity following the end of World War I put more disposable cash in their pocket, and they wanted a place to spend it. A new federal highway system was on the drawing board, and the open road was one natural destination. Department stores were another.

By 1919, a "camping craze" had taken the nation by storm, unleashing a wave of pent-up energy on the national landscape. Tin-can tourists, as they were called, began stopping for the night and pitching tents by the side of the road, avoiding big-city hotels for a more basic, do-it-yourself travel experience. Department stores were quick to exploit the trend, advertising stoves, tents, and

Kress, one of the most successful dime stores, or "five-and-dimes," may have sold its merchandise at a discount, but it didn't scrimp when it came to the exterior of this store in Greensboro, North Carolina. Stephen H. Provost, 2018.

other essential outdoor equipment for sale. But the changing face of retail and the expanding vistas of the American road were connected in an even more fundamental way: The auto camps of the early 1920s were like the general stores of the 1800s. They were only the beginning, and once they caught on with the general public, it was impossible to tell where they might lead.

It wasn't long before the auto camps morphed into permanent overnight stops. Savvy entrepreneurs built U-shaped motor courts, surrounded by small wooden cabins so tents were no longer needed. At first, these were bare-bones facilities: a cot, a blanket, and maybe a carport but not much else. Gradually, however, the traveling public demanded more amenities, things like running water, a bathroom that could be accessed without leaving their room, a queen-size bed, a telephone, air-conditioning, an alarm clock, a radio, a television, a swimming pool . . . the list got longer as time went by.

Before long, discount motels with "no-frills" names could no longer live up to them. A room at Motel 6 costs a lot more than $6 today; the same is true for an overnight stay at a Super 8. Meanwhile, however, there were those who still preferred roughing it. They bypassed motor inns and lodges in favor of campgrounds and RV parks, which remained far more reasonably priced.

This trend toward extremes—opulence on the one hand and thrift on the other—wasn't limited to vacation planning; it could be seen in the evolution of the department store as well. Some entrepreneurs realized that not everyone wanted to pay through the nose to shop at a store with escalators and marble floors and chandeliers. They'd rather save their money and get a good deal than wade through such extravagances, and they didn't want to order from a catalog and wait for their goods to arrive in the mail.

The Woolworth Building towers above the New York City skyline in 1913. Upon completion, it was the tallest building in the world. Library of Congress.

WOOLWORTH MAKES HIS MARK

To meet this need, retailers created the five-and-dime.

In many ways, it was a more direct descendant of the old general store than the giant "palaces of consumerism" epitomized by Marshall Field's and Wanamaker's. Goods weren't as neatly laid out, and atmosphere took a backseat to value at stores like Ben Franklin, Kress, S.S. Kresge, Sprouse-Reitz, and Walton's. Sometimes called variety stores or discount or dollar stores, they began as "five-and-dimes"—stores that sold items for a nickel or ten

A reconditioned soda fountain in a former Woolworth, Asheville, North Carolina. Library of Congress.

cents. The first store of this kind, and the first to make the low price a part of its nameplate, was Woolworth's Great Five Cent Store, which opened in 1878 in Utica, New York. The store failed, but owner Frank W. Woolworth teamed up with his brother Charles and tried again the following year in Lancaster, Pennsylvania. This time, he hit paydirt.

Woolworth's inventory when he opened included gravy strainers, schoolbook straps, apple corers, cake cutters, candlesticks, napkins, police whistles, baseballs, shaving lather brushes, handkerchiefs, and plates with rimmed with letters of the alphabet. One of the biggest attractions was candy, and children were among his most important customers. In fact, Woolworth believed each store could pay its rent with the money it made on candy alone.

"I don't pretend to know much about the candy business," he said, "but, in my opinion, if you want to make a big success of candy, put it in brass trays and put it up near the door, so that people can be reminded of it as they are [leaving], and take some home to the children."

Other stores opened over the next few years under the name 5¢ & 10¢ Woolworth Bro's Store, the first literal five-and-dime. And Woolworth insisted on adhering to that price code in the strictest sense. When a manager at one of his stores admitted he was selling some firecrackers for 3 cents and others for 15 cents a bunch, the boss set him straight. "That, in my opinion, was all wrong," he wrote in 1890, "as it is getting off the idea of strictly 5 and 10 cents business. Stick to the original idea."

By 1912, there were nearly 600 Woolworth stores, and the following year saw completion of Woolworth Tower, which would remain the world's tallest building until 1930. Woolworth paid for the entire thing in cash, and President Woodrow Wilson turned on the lights by pushing a button in Washington, DC.

While luxury department stores like Bullock's Wilshire and Lord & Taylor offered fine dining on their upper floors, Woolworth provided a ground-level, gut-level experience: the lunch counter. If candy could be used to attract youngsters, meals and snacks could serve a similar purpose for adults who might otherwise have left the store to head home, stroll across the street to a diner, or retire to the country for a picnic lunch. The lunch counter kept them in the building and within sight of the merchandise. If something caught their eye while they were eating, it might result in additional sales; meanwhile, the food they ordered would bring in revenue, too.

The tactic worked like a charm. In 1962, *Miami News* business columnist Agnes Ash noted that Woolworth's fed 750,000 people in its restaurants, ranging from lunch counter to table service: "Only the armed forces has more mouths to feed." Some stores had just a soda fountain, and Woolworth also had stand-alone cafeteria, but it seems almost everyone who grew up in that era has memories of visiting one of the chain's lunch counters.

"Woolworth's had a lunch counter that I so loved to sit at, order meatloaf, and drink coffee from those heavy white coffee cups," said Terri Martin of Fresno, where Woolworth's had a downtown location. "Their prices were good for young people just starting out."

A fifties lunch counter menu offered basic plain or toasted cheese and ham or egg salad sandwiches for 30 cents. Toasted, three-decker sandwiches were a little more expensive: 50 to 65 cents for bacon and tomato, baked ham and cheese, chicken salad, or ham salad/egg salad. Milkshakes or banana splits, each with two scoops of ice cream, would cost you a quarter, or you could pay 15 cents for a slice of apple pie or layer cake.

Laura Serna-Maytorena of Ohio remembered working at a Woolworth's lunch counter in Santa Cruz, California, when she was seventeen.

"When I was a teen (1985–86), I worked at a Woolworth's lunch counter in Santa Cruz, California, the big double-horseshoe kind," she said. "I waited on customers, cooked, rang up their sales, and washed the dishes. We were expected to follow each customer through the whole encounter/meal, which was quite different from any other restaurant I had worked in or would work in later in life. We had to wear the old-school uniforms and such—it was like being thrown back into the fifties."

Strict adherence to the store's proven formula was a must for employees. Woolworth didn't want know-it-all college grads who liked to think outside the box; it wanted managers who learned the system, stuck to it, and made it work. A high school grad was better than someone with a degree. Ability was less important than *reli*ability.

"We don't care how good you think you are. You've got to learn to do things our way," said Herbert Parson, who succeeded Frank Woolworth as company president.

Woolworth had strict standards for its employees. Drinking in public, for example, was grounds for dismissal, and employees were not allowed to engage in "games of chance." The standards at rival S.S. Kresge were similar; the company refused to hire smokers, drinkers, or gamblers. The rewards, however, could be worth the sacrifice. In the mid-twenties, thirteen of Kresge's top executives were millionaires, and a store manager in Kansas City was earning $26,000 a year—the equivalent of $375,000 in 2018.

Woolworth stores all looked pretty much the same from the street. They were called "red fronts" for the red signage on the front of their stores. The look wasn't exactly unique. Early Woolworth, Kresge, and S.H. Kress stores all used broad ribbons of red across their storefronts, embossed with the company name in gold using all capital letters and serif fonts.

Workplace attire at Woolworth was also standard into the second half of the twentieth century. Serna-Maytorena recalled that "the uniforms were light blue, fitted knee-length pencil skirts with matching short-sleeve fitted shirt with white cuffs and collar, hair up in a bun with a hair net, and white nurses' shoes."

She described the Woolworth's where she worked: "It was in a street mall called the Pacific Garden Mall, nicely landscaped, with benches and trees, flowering shrubs which bit the dust in an earthquake not long after. . . . I lived in the enormous and ancient St. George Hotel just up the mall. It rented out its rooms by the month like a big boarding house. . . . Every morning I would walk down to the café next door to Woolworth's, and a street person, nice old man, would sit down, and I shared my breakfast and a coffee with him. He'd wish me a good day, and I was off to the lunch counter."

Woolworth opened its first lunch counter in 1923 on Pearl Street in New Albany, and others soon followed. Department stores like J.C. Penney added lunch counters and cafeterias, too.

"In the seventies, I worked at the cafeteria in J.C. Penney at Fashion Fair" in Fresno, said Lora Simpson

The Kress chain of stores, such as this one in Knoxville, Tennessee, used gold lettering against a red strip just above the first floor, just as Woolworth did. The two companies were fierce competitors in the first half of the twentieth century. Stephen H. Provost, 2018.

Nordgreen. "We had a short-order and a cafeteria set up. The cook made the best Jell-O cheesecake. I remember the Sysco company truck drivers would sit and drink coffee for a good long while."

Brenda Lowe, from Huntington Beach, California, remembered telling her best friend she was pregnant at the lunch counter in J.J. Newberry's, another five-and-dime: "They had a small café in the store, and we often had lunches and sodas there on the weekends."

Melanie Marquis of Denver recalled eating at a Newberry's lunch counter in Douglas, Arizona: "I would get Slush Puppies to drink. I remember buying stuffed animals and these cool markers that were shaped like chubby little mice!"

DIMESTORE EXPLOSION

Unlike other US-based retailers, Frank Woolworth wasn't content to stay on this side of the Atlantic. In 1909, he converted pennies to pence and opened a Threepence and Sixpence store on Church Street in Liverpool, England. Three years later, he had a dozen stores in Britain under the direction of his cousin Fred, and by 1923, the number had grown to 150.

That's when something strange happened. An Australian company started using the name F.W. Woolworth & Co., Ltd., and formally applied to register it with the government there. The *real* Woolworth company, caught flat-footed, failed to raise any objection, and the name was approved for use by this entirely

W.T. Grant competed head-to-head with Woolworth, Kress, and Kresge, chains that offered a cheaper downtown alternative to more upscale department stores like Rich's and Macy's. Phillip Pessar, 1955. Creative Commons 2.0 license: https://creativecommons.org/licenses/by-sa/2.0.

unrelated "Woolies" (as it came to be known). The new store grew quickly and actually wound up outlasting the original Woolworth's, transforming itself into nationwide chain of grocery stores along the way.

Meanwhile, back in the US, Woolworth's was facing competition.

Many full-scale department stores traced their origins to Jewish immigrants from Eastern Europe, but the burgeoning five-and-dime craze attracted a different group of men: Protestants from the Northeast whose parents had been farmers with roots in Western Europe. A number of such men soon set out to replicate Woolworth's successful five-and-dime model, and new chains began to pop up across the country. The first of these was J.G.

McCrory, which was founded by a man named James Graham McCrorey. (Note the extra e. McCrory legally had it excised from his name so he wouldn't have to pay for the extra letter on his store's signs.)

McCrory opened his first store in 1882 in Scottsdale, Pennsylvania, and had added a few stores to form a small chain when he met a traveling salesman named Sebastian Spering Kresge some fifteen years later. The two decided to go in as partners on two stores but went their separate ways after eighteen months, each finding success. By 1917, the year of America's involvement in World War I, McCrory had 143 stores, and Kresge (now based in Detroit) had 164. Each company was enjoying sales of several million dollars, with Kresge's chain was the nation's second largest, behind Woolworth.

The brief Kresge-McCrory partnership also spawned a third successful entry into the increasingly crowded field of Main Street discount stores. When the pair opened one of their jointly owned stores in Detroit, they chose a man named George Clinton Murphy to manage it. Murphy didn't stay long, though. Instead, he left for Pittsburgh and founded his own chain of stores, which he sold to Woolworth before starting over in nearby McKeesport in 1906.

Murphy died in three years later, and his G.C. Murphy stores were purchased by two former McCrory's executives. Over the next sixty-seven years, the chain would expand to more than 500 locations.

Another successful chain also began in Pennsylvania, where Samuel H. Kress started a store of his own in 1896. When he and Kresge happened to cross paths on a train ride, they struck up an agreement not to operate in the same areas. Kresge took the Midwest, while Kress focused on the Southeast. This allowed them to avoid any confusion that might arise from their similar store names—S.S. Kresge and S.H. Kress.

A number of stores adopted similar formats: using their founder's first two initials and last name. In 1906, Boston-area businessman William Thomas Grant opened his first W.T. Grant discount store across the street from a Woolworth's and a Kresge store in Lynn, Massachusetts. But instead of limiting his price to nickels and dimes, Grant expanded his options by charging a quarter for some items. Grant also adopted a different approach to hiring than Woolworth's by pursuing college graduates, who filled 60 percent of the company's management slots in 1929.

By the mid-teens, Grant's approach had proved successful enough to create a chain of thirty stores with sales of $4.5 million, and by 1933, the Grant chain was the third largest in the country.

Other retailers also found success within the burgeoning discount marketplace. In 1911, John Newberry quit his position as an executive with Kress and teamed up with his brother Charles (an executive at Woolworth) to start the J.J. Newberry chain.

The Ben Franklin chain started off a little differently. It began in 1877 as a successful mail-order company called Butler Brothers and had built a customer base of 100,000 by the dawn of the twentieth century. As catalog sales started to wane, it followed a trajectory similar to Sears's by getting into the brick-and-mortar business in the mid-twenties. But instead of creating a mid-level department store, the way Sears did, the company changed its name and focused on discount products, adopting Benjamin Franklin's saying "A penny saved is a penny earned" as its motto.

Some Ben Franklin stores focused on crafts, such as needlepoint, quilting, scrapbooking, and sewing. The chain reached 2,500 stores at its peak and is now defunct, but two companies that survive today can trace their roots back to it. Sam Walton of Walmart fame was twenty-six when he opened his first store in 1945—a Ben Franklin in Newport, Arkansas. More than two decades later, in 1968, Michael Dupey bought a floundering Ben Franklin store in Dallas and appointed his son, Michael Jr., as manager. The younger Dupey brought in more craft supplies and eventually changed the name of the store to Michael's Arts and Crafts. By 2018, the company he founded had blossomed into the largest craft chain in the United States, operating more than 1,200 stores in forty-nine states and Canada.

Another notable five-and-dime chain was Sprouse-Reitz. Founded in 1909 in Tacoma, Washington, it grew at one point into a chain of 470 stores across eleven Western states. (A building in my hometown, Fresno, California, that once housed a Sprouse-Reitz store was later converted into a successful dinner theater.) The chain was still family owned in 1990 when it rebranded itself as Sprouse! and vowed to stop trying to be "all things to all people." Instead, it would focus on six specific areas—toys, housewares, crafts, home furnishings, family apparel, and paper products such as greeting cards and wrapping paper—even as CEO Robert Sprouse shopped around for a buyer.

"We can't have business as usual," he said.

But the new identity and tighter focus made little impact with the public and after the chain was, in fact, sold later in 1990, it survived just three more years before the last eighty-four stores were closed and liquidated.

It wasn't just Sprouse. The old five-and-dimes were clearly on their way out. It had been years since they'd even been five-and-dimes in anything more than name, anyway.

As inflation took its toll, many of the stores dropped the "five-and-dime" or "dime store" terminology and started calling themselves discount or variety stores instead. (Woolworth was among the last to drop the 10-cent limit, in 1932.) Although they were born mostly in rural areas, they soon invaded the big cities, finding a niche there as they challenged the big department stores' bargain basements. Woolworth opened stores in Brooklyn and the nation's capital; Kresge in Memphis and Detroit.

W.T. Grant stuck to rural areas until the twenties, and mid-market retailer J.C. Penney did the same: On the eve of the Depression, more than half of Penney's stores stores could be found in communities of 5,000 people or fewer. But even those two chains eventually established a presence in the nation's larger markets. Although hit by losses in the thirties, the businesses survived and, in some cases, thrived during the postwar period.

Many of the pioneers floundered in the twilight of the twentieth century, but they were replaced by others—no longer dime stores but dollar stores. Places like Dollar General, Dollar Tree, 99 Cents Only, and Family Dollar caught on during the Great Recession and continued to grow, although inflation meant that some offered items for more than a dollar, just as their predecessors had wound up selling goods for more than a dime.

Dollar General, which focused on rural areas, was operating a massive 15,000 stores in forty-five states as of 2018, replicating Woolworth's success of a century earlier.

The more things changed, the more they ultimately stayed the same.

The Woolworth store in Danville, Virginia, is vacant today, but this building on Main at Union Street was brand new when it opened in 1937. Stephen H. Provost, 2021.

8

SEPARATE AND UNEQUAL

As the retail world was changing, so was the world at large. But it was a gradual change, experienced in fits and starts, especially when it came to race relations.

Although many retailers were happy to accept money from black customers, most didn't want to see the customers themselves. They weren't outright banned from most stores, but they weren't sought after, either. Even in the North, stores largely ignored potential black patrons, and only Strawbridge & Clothier and Wanamaker's even bothered to advertise in Philadelphia's black newspapers. Once they walked through the doors, black customers were often treated like second-class shoppers, and the businesses didn't want them staying long. In the South, they had to use separate restrooms and separate drinking fountains, and at Rich's in Atlanta, they weren't allowed to try on apparel in the fitting rooms. Instead, they were forced to buy it, take it home, and then return it if it didn't fit.

The way department stores were set up made it easier for them to discriminate. Stores like Rich's, Burdines,

Four black college students started a revolution when they sat down at a "whites-only" Woolworth's lunch counter in Greensboro, North Carolina. From left: Joseph McNeil, Franklin McCain, Billy Smith, and Clarence Henderson. Public domain.

and Foley's weren't built on self-service like supermarkets or discount stores. You had to approach a sales associate for help and wait at a register in the department where you were shopping; there were no front-of-the-store cash registers. As a result, the sales staff had discretion about whom to help first. In the South, that meant *white* customers. Black patrons had to wait at the back of the line.

Another reason black patrons might not have felt comfortable there was no one looked like them on the other side of the counter. In 1946, Wanamaker's would hire black applicants for any job in the store except two: saleswoman and clerk. Translated: Wanamaker's didn't want black employees interacting with white customers, who they feared would be discouraged from shopping there. Wanamaker's personnel manager, Olive Leach, explained the rationale to Marjorie Swann and William

Hefner, who questioned the policy on behalf of the newly formed Congress of Racial Equality (CORE). Wanamaker's didn't want black employees to "scare off" customers. Leach appeared to think of "customers" exclusively as white patrons, which reflected a cold reality: The store didn't care about scaring off black patrons, because it wasn't interested in attracting them in the first place.

During the Depression, black picketers had protested in front of white-owned businesses that refused to hire them because of their race, vowing to boycott the stores. Their motto: "Don't buy where you can't work." As Wanamaker's policy made clear, the impact of that campaign had been minimal at best.

Black customers simply weren't valued, because most of them didn't have as much money to spend, and they were far more likely to shoplift than their white counterparts.

The Woolworth in Greensboro, North Carolina, where the first sit-in took place now houses the International Civil Rights Center and Museum. Stephen H. Provost, 2018.

Actually, that wasn't true. The stores simply believed it to be true. They saw what they wanted to see. A 1964 study of shoplifting in Chicago department stores during the forties found that black customers were "kept under much closer observation than whites" and juveniles were "under almost constant observation." The results were predictable. Black patrons were both detained by store security and referred to police at much higher levels than their white counterparts. Another study found more than two-thirds of suspected black shoplifters were turned over to police, compared with only half of whites.

In her meeting with Swann and Heftner, Leach argued that changes shouldn't be rushed and said she didn't expect to see black sales staff hired at the store during her lifetime. She passed the buck, saying the issue was out of her hands because the Market Street Store Managers Association had recently "decided against hiring Negro salesclerks." But she also sought to rationalize that decision by claiming that black women hired for other positions at the store during wartime had been "irresponsible," too frequently calling in with excuses for not coming to work. This, of course, overlooked the fact that the company continued to hire black employees for those "other" positions, just not for sales jobs.

Downtown department stores perpetuated the racist stereotypes that blacks were "lazy" and more likely to engage in criminal activity because their white patrons held those same stereotypes and put simply, they feared losing their core customers—shoppers who would soon desert them for the suburbs, anyway.

Meanwhile, the pressure continued to mount on society to change its ways, eventually coalescing around services and institutions that were visibly segregated: professional sports, public transportation, and lunch counters. Kenny Washington broke pro football's color barrier in 1946, and his former UCLA teammate Jackie Robinson did the same in baseball a year later. Rosa Parks refused to give up her seat on the bus in 1955, and five years later, black students refused to do the same at a Woolworth's lunch counter.

Sit-ins

Many remember the Woolworth's lunch counter fondly as part of a simpler time, when shopping included a midday stop for a grilled cheese sandwich or an ice cream sundae. But to others, the times were anything but simple, and the memories were anything but fond. Black patrons weren't allowed to sit, let alone eat, there or at most other retail cafés and lunch counters in the fifties.

But on February 1 of 1960, four black freshmen at North Carolina A&T sat down at the F.W. Woolworth counter on Elm Street in Greensboro and asked for a cup of coffee. They were refused service and asked to leave, but Ezell A. Blair Jr., Franklin E. McCain, Joseph A. McNeil, and David L. Richmond remained in their seats until closing time.

There was a reason college students were at the forefront of the protests, Blair—then seventeen years old—told the Associated Press that spring. "I don't like having to go to a separate section of a public place," he said. "Older Negroes have always put up with that because they were afraid of losing their jobs. As college students, we have no jobs to lose."

The following day, more students arrived to continue the protest, which swelled to 60 people by the third day and 300 on the fourth. The movement quickly spread to a lunch counter at the Kress five-and-dime in Greensboro, and after that to Winston-Salem, Durham, Raleigh, Charlotte, and beyond the North Carolina state line. Sit-ins took place in Baton Rouge, Louisiana; Charleston, South Carolina; Lexington, Kentucky; Nashville, Tennessee; and Richmond, Virginia, among other places.

At S.H. Kress in Charleston, someone phoned in a bomb threat, and the store manager asked twenty-four protesters to leave. They refused, and police arrested them on suspicion of trespassing. No bomb was ever found.

By April 28, more than 1,000 demonstrators had been arrested. But still, the segregationists held firm. Managers of the Kress and Woolworth stores in Greensboro rejected a compromise plan floated by city officials that would have allowed people of color to be served at a portion of the lunch counter, while reserving the rest for white customers.

The protests weren't limited to variety stores. They also targeted segregated lunch counters at major department stores such as Foley's in Houston and Burdines in Florida, where police barred entrance to eight black pastors in early March of 1960. Baptist minister Edward Graham, an imposing man at 6 feet 3 inches, objected when a store detective himself pushed past him: "Don't you push me around. Tell me who you are, and if you have any authority, I will respect it."

The officer, however, refused to identify himself: "You're blocking our way."

Graham: "Sir, you have been blocking our way for 300 years."

Carl Yaeger, a physician and associate minister from the same congregation, pulled out his metal Burdines Charga-Plate and asked if he would be allowed to go inside and use it. When he was denied, he crumpled the plate up in his fist and threw it to the ground, declaring, "I have no further use for this."

At Rich's in Knoxville, the basement snack bar was also "whites only," as were lunch counters a few blocks away in the main shopping district on Gay Street.

Knoxville's mayor worked toward a deal with city leaders in Nashville and Chattanooga to end segregation at lunch counters in those cities, but the stores themselves demurred, saying they needed approval from corporate headquarters. So, the mayor took his campaign over their heads, traveling to New York with the president of Knoxville College and two black students to present his case to company leaders. The bigwigs, however, refused to even see them.

Soon, sit-ins began at Rich's, W.T. Grant, Sears, S.H. Kress, and other Knoxville businesses, but Rich's tried to keep protesters away from its lunch counter by building

Lunch counter sit-ins quickly spread to other five-and-dimes and department stores with segregated service, including this Kress store just down the street from Woolworth in Greensboro. Stephen H. Provost, 2018.

a barricade around it, leaving only a narrow entrance. A Knoxville College professor and student managed do make it through, anyway, and conducted a forty-five-minute sit-in, but the store responded by closing the area altogether and removing the stools. Black customers moved their protest upstairs to the sit-down Laurel Room, but those waiting to be served there were simply ignored.

More than two weeks later, on June 27, several hundred protesters gathered outside Rich's, carrying signs with messages like "We just can't shop on an empty stomach" and "Rich's likes our dollars . . . standing up!!" One man grabbed three signs from the protesters and smashed them over his knee; a teenager splashed water from the store's fountain on demonstrators; several eggs were thrown, and one of them hit a student from the University of Tennessee.

The following month, five downtown stores agreed to integrate their lunch counters, but Rich's stood firm until October, when it finally relented—temporarily. It promptly reversed course again after Martin Luther King Jr. was arrested during a Magnolia Tea Room sit-in at the Atlanta flagship store. King vowed "jail instead of bail" after being arrested with dozens of other protesters; all were charged with violating a three-year-old misdemeanor statute by refusing to leave private property upon request. Just three months later, Rich's announced it was leaving Knoxville altogether. At a court hearing, King said his family had spent $4,500 at Rich's in 1959, adding that "we are welcome at all counters but the lunch counter."

Just three months later, Rich's announced it was pulling out of the Knoxville market, selling its six-year-old building to local rival Miller's. If the lunch counter protests had any role to play in the decision, the company didn't say, only declaring that it wanted to focus on expansion closer to its base in Atlanta.

There's no doubt, however, that Southern stores were loath to change their ways. When Sears started sending out its catalog in the 1890s, it proved to be a great equalizer because anyone could order from one. No one at the Sears warehouse in Chicago was checking on the color of a recipient's skin; a black customer could order the same jacket or dress or hat as a white customer, no questions asked, and get it in the same amount of time.

Some store owners were so livid they burned Sears catalogs in public bonfires to protest the equal access to merchandise they allowed black customers to enjoy. They even spread a rumor that Richard Sears and Aaron Montgomery Ward were black; this was, supposedly, the reason they didn't include their photos in the catalogs bearing their names. (They responded by doing exactly that.)

If they couldn't keep black customers from getting the catalog, they tried to keep them from ordering any merchandise, especially in rural areas.

"If they controlled the mail service, as they did in many small towns, then they would refuse to sell stamps to black people," Cornell professor Louis Hyman explained. "They would refuse to sell them money orders or even write purchase requests, since so many people were illiterate." This kind of interference happened so often that the catalog included a section telling customers how to deal directly with the post office—and encouraging them to do so:

"Just give the money to the mail carrier, and he will get the money order at the post office and mail the letter for you."

Woolworth, meanwhile, finally allowed its lunch counter in Greensboro to desegregate, but only after the store suffered an estimated $200,000 in losses. (The site is now preserved as the International Civil Rights Center and Museum.) Other Woolworths followed suit, along with Kresge and Grant stores in Norfolk and Portsmouth, Virginia, but some lunch counters persisted in refusing service to people of color for some five years. Rich's in Atlanta, for example, didn't integrate its Magnolia Room until the summer of 1961. It wasn't until two years later that Loveman's department store did so along with other shops in Birmingham, Alabama. Two weeks after that, a white customer dropped a smoke bomb in a trash can, and the building had to be evacuated after the gas got into the ventilation system and reached all four stories. Twenty-two people were taken to the hospital.

Karen Redding, from Franklinville, North Carolina, remembers going shopping at the nearby Greensboro Woolworth's with her grandparents as a child.

"There were no Walmarts or malls," she said. "We regularly went downtown to the stores there and to the Woolworth's, and ate at the now-famous lunch counter.

"I remember the merchandise counters that were even with my eyes. They were like tables with short sides around their edges to keep the merchandise from falling off. There were no shopping carts, and I walked around with either Grandma or Grandpa, but usually her, as they shopped—or, rather, she did. (He usually found a seat to sit on somewhere and smoked his pipe and observed the other shoppers.) I can see it all vividly from my five-year-old perspective. And I will never forget, and will be forever grateful for, them teaching me about the awesome history that it held, and what it meant. I treasure these memories and the fact that I actually ate at that very same lunch counter with the two people who had the most influence on who I am today."

She added: "In a world surrounded by prejudice, they [my grandparents] taught me so much about acceptance. Of everyone regardless of their race, religion, sexual orientation. They taught me that every person is valuable and has something to offer. They instilled in me a love for learning and a thirst for knowledge."

Woolworth's survived the controversy and continued to prosper. At its pinnacle, Woolworth was opening a new store every seventeen days. In the late seventies, it was bigger than Sears, Montgomery Ward, or any other retailer in the world.

9

SPEND MORE, SAVE MORE

Sales and discounts have always played huge roles in the culture of the American department store. From bargain basements in the big cities to Blue Light Specials at Kmart, retailers have always looked for new ways to accomplish the same old goal: attract customers by promising them more for less and by offering them creative ways to pay.

One of those ways was credit cards. If you watched *The Flintstones* in the sixties, you might remember a scene in which Wilma and Betty shout, "Charge it!"—then run to the store to do just that. At the time (the sixties, not the Stone Age), credit cards were relatively new; buying on credit, however, had been around a long time.

"'Charge it, please.' That's all you have to say," read a 1935 newspaper ad in extolling the virtues of an innovation called Charga-Plate, which evolved from charge coins used in the nineteenth and early twentieth centuries.

The first charge coins were made of plastic, but later versions were typically fashioned from copper, steel, or aluminum. Department stores started issuing them about 1865, and they were still in use during the Depression.

An old, rusted sign inviting the use of BankAmericard, the predecessor of Visa, still hung outside the closed Shamrock Dinners restaurant in Northern California recently. Stephen H. Provost, 2016.

Compared to credit cards, they were pretty simple: no chips, metallic strips, or personal information. Not even the customer's name. Just a number on the back of what otherwise looked like a dog tag (some even had a hole punched in the top so they could be attached to a key ring, just as some plastic loyalty cards do today).

Charge coins were usually round but came in other shapes, too. They made it easy for stores to look up a customer's account by cross-referencing the numbers with their records. Unfortunately, they also made it easy to rip people off—especially as cities got bigger. When charge coins first appeared, most store employees recognized the customers who frequented their business. They probably even went to church with Mrs. Thomas or had taken tea with Mrs. Jones. But then cities grew and stores began to serve people traveling via that new innovation called the motorcar—people from outside the immediate neighborhood. By the turn of the century, Boston was a city of more than half a million people, and it was no longer possible to know every customer by sight.

This made it a simple matter for anyone who came into possession of a charge coin to use it, no questions asked. If you found it lying on the street, you could pick it up and take it to the store that had issued it, the name of which was embossed in a seal on the coin. Identity fraud was a problem back then, too.

The lost-and-found section of the *Brooklyn Eagle* in 1907 contained a classified ad seeking the return of a purse containing money and a Wanamaker charge coin. No word on whether the purse was returned, but chances were equally good that the money and charge coin would have been removed if it was.

In 1931, a Boston woman spent three days in the hospital and gave her housekeeper a charge coin to buy a bathrobe and a pair of slippers. Not only did the housekeeper make those purchases, she also spent $315 on a fur jacket, a dress, some jewelry, and toys for herself. She was convicted of larceny, told to make restitution, and sentenced to an indefinite term at the Home of the Good Shepherd, in lieu of a stay at the women's reformatory.

To guard against fraud, some department stores started asking customers to confirm their identity verbally at the cash register, slowing service as patrons spelled their names, provided their addresses, and so forth.

FROM CHARGA-PLATES TO CREDIT CARDS

Clearly, a better system was needed. Enter the Charga-Plate, a product introduced in 1928 by Farrington Manufacturing. These rectangular pieces of metal came with a vinyl or leather sleeve and contained a good deal more customer information than a charge coin, such as the cardholder's name and address in raised lettering on the front

This ad for Charga-Plates appeared in the *Boston Globe* in 1934. Unlike modern credit cards, you couldn't carry a balance; the entire debt had to be paid at the end of each month.

of the card, which could be used to make an impression on the sales slip. The cards were also backed with a piece of thin cardboard with a place for the customer's signature, and merchants made notches in the metal to indicate the month in which they'd been used. This was important because they weren't credit cards in the modern sense: You couldn't carry over a balance; you had to pay it all off at the end of the month (or weekly, if you preferred).

Another safeguard against fraud, available at Bloomingdale's, was the "planned charge account" that allowed cardholders to limit purchases to any amount up to $30 a month, thus eliminating the threat of a thief using the cards to run up hundreds of dollars in debt.

An ad for Horne's Department Store in the 1935 *Pittsburgh Press* called the Charga-Plate the "latest innovation" in shopping convenience. "It does away with giving name and address, and the possibility . . . [of] misspelling, when making a charge purchase. You simply hand your Charga-Plate to the clerk. It requires the salesperson only a few seconds to automatically print your name and address on the sales check, and to return the plate with a 'Thank you.'"

The ad was sure to point out that the cards were available in Pittsburgh exclusively at Horne's, but a number of stores in Boston took a different approach. Instead of going it alone, they banded together in 1934 to accept the same Charga-Plate at all their locations. Seven stores were part of the agreement, including two major department stores: Filene's and R.H. White, which occupied a five-story building on Washington Street that Filene's had purchased six years earlier.

The stores advertised ten "cardinal virtues" of the Charga-Plate, emphasizing security and convenience. Most importantly:

"You are sure YOUR purchases and ONLY your purchases go on the bill."

"You don't need to spell out your correct name and address, repeat correct and so forth."

"You are protected against others using your account."

"You don't have to announce who you are in public."

The stores maintained that it took just one-fifth as long to pay by Charga-Plate as it did with a traditional charge coin. And, because several stores accepted the same card, "you no longer have to dig in your bag for this, that, or the other coin." You could even have separate plates for every family member "to avoid family arguments," and having the correct address on the card helped ensure prompt and correct home deliveries.

Charga-Plates remained in use through the fifties, but businesses kept looking for ways to improve on the process. One of their most important goals—creating a card that could be used anywhere.

The first step in that direction came in 1946, thanks to a man named John Biggins. He wasn't a department store guy, but a banker working for Flatbush National Bank in New York. He came up with a card called Charg-It that allowed local stores to offer credit to the bank's customers. The bank was effectively using the card as a means of lending money to consumers (who would have to repay it with interest). It was a good deal for consumers, who expanded their buying power throughout the Flatbush neighborhood. It was a good deal for the stores, because the bank took on the task of collecting cardholders' debt. And it was a good deal for the bank, which collected interest on that debt.

But the card was limited, because the bank's clientele was strictly limited to the Flatbush area.

More widely used was the Diners Club card, created in 1949 after a businessman named Frank McNamara forgot his wallet while out to dinner with clients. His wife, fortunately, had remembered to bring *her* wallet and was able to pick up the check. Embarrassed at his own absentmindedness, McNamara came up with a solution: a cardboard card he called Diners Club. The following year, he returned to the restaurant and used the card to pay the tab. (The legend conveniently overlooks the fact that the card—had it existed—would have been left behind with the forgotten wallet a year earlier.)

But there was another advantage of using the card: It established a paper trail. Business professionals were now automatically given receipts they could use to document expenses with the IRS.

Launching Diners Club was no easy task. It took an investment of $250,000, and the initiative made just $1,200 in billing during its first month.

Bank of America test-marketed the first-of-its-kind credit card in Fresno, California, in 1958. Stephen H. Provost, 2014.

At the outset, twenty-seven restaurants signed on to accept the card, which was distributed to 200 of McNamara's friends for a modest membership fee of $3. By the end of 1951, its ranks had swollen to 60,000, and the cost of membership had risen to $5. Still, Diners Club made the bulk of its money from the 7 percent fee it charged establishments for using the card to accept transactions. At that point, 700 restaurants, hotels, and car-rental agencies were taking payments via the card. Billing via Diners Club had reached $700,000.

"It saves the customers the trouble of carrying around cash, and it saves restaurant owners a lot of bookkeeping and the bother of collecting bad debts," McNamara said. "It's so simple that at least 25 people have told me they had the same idea before me, but they didn't follow through."

While Diners Club remained popular with business professionals, most of the charges went for travel expenses, entertainment, and, of course, dining. American Express introduced a similar card in 1958, but both cards required holders to pay their entire balance every month. That same year, however, Bank of America had a different idea. It conducted a large-scale test to see whether the public was ready for a national credit card that would work at all kinds of businesses. Unlike Diners Club, there wouldn't be an annual fee for cardholders, but merchants would have to pay Bank of America 6 percent of each purchase price. Another difference: Users would be able to carry over their balances from one month to the next, as long as they made a minimum monthly payment.

The ideal guinea pig for this experiment was Fresno, California, a middle-size city with the kind of middle-class clientele that the bank wanted to target. So, it sent 60,000 residents of the city—nearly half its population—a piece of plastic in the mail. The BankAmericard, as it was called, came with no strings attached. You didn't have to prequalify. You didn't even need to fill out an application. The card itself simply appeared in mailboxes, with an invitation to start using it. Each person got a credit limit of $300 to $500 to spend however they wished at any of the 300 merchants that had signed up to be part of the experiment.

There wasn't much publicity surrounding the test, and the bank probably wanted it that way. That's another reason it made more sense to "drop" the card in Fresno, not Los Angeles or New York. If it made a big splash and the idea didn't work, the bank's reputation might be tarnished, and it wouldn't be able to go back to the drawing board and try again without added public scrutiny.

But the plan *did* work—so well, in fact, that it was quickly implemented in Stockton and Sacramento, then ultimately rolled out across California in 1959. A year later, some 30,000 merchants were accepting the card from almost a million Americans, and after two and a half years, the card was turning a profit.

In 1966, Wells Fargo and three other California-based banks announced plans to form a competing card called Master Charge. The new card was to be tied into the Interbank Card, which was being offered by New York's Marine Midland Bank; altogether, the new card was backed by $17 billion in deposits, just slightly less than BankAmericard's $17.5 billion.

Coincidentally (or not), Bank of America opened its own program up to other banks that same year, and BofA president Rudolph Peterson declared the "great credit card race" was on.

In the next two years forty more banks started issuing the BankAmericard. By 1970, more than 100 million cards were in circulation, and a few years later, the multibank program rechristened itself as Visa. Master Charge became MasterCard in 1979. Meanwhile, individual department stores were issuing their own credit cards, which were less flexible but helped encourage customer loyalty.

One of them, Sears, tested its Discover Card in Atlanta in 1985 and then rolled it out nationwide. Distinguishing itself from Visa and MasterCard, it offered a "cash back" incentive, refunding a small percentage of the total amount a customer charged on the card at the end of each year. Sears president and CEO Edward Brennan predicted: "Consumers will be attracted because Discover will help them save—as well as spend and invest."

By 1978, when this photo was taken, Kmart virtually dominated the retail landscape, its stores anchoring strip centers across the country. This one was in New Orleans, but nearly identical buildings could be found in hundreds of other cities and towns. Phillip Pessar, 1978. Creative Commons 2.0 license: https://creativecommons.org/licenses/by-sa/2.0.

Because of Sears's broad national footprint, Discover had a built-in advantage over other would-be "universal" cards. Another plus: It was the only card accepted by Sam's Club, the membership store affiliated with Walmart. Brennan had other reasons to be optimistic that the card would turn a profit quickly, citing surveys that found 38 percent of Sears cardholders had agreed to sign up for one, and that nearly one-third of those who didn't have a Sears card would welcome it. But the card wasn't a financial boon for Sears, which lost $25.8 million in the first quarter of 1987, up from $22 million the previous quarter. Six years later, it sold Discover Card and got out of the financial services business.

LAYAWAYS AND BLUE LIGHT SPECIALS

During the Depression, department stores started experimenting with the concept of layaway. This allowed customers to reserve an item for purchase, make payments over a set period of time, and then pick it up when the item was paid off. Even as the economy improved, layaway remained an option at many retailers until credit cards made it less attractive. Why wait to take that TV home with you when you could put it on plastic and cart it away the same afternoon?

From the eighties onward, few retailers saw any reason to continue the practice, which required warehouse space and employee time. Kmart and a handful of others did, and it enjoyed a brief resurgence in the early twenty-first century when the Great Recession killed off credit as an option for many consumers. Mostly, it was the province of large-scale discounters and closeout chains such as T.J. Maxx, Marshalls, and Burlington Coat Factory.

Kmart was known (and sometimes mocked) for its Blue Light Specials, the brainchild of a twenty-four-year-old assistant manager named Earl Bartell. He wasn't trying to start a marketing revolution; he just wanted to help customers find Christmas wrapping paper in his Fort Wayne, Indiana, store. The year was 1965. Bartell had ordered the paper, but it wasn't selling, so he hit on the idea of holding a fifteen-minute special sale, marking the price down from 86 to 56 cents. Unfortunately, he had stocked the paper on a different aisle than the regular Christmas paper, so customers were having a hard time finding it. So, Bartell took a flashing lantern from the sporting goods section, strapped it to a two-by-four, and taped it to a stock cart. "Everybody went to the right place," he told the Akron Beacon Journal in 2001. "I thought, that's not a bad idea."

Bartell refined his idea a week later by installing a police light atop a pipe and attaching it to a 12-volt battery. What many people don't know is that the original light was red. The color was too jarring, however, so it was changed to amber, then to blue.

He tracked the results and reported them to the company, and within six months, Kmart had adopted Blue Light Specials across the chain. His reward for this classic bit of ingenuity? Company headquarters sent him $25.

It wasn't long before the promotion became part of American culture. Accompanied by the legendary loud-speaker announcement, "Attention, Kmart shoppers . . . ," the flashing blue light was a signal to make a beeline for a particular aisle that was offering a brief mini-sale on a particular item.

Honolulu Advertiser reporter Will Hoover described it as "that brief interlude when prices on items in one part of a Kmart store are drastically reduced and shoppers are whipped into a needing frenzy."

Hoover quoted regional manager Dale Fishell's impression of a typical Blue Light Special: "Attention, Kmart shoppers. For the next 10 minutes in our cosmetics department, we've got a blue light special on Crest toothpaste—while it lasts!—regularly priced at $2.20, we've got it on special for a buck eighty-eight! Come on over!"

Blue Light Specials encouraged two things. First, they got the customer into the store. You had to be there in order to take advantage of the sales, which lasted only a few minutes each. You didn't know what was going to go on sale and when, unless the store gave you a heads-up in the morning newspaper. For instance, a 1969 ad in Port Huron, Michigan, touted fifteen-minute Blue Light Specials every hour throughout the day one Saturday, listing big price cuts on (among other things) beach bags at noon, Acme exterior house paint at 2 p.m., and Kodak Instamatic cameras at 7.

The first sale of the day was on one group of gold polished wrought-iron Italian provincial table lamps. Regular price $12.96 to $13.96, on sale for just $5. That

A sign promises S&H Green Stamps to customers of a now-abandoned gas station along Route 66 in Valentine, Arizona. Stephen H. Provost, 2019.

particular special was limited to the first ten customers, which brings us to the second consequence of Blue Light Specials: stampedes to procure the sale-priced items.

In one case, there was a literal run on Crest toothpaste, which was marked down to a nickel a tube as long as fifty tubes would last. "People were pushing and shoving, and 50 tubes lasted all of two seconds," said William Reynolds, district manager for west Texas and southern New Mexico. According to legend, another Blue Light Special resulted in chaos when customers armed themselves with ironing boards.

Blue Light Specials became so ingrained in popular culture that they spawned an independently produced album from blues singer-pianist Kelley Hunt and her band, the Kinetics. Lyrics to the song "Discount Store" from the album poked fun at "how all these shoppers . . . made a beeline for these specials." She described it as

"sort of mayhem" and compared it to "a sound like the theme song from *Jaws*, where all these shoppers are . . . 'I gotta get that.'"

The Blue Light Special even spawned a board game that Kmart carried in 800 of its stores during the late eighties. Designed by a former toll-road dispatcher named Larry Johnson, it was described as a "standard board game in which the player tosses a die, selects a card and moves the blue light icon a specified distance around the board."

Blue Light Specials were discontinued in 1991 but have been revived periodically since then, in 2001, 2005, 2009, and 2015—when they were also offered online.

Trading stamps

If Blue Light Specials were designed to get customers into the store, another sales gimmick was meant to keep them coming back. Loyalty rewards are still a standard at places like grocery stores, many of which offer "rewards cards"; and coffee shops distribute punch cards that give you a free cuppa joe on your tenth visit. Hotels.com even has an online incentive that gives users who book rooms through the site a free night's stay after they've made ten reservations.

The first widespread use of loyalty rewards, however, came in the form of something called trading stamps, and a department store was the first to use them. Ed Schuster had started Schuster's department store in Milwaukee in 1883 and was looking for a way to keep patrons coming back. It came in the form of what he called Blue Trading Stamps. Customers received one for every dime they spent at Schuster's, pasted them into a booklet, and exchanged them for items carried by the store.

The program expanded, and Schuster's stamps were offered at more than 300 outlets, including food markets, butchers, service stations, and hardware stores.

A Michigan silverware salesman named Thomas Sperry who traveled to Milwaukee on business got wind of the idea and took it a step further. What if he were to start his own stamp company and recruit a number of retailers to participate? The stamps would offer customers at these stores an incentive to shop there, but they'd redeem the stamps with Sperry's company rather than at the stores themselves. Shelly Hutchinson, a Michigan businessman, liked the idea enough to back Sperry's idea and, in 1896, S&H Green Stamps (for Sperry and Hutchinson) were born.

The company opened its first redemption center, called a "premium parlor," a year later in Bridgeport, Connecticut. Retailers quickly signed on, and the company was such a success that it had accumulated capital of $1 million after just eight years in business.

That kind of success, predictably, spawned imitators, and trading stamp companies quickly sprang up across the country. An ad in the *Buffalo Evening* included this anecdote about a dental patient in January 1905.

"One moment, doctor," said the woman in the dentist's chair. "I am not sure I can stand the pain. Folks have died in the dentist's chair. Don't you think I would better wait until tomorrow?"

"Madame," sternly replied the dentist as he winked at his assistant, "let me say that I am giving 300 trading stamps to every woman who has a tooth pulled today, and the offer won't hold good tomorrow! Therefore"—

"Therefore go ahead and pull it as quickly as you can!" she said, as she leaned back and opened her mouth and shut her eyes.

Trading stamps were all the rage among consumers, but there was a downside. If a company went out of business, people were left with books of now-worthless stamps. When news broke that a stamp company called Benedict & McFarlane had gone belly-up in the spring of 1905, it caused a run on the company's New York redemption center.

According to a report in the *Chicago Tribune*, a crowd "besieged the [company's store] and finally became so insistent that police reserves were called out. Excited women from Staten Island, Jersey City, Brooklyn, and other places flocked to the store with stamp books, eager to redeem them before Benedict & McFarlane's supply of desks, baby carriages, chairs, and numberless other articles gave out."

The throng was so insistent that the company stationed guards at the door and let only three women in at a time. Some of the voices heard amid the chaos:

"Stop pushing me!"

"I didn't push you!"

"I got here before you. It's my turn to go in!"

"They're tearing the baby carriages all to pieces!"

Things only got worse, and customers had claimed so much of the store's stock by late afternoon that an employee emerged to post a sign: "This store closed on account of taking stock." The women responded by rushing the door in what the article described as "a sort of flying wedge," but they were rebuffed by the employee, who was able to bolt the door shut before they could gain access. By this time, all that remained inside were large pieces of furniture too big to be carried away.

Established just two years earlier, in 1903, the company had set up shop in Baltimore, Boston, Chicago, Denver, St. Louis, and elsewhere. Its demise provided fodder for the critics of trading stamps, who argued that trading stamps were a boondoggle. The stamps became the bitcoin of their day, attracting scalpers and profiteers seeking to make a quick buck at customers' expense.

But you never got something for nothing. Retailers had to buy the stamps from companies like S&H, and the cost of doing so forced them to raise their prices. Some retailers made a point of telling customers they were able to offer low prices because they *didn't* give out the stamps. J.N. Adam in Buffalo ran an ad declaring "no trading stamp prices here."

"We sell the best; we sell the most; we charge the least because we do not pay for trading stamps—nor do you, if you buy here."

Two ads in a New Jersey newspaper appeared on top of one another in April of 1905. Woodhull & Martin touted "no trading stamps . . . but extra values" while S. Mann offered free green, red, gold, and blue stamps.

Some retailers continued to offer the stamps while looking for ways around the cost of carrying them. They turned to scalpers, who fished discarded stamps out of trash cans and bought them for pennies from customers who didn't plan to use them. These unscrupulous types then resold the stamps at a discount to stores under contract to offer them. It saved the stores money and allowed them to hold prices down, but it wasn't any good for the stamp companies, which didn't make any money off such under-the-table deals. They quickly learned to destroy any unused stamps instead of throwing them in the trash.

States from Kansas to Wisconsin to Idaho sought, at various times, to ban or heavily tax the stamps as a means of unfair competition. Trade associations, unions, and some merchants opposed them.

In Paducah, Kentucky, the Retail Merchants Association took out a full-page newspaper ad in 1955 condemning the stamps as "playing on the housewife's weakness for giveaways" and quoting a study that found most retailers had to raise their prices by 4 percent to cover the expense of carrying them.

When Wyoming introduced a bill to outlaw them that same year, supermarket owner E.H. Hatch argued that consumers not only wound up paying for the stamps, but that the profits ended up out of state. Stamp companies reaped the windfall because 30 to 50 percent of the stamps were never redeemed, he argued. On top of that, if all the retailers in town felt pressured to carry the stamps, no one would have any advantage—or any increase in revenues. They'd be right back where they started, except now they'd be dealing with the extra cost of carrying "those little pieces of gummed paper." Promises of a 15 to 20 percent bump in business were fiction, according to Hatch, and the stamp companies were the only ones making a profit.

Consumers, however, loved the stamps. In a hearing on the Wyoming case, an attorney claimed to represent "the 25,000 Cheyenne housewives who want trading stamps."

Opponents said he was really working for S&H.

He denied it.

Lawmakers claimed to have received more mail about the legislation than any other bill, which passed the state senate by a single vote but was killed in the house. That wasn't the end of it, though, as a new stamp ban was introduced—and passed—in Wyoming four years later. The stamp companies promptly sued in an attempt to nullify it, but the state's high court upheld it, with the chief justice writing that "the lure of trading stamps is an evil, and the legislature has every right to suppress it."

As early as 1916, the US Supreme Court had agreed, calling the stamps "an appeal to stupidity," but some states hesitated to outlaw them because of their popularity and courts in other states struck down laws restricting them. The Iowa Supreme Court, for example, ruled that stamp bans were "unnecessary restrictions on the right of contract" and interfered with "a natural right to attract custom." They were, the court found, "not the proper exercise of police powers."

Amid all the controversy and legal maneuvering, the stamp trade grew and flourished—especially after World War II. Stamps had begun as a department store gimmick, but more and more, they were being marketed through grocers, drugstores, and gas stations. In 1958, according to one estimate, stamps were used in as many as half of supermarket food purchases. The founder of Big Bear Stores, Wayne Brown, started his own trading stamp company called Buckeye Stamps, distributing orange-and-blue stamps that could be turned in at a redemption center in downtown Columbus, Ohio.

In 1960, there were 200 to 400 trading stamp companies, an estimated 77 percent of American families were saving the stamps, and firms reported gross income of $650 million. That figured passed the $1 billion mark five years later. One company offered such pricey items as Cadillacs, powerboats, and mink stoles in exchange for the stamps, which were used to buy school buses and planes for Christian missionaries abroad; church pipe organs; and even two gorillas for the zoo in Erie, Pennsylvania.

S&H remained the industry leader, with 560 redemption centers in the sixties. I remember seeing one on Shields Avenue, west of Blackstone, when I was growing up in Fresno, California. Overall, the six largest companies accounted for more than 80 percent of the business. Other leading firms included King Korn and Gold Bond. Blue Chip Stamps accounted for about three-quarters of the stamp business in California; Top Value Stamps were popular in the Midwest, and Plaid Stamps in the East.

The stamp companies' decline began with the oil crisis of the early seventies. Gas stations, strapped for cash, stopped offering them, and supermarkets turned to other strategies: rewards cards, in-house games, double coupons, and so on. By 1999, only 100 stores were still offering S&H Green Stamps. The last trading stamp company, Eagle Stamps, was out of business by 2008, although S&H remains in business online as S&H Greenpoints. As of 2017, the program allowed people to convert their old Green Stamps into Greenpoints (two stamps could be exchanged for one point), but only if they had at least sixty full books of stamps.

10

SUPERMARKET SPREE

At first blush, grocers and department stores might seem to be like apples and oranges—or perhaps apples and leisurewear. Still, they share a common heritage—the old-fashioned general store—and even when they tried to go their separate ways, they never quite got over each other. Downtown department stores tried to be all things to all people. In addition to selling apparel, jewelry, fragrances, furniture, and just about everything else, most were in the food business. In addition to their tea rooms and restaurants, Jordan Marsh sold famous blueberry muffins from its bakery and Bamberger's had its Fruitador line.

Food shops were slow to catch up.

Nonetheless, grocery sales evolved along much the same lines as dry-goods retailing had in the latter half of the nineteenth century.

Just as immigrants like Adam Gimbel had started out as itinerant peddlers in that era, a new wave of immigrants—this time from Western Europe—gravitated to the grocery business as food-cart vendors in the early wentieth century. But unlike a dry-goods salesman, who might travel hundreds of miles in search of customers, they generally stayed close to home. The produce they sold was perishable and couldn't be taken long distances, and they usually weren't welcomed outside the ethnic neighborhoods they served.

Piggly Wiggly, the nation's first self-service market, remains in business today and has more than 500 stores in seventeen states as of 2019. This one is on U.S. Highway 58 near Danville, Virginia. Stephen H. Provost, 2018.

The corner grocer, which evolved from the old greengrocer, could still be found in many places during the Depression, when supermarkets were just taking off. This one in Grundy Center, Iowa, put produce front and center, offering potatoes for 21 cents a peck. Library of Congress, 1939.

Supermarkets, as such, didn't even exist before the Great Depression. If you wanted canned goods, you could get them at the corner grocer, but you had to make separate stops to pick up meat (at the deli or butcher shop), bread and baked goods (at the bakery), or fruits and vegetables (at the greengrocer).

The dominant grocer of the early twentieth century, the A&P, was the opposite of a supermarket. Most locations were in narrow, confined spaces on side streets and had only a couple of employees.

The format worked well and helped the chain expand to the West Coast by the early thirties, finally living up to its name—the Great Atlantic and Pacific Tea Company—more than seven decades after it took that name. It sold a lot more than warm beverages by that point (like some other early grocers, it had started as a mail-order tea business). But it still was a small corner grocer carrying mostly canned and boxed goods and not much in the way of produce.

What set it apart was the scope of the business. In 1930, it was the nation's largest retailer with nearly 16,000 stores. A&P's strategy was more like Starbucks than Marshall Field's: Instead of focusing on a few huge

locations, it wanted a store on virtually every corner—and in some places, it achieved that goal. By 1921, there were 98 A&P outlets in Chicago alone, including one on every block in a four-block stretch of Ponce de Leon Avenue. At its peak, A&P had more US stores than either Starbucks or McDonald's hamburgers (about 14,000 each) had in 2017, at a time when the US population was just one-third as large.

As late as 1965, A&P was still the largest retailer in the country. Its initial success helped mark the ascent of a new kind of retailer: the chain store. This concept had already gained traction among five-and-dimes such as Kress and Woolworth's and was spreading to department stores as well (Sears and Montgomery Ward would open up hundreds of stores during the 1920s).

The chains promoted themselves as modern, clean, and predictable. One store in a chain could be counted on to carry the same brands, offer the same layout, and provide the same level of service as the next. The chains also marketed themselves as thoroughly *American*, in contrast to the street vendors and mom-and-pop shops run by immigrants. Christine Frederick, writing in the June 1925 issue of *Chain Store Age*, maligned the

This is what the Piggly Wiggly in Memphis, Tennessee, looked like a century ago. Customers entered at left, zigzagged through the store aisles, and then paid at the checkstand, center. Library of Congress.

typical owner of such a businesses as "a dirty, illiterate, short-sighted, half-Americanized foreigner, or a sleepy, narrow-minded, dead-from-the-neck-up American."

Increasingly strict limits on street vendors in the twenties and thirties curtailed street peddlers, and the chains took a heavy toll on mom-and-pop stores, but new generations of immigrants have continued to gravitate toward such businesses. The large number of South Asian immigrants operating convenience stores in the early twenty-first century earned a send-up from *The Simpsons*, where an Indian American character was introduced as owner of the fictional Kwik-E-Mart. In the Southwest, taco trucks run by Latino immigrants emerged during the same period as an alternative to corporate fast-food outlets like Taco Bell.

Today's chains have lobbied against taco trucks and other mobile food vendors. A 2008 ordinance in Los Angeles County threatened such vendors with $1,000 and six months in jail if they stayed parked in a single location for more than an hour—or returned sooner

than four hours later. In the same way, food peddlers in the thirties faced ever-expanding "no peddling" zones in Chicago and an outright ban in New York.

But the chains faced opposition, too, especially when their policies ran afoul of local customs and traditions. When A&P decided to flout local ordinances in Ohio and Wisconsin by staying open on Armistice Day in 1930, a group of "Merchants' Minute Men" from the American Legion protested outside, decrying what they called "foreign-owned" chain stores. A North Carolina mayor threatened to fire city employees seen shopping at a chain store, and a group in Nashville offered prizes to high school students who wrote an essay on "Why My Parents Trade with the Independent Merchant."

PIGGLY WIGGLY

Chain stores, however, were here to stay.

The next big development in grocery shopping took place in 1916, thanks to a store with the rather humorous name Piggly Wiggly. The origin of the singsong name is a bit of a mystery; according to one story, founder Clarence Saunders simply wanted a quirky name so people would "ask that very question."

What wasn't in question was Saunders's foresight in creating the system that made Piggly Wiggly a success: self-service. Until that time, shoppers had relied on clerks to measure out dry goods like sugar, flour, coffee beans, spices, and baking powder. This was both time consuming for the customer and expensive for the store. Patrons had to wait their turn to be served, and the store had to pay a large number of employees to weigh and package the goods.

When Saunders opened his first store, he hired fewer clerks; those who were on duty politely declined to help shoppers pick out their food. Instead, customers were directed to a pile of wicker baskets in which they would collect the items they wanted as they moved throughout the store.

"His disdain for clerks is palpable—nothing can be allowed to stand in between 'Mrs. Consumer' and the goods on the shelf," explained Paul Gilmore, history professor at Fresno City College and an expert on the evolution of retail grocery stores. "Salespeople were seen as only encouraging resistance" to buying. A clerk standing between a customer and an impulse buy made that customer think twice—and perhaps decide *against* laying down her money.

"With salespeople removed from the floor, and the shopper doing the [formerly paid] work of compiling orders for free, there was an incentive built in to encourage the shopper to linger, even get lost, through the placement of items and the enticement of spontaneous sales. That left the check stand [as] the only place on the sales floor where actual paid clerks came into contact with customers." TThose clerks "should do as little of the work as possible—just add up the price, collect money, and make change."

Not only would Saunders's self-service system become the model for supermarkets across the country, it would also be used by discount department stores when they began to proliferate at mid-century.

At its Memphis opening in 1916, Piggly Wiggly admitted that "we don't expect to appeal to everybody's taste."

"But if you want to trade with a store that has cut out all the frills of merchandising and a store that offers food products to you minus the expense of credit, minus booking, minus clerks as salesmen, minus useless waste of paper and twine, minus delivery expense entirely. . . . If you do really want to get groceries at prices minus all of this wasteful expense, then The Piggly Wiggly will suit you."

There were a couple of extra fees. Shoppers had to pay three cents for a take-home basket (not to be confused with a shopping cart, which had yet to be invented) and were also charged for paper bags, depending on how big they were. If they'd been shopping somewhere else beforehand, they couldn't carry their packages with them while they shopped but had to leave them at the door.

Everything in the store was prepackaged; nothing had to be measured out or weighed ahead of time, whether it be bacon or butter or tomatoes. It was like fast food for the grocery shopper. The owner of Big Bear Stores, the first supermarket in the Midwest, had workers down in the basement dividing up 100-pound bags of flour into 5-pound bags, then carting them up to the main floor for display. Piggly Wiggly pioneered the use of such prefab products, the way chains like White Castle and McDonald's pioneered selling processed food on the go.

At Piggly Wiggly, any shopper could get a price list upon request.

What did they get for trying out Saunders's new system? Piggly Wiggly's ad the day after it opened in Memphis had a little fun at the expense of the delivery boys who worked for those competing, full-service markets. By contrast, the store boasted, the sixty-eight people who bought groceries that first day at Piggly Wiggly received goods that had not been:

- "Dropped on the floor, trampled on, [or had] dirt spilt into them."
- "Mashed by someone sitting on them in or stepping on them . . . in a delivery wagon."
- "Left on the back porch step because nobody was home, and there to be at the mercy of a 'hide and seek' game played by the cats and dogs of the neighborhood, who raced and jumped and smelt and licked and bit into some of the things."

- "Thrown into a half-open door of someone's kitchen by the impatient, tired and reckless delivery boy who 'skated' them clear across the floor and possibly mixed rice and coffee and potatoes with molasses as he ran down the driveway to get in a hurry to the next stop, where he could make another 'skoot' along the kitchen floor with somebody else's things to eat."

Did any of those things happen? "No, Ma'am: 'ree bob tail-cat tail!'" came the emphatic if folksy rejoinder.

Saunders lost control of Piggly Wiggly after a stock scheme backfired, and his next big idea didn't work nearly as well. Keedoozle, as he called it for "key does all," was designed around an electric key that shoppers would use to select items from display cases; a conveyor belt would carry them to the cashier, where the shopper would present her key and pay for them. But the automated system proved too complicated—especially during peak shopping hours—and repeated malfunctions short-circuited the idea after only three stores were opened.

Piggly Wiggly, on the other hand, kept going strong. Its success soon spawned a number of imitators called "groceterias"—cafeteria-style grocers. Loblaw Groceterias took the concept north of the border into Toronto in 1919, and the founders of Alpha Beta (which later morphed into a supermarket) started using it in Southern California at their Triangle Groceteria about the same time Saunders was patenting his system. The store established other locations and adopted the name Alpha Beta in the next couple of years, based on Triangle's system of arranging its groceries alphabetically.

Apparently the Piggly Wiggly name was so catchy that other stores sought to emulate its rhyming two-step. In 1924, a store called Nifty Jiffy—whose vice president was a former Piggly Wiggly executive—opened in Atlanta, while Texas welcomed Handy-Andy in the late teens and Helpy-Selfy during the twenties. All were self-service grocers in the mold of Saunders's store.

None of these stores were supermarkets; they weren't nearly that big. In fact, Nifty Jiffy crowed that its store was so "compact in size" that "every item, with its price clearly marked, is in plain view from the entrance." The first Piggly Wiggly opened in a typical Main Street type storefront, with display windows on each side of a central door, and a floor plan that was three times as deep as it was wide. Inside, it was laid out in a sort of mini-labyrinth that resembled a one-way street snaking through the store. As Gilmore put it, "customers were herded along a specified route and past the checkout counter like hogs in a pig run." The idea was to guarantee that the customer "became acquainted with the entire assortment of goods in the store." There was a turnstile at the beginning, where you picked up your basket, and another at the end that, as one observer put it, "lets you out, but won't let you back in." All this was in less than 2,000 square feet, with a single cash register at the front.

The result was a sort of human assembly line of shoppers. According to Saunders, the system made it possible for 100 people to shop at once at a Piggly Wiggly and for a satisfied customer to exit every forty-eight seconds.

THE NEW FRONTIER

In addition to reducing costs by hiring fewer clerks, self-service stores saved money by being "cash-and-carry" operations: They didn't sell anything on credit. Saunders patented the Piggly Wiggly format and even sued another store, the alliterative Jitney-Jungle of Mississippi, which took its very name from a reference to coins—playing off the then-popular phrase "jingling of jitneys in your pockets" (jitneys being an old-fashioned name for nickels).

Saunders claimed Piggly Wiggly had exclusive rights to the cash-only format.

He lost his case.

But none of these early self-service stores were responsible for taking the next step in grocery-store evolution: inventing the supermarket. There's a debate over who gets credit for that, but as Piggly Wiggly was revolutionizing the grocery business in the South, innovators were upping their game out west, too.

Safeway, a chain ultimately backed with the capital from Merrill Lynch, chose its name based on the very concept of cash-and-carry. Its motto, "Drive the Safeway; buy the Safeway," told customers they could rest easy when they went grocery shopping. They couldn't put themselves in a financial bind by overextending themselves, because buying on credit wasn't an option.

The Ralphs store in the Westwood Village neighborhood of Los Angeles was supersized, making it one of the first true supermarkets. Wikimedia Commons. Creative Commons 3.0 license: https://creativecommons.org/licenses/by-sa/3.0/deed.en.

The Safeway chain was the product of a merger involving Los Angeles–based Seelig markets, founded in 1911 by Sam Seelig. Under his leadership, the Seelig chain (where "cash is king") grew to 270 stores in fourteen years before he sold it and the new owner rechristened it as Safeway. A year later, the chain was sold again, to a group of investors organized by Charles Merrill of Merrill Lynch fame. A merger with Skaggs of Idaho—another cash-and-carry chain with several hundred branches of its own—created a super-chain of 750 grocery stores, 114 meat markets, and five bakeries across ten western states.

Marion Skaggs remained on as CEO.

Shortly afterward, Merrill purchased chains owned by Ross McIntyre of Portland, Oregon, and Charles Marr of Spokane, Washington. Both owners wanted to stay with the new company, but neither wanted to work under Skaggs, so Merrill created a *second* business

called MacMarr. The two companies grew further with subsequent mergers, absorbing Piggly Wiggly stores in Los Angeles, Fresno, Modesto, San Francisco, Seattle, and Tacoma along the way as the company founded by Clarence Saunders exited the western market. Some of the stores were co-branded as "Safeway and Piggly Wiggly" for a brief period before ultimately adopting the Safeway name alone.

Merrill's two chains also gobbled up a series of municipal and small regional brands, such as nearly forty stores operated by Economic Food Co. (the dominant chain in Fresno, where it had fifteen locations). By 1930, Safeway and MacMarr had a total of 2,372 grocery stores and 1,422 meat markets, including twenty-six stores in San Francisco alone. The two chains were consolidated under the Safeway name in 1940.

Safeway had some stiff competition in the form of Ralphs. One of the oldest grocery chains still operating,

Ralphs traces its history back to the nineteenth century, when a twenty-two-year-old bricklayer named George Ralphs decided to go hunting with his brother Walter. The pair had a side business where they would sell the game they shot to local butchers, charging 15 cents for two doves or a pair of quail and a quarter for three ducks or cottontails.

As he drove the wagon, George Ralphs unwisely decided to rest his left arm on the barrel of his shotgun, and when the wagon hit a deep hole, the gun went off. Ralphs arm was shattered and had to be amputated at the elbow, which put an end to any future he might have had as a bricklayer. But the brothers had already been making money in the food business, so George Ralphs took a job as a grocery clerk in downtown Los Angeles and used the money he earned there to buy a partnership in a second store. Shortly afterward, his boss sold his own share of that store to Walter Ralphs, and the brothers were in business as Ralphs Bros. Grocers.

They didn't open a second store until 1911, but it was quite a project. At 15,000 square feet, including a basement, it even had stables for farmers making deliveries via horse-drawn wagon. The brothers also provided the farmers with free lodging, allowing Ralphs to increase its supplies and charge lower prices as a result. Walter Ralphs used his share of the profits to buy up land in Southern California, including the entire town of Gorman in the Tehachapi Mountains between LA and Bakersfield.

George Ralphs died three years after that second grocery store opened in another freak accident. While hiking with his family near Lake Arrowhead, a three-ton boulder came loose and crushed his leg. It, like the arm, would have to be amputated. But the doctor ignored Ralphs's pleas not to use ether and, after he went under, he never regained consciousness.

His son and nephews took over the business and continued to innovate. The car was quickly supplanting the horse and buggy as the preferred means of travel, so the company came up with another concept: a "drive-in" grocery store attached to a gas station. But what was really needed in the fast-growing and increasingly sprawling Los Angeles was parking—space for enough cars to support the larger stores the company wanted to build. That kind of parking couldn't be had curbside on congested downtown streets, so Ralphs opened larger markets with parking "lots" on the new frontier of suburbia.

By 1928, Ralphs had ten stores and decided to end its home delivery service, adopting the cash-and-carry model instead. The following year, it commissioned two new stores in Pasadena and Alhambra and a third in Westwood Village. These wouldn't be just grocery stores but supersized markets. Or supermarkets. The Alhambra and Pasadena stores would each have 9,000 square feet of store space and warehouses that checked in at 11,000 square feet. *The Los Angeles Times* reported that they would be "modern, providing lounging rooms for patrons, parking space for automobiles, as well as complete market facilities."

Grocery stores were following the same trajectory as department stores in moving away from the city center. The Ralphs Westwood Village store opened the same year Bullock's Wilshire debuted about a half hour away in another suburban setting. The Ralphs store, built in Mission Revival style, featured a corner entrance in a distinctive short rotunda tower. It was right next to a brand-new Safeway and was one of six original buildings in Westwood Village, adjacent to the UCLA campus. Other stores in the development included a men's clothier called Desmond's, a drugstore, a music shop, a sweet shop, a barbershop, a dry cleaner, a bookstore, a shoe repair, and a beauty shop.

The lineup of shops didn't include a department store, but it was very much a suburban mall nonetheless.

Whether the three new Ralphs (or the one built in 1911) were in fact the nation's first supermarkets is open for debate. At the dawn of the Great Depression other grocers in the Northeast and Midwest were moving forward with similar plans: to create large-scale grocery stores that maximized profits by buying in bulk and keeping their costs at a minimum.

Soon, they would be everywhere.

EAST COAST KINGS

Back east, Michael Cullen was working in Illinois for a branch of the Kroger chain.

The Cincinnati-based business founded in 1883 by Bernard Kroger would eventually buy Ralphs and would become the largest supermarket chain in the country by the early twenty-first century. Kroger's success, however, came despite a significant misstep in 1930. Management didn't listen to Cullen. The former A&P clerk had been with Kroger for eleven years when he approached his boss with a suggestion: open five prototype stores that would apply the principles pioneered by Piggly Wiggly (self-service, cash-and-carry) but be "monstrous in size." This high-volume approach could maximize profits, he contended.

"Can you imagine how the public would respond to a store of this kind?" he asked. "To think of it—a man selling 300 items at cost and another 200 items at 5 percent above cost—nobody in the world ever did this before. Nobody ever flew the Atlantic either, until Lindbergh did it. . . . I was never so confident in my life as I am at the present time; and in order to prove to you my sincerity and my good faith, I am willing to invest $15,000 of my own money to prove that this will be the biggest money maker you have ever invested yourself in."

Cullen proposed moving the store two or three blocks away from the city center, so he could provide customers with ample parking space. "The public will walk an extra block or two if they can save money," he argued, "and one of our talking points would be, the reason we sell at wholesale prices is that we are out of the high-rent district.

"Before you throw this letter in the wastebasket, read it again and then wire me to come to Cincinnati, so I can tell you more about this plan, and what it will do for you and your company."

But his boss wasn't interested, and the proposal never made it to company president William Albers. So, Cullen quit and moved to New York City, intent on making his vision a reality.

In a move that foreshadowed the approach taken by discount department stores a couple of decades later, he leased an abandoned garage in Queens with 6,000 square feet of space—three times the size of the first Piggly Wiggly. He stocked the space with more than 1,000 items and not just groceries; he threw automotive goods and hardware into the mix for good measure. Cullen called the store King Kullen.

"Tell your friends and neighbors about this great price-wrecker," an early ad read. "Tell 'em it's the lowest price grocery in all America. Tell 'em our prices are not

for a day or a week, they are our regular everyday prices. Save 10% to 50%."

The first King Kullen store opened in 1930 and was a big success. Another one, in Brooklyn, opened in an old car barn, and according to one observer, it still had a working fire hydrant in the middle of the store as of 1937. Cullen died a year earlier, in 1936, at the age of fifty-two, by which time the company had sixteen or seventeen locations and was doing $6 million in business annually.

Just as other markets had copied Piggly Wiggly, imitators were quick to jump on the King Kullen bandwagon, opening larger-scale stores across the country. Tellingly, Albers—the Kroger president who never saw Cullen's proposal—stepped down three years after Cullen opened his store to start a chain called Albers Super Markets. Apparently, he had fished Cullen's idea out of the proverbial wastebasket and decided it was worth pursuing after all. King Kullen's success was evidence enough of that.

Others were following Cullen's lead, too.

In Hackensack, New Jersey, Frank Packard opened the Packard-Bamberger supermarket with a partner in 1932. (Edgar Bamberger had no connection to the Newark-based department store; three years later, Packard bought him out.) .) The goal was to create a store where he could sell all kinds of goods under a single roof. And a big roof it was. The 40,000-square-foot store had once been the ground floor of a factory building, and it sat on a ten-acre site with parking spaces for 3,000 cars. Some of the groceries were eclectic. Rye flour, turtle soup, and reindeer meatballs were among the items sold there, along with thirty-two brands of canned peaches.

Then again, the entire store was eclectic. In addition to groceries, Packard's sold items ranging from wallpaper to fur coats, from lingerie to hardware. Even cars. The second floor of the three-story building was devoted entirely to women's fashions. There was a barbershop, a garden shop, a shoe repair, and even, for a time, a post office.

"I guess you could call it an old country store, gone modern," Packard said in a 1951 interview in which he speculated that his store was the largest food business under a single roof in the United States. "I can't prove that, of course, but whenever anybody else makes that claim, I challenge them to compare figures. So far, I've had no takers."

Packard himself was an interesting character. He placed second in the 1923 national junior tennis championship and became a formidable golfer later on. He even claimed to have taught Joe Louis how to ride a horse. A wine connoisseur, he once proclaimed during a lecture that "Noah became a wine drinker after the flood because he found water unpotable. It tasted of sinners." He must have thought Noah had good taste, because he opened more than twenty stores selling fine wine, traveling to France each year to select which vintages his stores would stock. In 1961, the French government awarded him the Ordre du mérite agricole for his role in promoting French wine.

He was also the stepfather of actress Lee Remick.

The Packard building was as distinctive as its owner, with its external staircase and the name Packard's written in white script across a giant green billboard between two oil derrick–shaped radio towers. During the holidays, the towers would be lit up like a pair of Christmas trees. Between them, a string of illuminated reindeer pulled Santa's sleigh upward into the night.

Packard sold 3,000 cases of beer and two tons of frankfurters in a week's time, hosting 30,000 customers on an average weekend. In 1958, Packard's and Sears teamed up to run joint ads on sales being offered at the same time in both Hackensack stores: Sears was promoting its annual Sears Days, while Packard's was celebrating its twenty-seventh anniversary. "We're not afraid of each other. We admire each other," Packard said. "We have implicit faith in Hackensack, and this plan of advertising is our best way of giving the public the best offering we can."

Packard's finally closed its doors in 1991, and a Target later opened on the site.

THREE BEARS

A number of entrepreneurs seem to have gotten the supermarket idea at the same time. Either that or they copied one another, opening similar stores in the early thirties. Three of them, confusingly, chose the same name: Big Bear.

A Durant automobile plant in Elizabeth, New Jersey, had closed down when a pair of entrepreneurs decided to put its 50,000 square feet of space to a different use. In 1933, they moved in and opened up their Big Bear,

which sold food in the center and had eleven specialty departments (selling hardware, paint, electronics, and other items) arrayed around the sides. It was as much like a yard sale as a supermarket. Products were laid out on pine tables and stocked in heaping displays.

Shoppers came from fifty miles away, and the store sold as much in its first three days of business as the average A&P store made in six months. Competitors, livid about being undersold, fought back by decrying the new approach and lobbying newspapers to ban Big Bear's ads from their pages. Instead, the store started distributing four-page fliers to every home within ten miles of the store.

The owner of the second Big Bear business, this one based in Somerville, Massachusetts, faced a similar backlash after he opened in a five-story building in 1933. Arthur Smith operated the grocery section and leased out floor space in the 150,000-square-foot structure to concessionaires who sold flowers, tobacco, paint, shoes, auto supplies, electronics, linoleum, appliances, and other items. Services were offered at a beauty parlor, a barbershop, and a soda fountain.

Smith's business was so successful he once sold 48,000 cans of Campbell's soup in five days and 24,000 cans of Maxwell House coffee in just two.

Still, even that couldn't match the success enjoyed by Wayne Brown when he opened the first of his Big Bear Stores in February of 1934. For his site, he chose a building that had been used previously as a dance hall, then a roller rink, and finally a horse-show ring. The store, in Columbus, Ohio (next door to Ohio State University), has been generally recognized as the first supermarket in the Midwest.

Before he opened Big Bear, Brown had floated the self-service concept to A&P, where he even opened a couple of experimental stores using that model. His initiative didn't sit too well with the mothership, though, and A&P demanded that he change them back. The company feared that customers, if left to their own devices, would go on a shoplifting spree.

Piggly Wiggly had faced similar criticism and even took out a newspaper ad to rebut it: "There may be some downright thievery in the world, but we don't hold the average opinion that everybody is a thief excepting ourselves. On the contrary, we KNOW that most everybody is honest and [we] are willing to take our chances on the honest folks being in the large majority."

Despite Piggly Wiggly's assertion that "we place every person on her honor that enters our store," that wasn't entirely true. The turnstiles at both ends of the shopping area, along with the store's insistence that customers leave any bags they brought in by the front door, showed Piggly Wiggly worried about theft just like A&P or anybody else. Owner Clarence Saunders even designed his stores with a back entrance that allowed employees access to the top of the shelves, a vantage point from which they could make sure there wasn't any funny business going on below.

Even though he empowered customers to "do it themselves," the irony is that Saunders was a control freak. He insisted that all his Piggly Wiggly stores be laid out exactly the same way, and he lost his fortune in a failed attempt to corner the market on the store's stock.

But the A&P was even more conservative. Safeguards such as those Saunders put in place weren't enough; it didn't want to take any chances at all.

Before long, however, even A&P had to bow to the inevitable. A few short years after it had rebuked Brown for his temerity in trying his newfangled supermarket approach, the company saw the light about high-volume retail. It opened 400 self-service supermarkets of its own in 1936.

Brown, however, had a head start with his Ohio-based Big Bear, the first supermarket to open in the Midwest. With 47,000 square feet of floor space, it was immense by the standards of the day, dwarfing even the first King Kullen location. In a move that foreshadowed the arrival of big-box discount department stores, he didn't bother to put in a ceiling; he just hung rows of fluorescent lights from the rafters to provide illumination for shoppers.

When it came to the products, however, Brown made sure merchandise was pleasing to the eye. Seemingly endless rows of canned goods were stacked along the walls and in elaborate displays—the kind that inspired those now-familiar slapstick scenes in which neatly stacked pyramids of grocery items are toppled by a "careless" comedian. Some of them were more than 10 feet high and contained seemingly thousands of cans or boxes.

The gigantic A&P corner grocery chain initially resisted the idea of the supermarket but eventually followed the crowd—and the profits—to the larger format. This store was in Montreal, Quebec, Canada. Conrad Poirier, 1941, public domain.

The merchandise sold itself. This had been an aspect of self-service from the beginning, since clerks were no longer around to call customers' attention to the "best" products (the ones they store wanted to promote).

"With self-service, there was much less person-to-person attention, much less selling and more concern with packaging—merchandising," Fresno professor Paul Gilmore said. "Of course, this meant that an entire industry of packaging-as-advertising rose up, along with more general broadcast advertising of packaged foods."

The concept really came into its own with supermarkets, where everything was done on a much larger scale. At the Ohio Big Bear, banners that spelled out FOOD

SHOW and hawked cleaning items like Vel, Fab, Ajax, and Palmolive hung from the rafters, heralding the store's opening as the "Greatest Show on Earth."

The signs helped serve notice that there was more than food to be had at Big Bear. Things like housewares, appliances, tricycles, and baby carriages were also on display. There was a candy department, a pharmacy, and a lunch counter. There was even a shoe-repair service. In effect, Big Bear was a proto-hypermarket.

The store was such a hit that some say 200,000 shoppers thronged to the store during its first three days in business. A second location opened the following year, and a third the year after that. The store offered shoppers up to $25 to mix six words with "Big Bear" and "low prices" to create a slogan for the store. It came up with several of its own through the years, such as "Get the bear minimum price!" and "Give 'em a Big Bear hug!"

Established grocers, chagrined at being beaten to the punch, looked down their noses at upstarts like the Big Bears when they started building bigger stores themselves.

In 1938, M.M. Zimmerman, executive secretary of the Super Market Institute, disparaged "the type of store which is set up in an unattractive building, stocked with odds and ends of merchandise with only limited stocks of popular brands and with ballyhoo circus appeal." Such establishments, he said "will attract only the class of crowds looking for bargains and will reflect unfavorably on all supers."

He predicted that such endeavors would result in bankruptcies, credit losses, and weakened distribution. But all the customer could see was the vast selection and, even more important, the bargain prices. During the Depression, especially, that was the clincher.

Roy Dawson, one of the founders of the New Jersey Big Bear, had a different prediction: "Someday, supermarkets will do nearly all of the business all over the country. It's inevitable because it's cheaper, because people have automobiles, and because they like to shop. It's the new method of retailing."

He could have just as easily been talking about discount department stores.

Either way, he was right.

DEALING WITH DISCOUNTERS

Brown's Ohio-based Big Bear was a trailblazer in several areas. It had a store in Columbus's first regional shopping center, Town and Country, and in 1955 it served as a testing ground for IBM's massive RAMAC mainframe computer, which it used for accounting and inventory. But one of its most lasting contributions to the retail trade was its role in merging the grocery and discount department store businesses.

One such store, Harts, had stores in the basements of two Big Bear locations when the supermarket chain purchased it. Big Bear went on to open several Harts Family Centers, as they were called in the ensuing years, often adjacent to its own stores. In 1988, it merged the two operations into a full-fledged hypermarket called Big Bear Plus—stores that were stocked with 40 percent food and 60 percent general merchandise.

Discount houses, meanwhile, were starting to proliferate, often taking over large vacant sites that had been built with something else in mind: warehouses and, especially in New England, abandoned textile mills. In the fifties, the Super Market Institute asked its members whether discount houses were a threat to grocers. Almost all of them said no. But the same survey in 1960 produced the opposite result—three in five saw the emerging retail trend as a threat.

Many supermarkets began to think about making preemptive strikes, getting into the discounting field by buying out their would-be rivals. One such deal involved a former mill store called J.M. Fields, which had a longer history than most of its contemporaries. Phillip Feldman had begun the business as Enterprise Stores in the early 1900s, but son Joseph M. Feldman changed it to J.M. Fields (an anglicized variation on his own name) in the fifties and decided to expand. The first store opened in a 30,000-square-foot mill building in Salem, Massachusetts, and two more followed in former car barns over the next two years.

By 1961, J.M. Fields had grown to a chain of thirty-three stores in eight states up and down the Eastern Seaboard, from New Hampshire all the way to Florida. It was at this point that it attracted the attention of grocery retailer Food Fair, which purchased the chain and opened new branches adjacent to its supermarkets,

You could find a lot of merchandise crammed into a small space at Katz in Kansas City. The store's "19th Annual Million Dollar Sale" took place around 1950. Public domain.

creating the kind of mega-retail centers that foreshadowed those of Target and Walmart. The combined chain lasted until it declared bankruptcy in 1978, at which time Kmart (naturally) took over many of the locations.

Also in 1961, another discount department store, Bradlees, was gobbled up by the much older food chain Stop & Shop, while Jewel Food Stores acquired a four-year-old Boston chain of four stores called Turn Style. At the same time, it bought the Osco drugstore chain, which enabled Jewel to package the two companies together as it expanded Turn Style beyond its New England base. The resulting chain grew as large as fifty stores in the Midwest (Illinois, Iowa, Nebraska, Indiana, and Michigan) in addition to its original Massachusetts base. That figure

was down to twenty-two by 1978, when Jewel sold nineteen of the stores to May Department Stores, which had its own ten-year-old discount chain called Venture and was looking to increase its presence in Chicago. Venture, created to compete with Kmart, never posed a threat to the then-industry leader. In fact, the same year it acquired Turn Style, the company chairman said it was "choking" on its Chicago-area Venture stores. He had hopes that things would turn around, but Venture went out of business in 1998, taking the last remnants of Turn Style with it.

May itself was sold to Macy's a few years later.

MORE THAN JUST DRUGS

While supermarkets were dipping their toes into the discount market, drugstores were doing the same: evolving from simply pharmacies into one-stop shops that began to overlap with dime stores and larger discounters. One example was Katz Drug Stores in Kansas City, which was founded in 1914 and evolved into a chain with sixty-five stores in five states and $100 million in annual sales. Katz's business didn't start out as a drugstore, but as a cigar shop. When the government imposed wartime restrictions on businesses, however, founder Ike Katz started looking for a loophole. And he found one. Wartime policy required all businesses to close by 6 p.m. except for drugstores. So, Katz hired a pharmacist and started filling prescriptions, which allowed him to sell everything else he had in stock as well. Over time, the selection grew from cigars to a vast array of items ranging from appliances to exotic pets like monkeys and baby alligators. Yes, alligators!

Katz also lured customers by eating the 10 percent tax on cigarettes, leading the company to adopt the slogan "Katz pays the tax!" Discounting was the name of the game, and Katz was big on sales: "Not a regular price in the entire store!" one ad proclaimed. It was also big on self-promotion. New stores would open to great fanfare, with searchlights, marching bands, magicians, clowns, and giveaways. There were balloons for the kids and orchids for the ladies. In 1970, it brought in "Flapper the Million Dollar Dolphin" (not to be confused with Flipper) to perform in a 20,000-gallon tank at its store.

As the attractions got bigger, so did the stores themselves. In 1957, a Katz store opened in Des Moines, Iowa, with twenty-six departments covering 38,000 square feet. Just four years later—a year before Kmart, Target, and Walmart burst onto the scene—Katz opened its largest store yet: a 75,000-square-foot site in Springfield, Missouri. The store looked like a discount center with a pharmacy attached, and the name reflected that: Katz Discount City, described by the company as a "one-stop shopping colossus." The long, single-story glass front was topped by zigzagging series of connected, angular canopies that looked like a range of origami mountains.

Katz ultimately ceased to exist in 1971 when it was merged into the Skaggs Drug Company to create what was then the nation's third-largest drugstore chain.

The store with the grinning black-cat mascot wasn't the only drugstore to become much more than just a pharmacy. At Thrifty Drugs, ice cream was the best medicine. Thrifty sold ice cream from outside suppliers in 1933, but seven years later it decided to start making its own, plunking down $250,000 for a former Borden plant in Southern California. The ice cream it produced there quickly earned a reputation as some of the best around, even winning the "Great Summer of '87 Ice Cream Taste Test" in Fresno against the likes of Baskin-Robbins, Swensen's, Dreyer's, and Häagen-Dazs (which finished in a tie for second with Skyler's).

Thrifty's brand of ice cream became so well known that it remained a centerpiece even after Rite Aid bought the chain in 1996.

Thrifty, like other drugstores, grew to offer items ranging from makeup to instant cameras to Christmas lights and Halloween costumes. It ultimately merged with PayLess, which had evolved much the same way. In northern Fresno, a PayLess store stood across Blackstone Avenue (the main north-south thoroughfare) and just south of Kmart in the 1980s, providing a similar selection of products. PayLess was even a Kmart subsidiary for a few years starting in 1985, before the Thrifty merger.

Drugstore chains, even regional ones, weren't small potatoes. Longs, another company that had a major presence in Fresno, once had 500 in the eight western states before it was acquired by CVS. (You can still find Longs in Hawai'i, where the new parent company had no name recognition and kept the brand intact.) Longs started out as an early self-service drugstore and even had that phrase as part of its name, opening in 1938 as Longs Self-Service Drugs on Oakland's Piedmont Avenue. One of its original owners was the son-in-law of Safeway cofounder Marion Skaggs.

11

DOWNTOWN DOWNTURN

The end of World War II marked the beginning of the end for downtown dominance in the world of retailing. You just wouldn't have known it at the time. On the surface, everything seemed normal—better than normal, in fact. The new peace had unleashed a torrent of pent-up shopping zeal that had lain dormant during an era of buckling down and rationing.

According to the Federal Reserve, department store profits for the first quarter of 1947 rose by 100 percent over 1945, when the US remained at war through the summer. That was the good news. But there were signs of trouble, too. During the same year, mail-order profits rose by three times that much. A lot of people preferred to do their shopping from home rather than drive into the city and contend with the congested streets and scarce parking—parking you had to pay for.

There was a reason the roads were so crowded. Two months after the bombing of Pearl Harbor, US automakers had stopped producing new cars. Assembly lines were dedicated to making tanks, planes, personnel

Empty storefronts line Scales Street, the downtown business strip in Reidsville, North Carolina. Stephen H. Provost, 2019.

carriers, and the like, not Fords and Chevys. (Chevrolet made 500,000 military trucks and 60,000 planes between 1942 and '45.) By the time new cars started rolling off the lines again, there was plenty of pent-up demand. They started selling like hotcakes, with sales quadrupling in the decade after the war, and their owners started driving them to the place most people shopped: downtown.

For the moment, downtowns had a near monopoly on major retail. Sure, a few suburban department stores had gotten started before the war (Bullock's Wilshire being a prime example), but as of 1945, most shoppers who wanted to visit their local department store had to take a trip downtown. Still, even with rationing behind them and more cash in their pockets, many seemed unwilling to do so.

The bottom line told the story. That postwar spike in department store sales? It all but evaporated after a single year. It was one thing to compare postwar profits with wartime figures, but year-over-year sales gains slowed to a crawl during peacetime. And profits were headed in the other direction, driven downward by increased expenses. Comparing the first half of 1947 to the first full year after the end of the war, the National Retail Dry Goods Association reported that department store profits were down by 21 percent. The trend continued the following year, as profits fell an additional 27.5 percent.

FAIR PRICES?

Results like that had to be discouraging for big department stores. Profits had been scarce during the Depression, and many stores had survived by merging with rivals or banding together in holding companies. The chains they formed used their combined purchasing power to buy in bulk from manufacturers, which allowed them to keep prices down and revenues up—at least enough to stay in business.

But smaller, mom-and-pop stores couldn't afford to do that. Even if they'd survived the Wall Street crash of '29, they were still perpetually at risk, in part because they couldn't compete with the big chains' prices. Seeing few other options, they sought protection from lawmakers, who responded by passing "fair trade" legislation, creating a basis for setting minimum prices on various goods. This kept chains from undercutting mom-and-pop stores with prices their smaller competitors couldn't afford to match.

California was the first to pass a fair-trade law, two years after the crash. That law, however, had little effect because it dealt only with one-on-one price agreements between a manufacturer and a specific store. Few retailers cared to strike such a deal unless it applied to *everyone* who carried the item(s) in question. So, in 1933, the California Legislature amended the law to include a "non-signers clause," which meant even stores that *hadn't* signed the agreement were still bound by it.

All but eight other states had passed similar laws by 1936, when the US Supreme Court ruled them constitutional. A year later, Congress passed the Miller-Tydings Act, explicitly exempting fair-trade agreements from the Sherman Antitrust Act.

All this was a boon to manufacturers, who could set minimum prices for their goods. But the laws were bad news for department stores, who found their superior purchasing power negated by the laws. All of a sudden, they were back on a level playing field with downtown mom-and-pops.

Some retailers, however, refused to play by those rules. Frank Packard in New Jersey was among them. In 1938, he took out a newspaper ad proclaiming, "We are willfully violating the most pernicious law ever passed in the State of New Jersey." And he did just that, selling what he said was 83 cents' worth of merchandise for a customer's dollar. The case went to court, and the New Jersey Supreme Court sided with Packard.

Because the fair-trade laws were all *state* laws, such as New Jersey's, they were also vulnerable to challenge at the federal level when the goods being sold crossed state lines, and just such a challenge arose in 1951. Schwegmann Brothers, a New Orleans supermarket, refused to sign a minimum-price deal for whiskey that had been imported from out of state. Instead, it sold the liquor for less than what 100 other Louisiana retailers were charging. The distributor, predictably, sued. And lost. The Supreme Court sided with Schwegmann Brothers, saying that nonsigner clauses in state law didn't apply to interstate commerce.

This was a victory not only for Schwegmann Brothers but for major retailers across the country.

Macy's was busy on this day in 1964, but it was nothing like 1951, when the store cut prices drastically to compete with other retailers after the courts nullified a fair-trade law. The deep discounts drew Christmas-like throngs to department stores across the country. Library of Congress.

Just days after the decision was handed down, Macy's, Gimbels, and other big department stores started slashing their prices. A seismic shakeup had begun, and New York City was at the epicenter. Macy's fired the first shot, announcing in a double-page newspaper ad: "You can now buy 5,978 'price fixed items' at less than price-fixed prices—at Macy's."

The Gimbels controller responded: "If Macy's cuts prices, we'll go right there with them. It looks like we are in an old-fashioned price war."

Abraham & Straus slashed prices by 10 percent across the board. Bloomingdale's said it would not be undersold, and Hearn's department store declared that "if there is a price war, we'll be right in the middle of it." Like Gimbels, Hearn's extended its hours to 8 p.m.

When Gimbels' price for Mixmasters plunged to $29.95, less than two-thirds the previous fixed price of $46.50, Macy's responded by cutting *its* prices to $29.64, six cents below cost. Both stores added several hundred people to their comparison-shopping staffs just to keep an eye on competitors' prices.

Shoppers, predictably, swarmed the stores. One newspaper compared them to locusts. A counter clerk said the crowds were as thick as they were at Christmas. Customers trying to push their way through the "in" and "out" sides of the revolving door at Macy's wound up knocking it over. Inside, they mobbed sales counters. Gimbels sold 5,100 Palm Beach suits over three days, more than ten times as many as normal. Macy's, which sold an average of ten Mixmasters a day, sold 400 of them in just forty-five minutes.

Some manufacturers, taken by surprise and fearing their products might be defined as "cheap," threatened to stop delivering them. Palm Beach suits threatened to cut off Macy's supply if the store didn't rescind its price cuts, while Sunbeam sued Macy's for $6 million, alleging damage to its trademark under the Sherman Act.

Meanwhile, the price war spread. An ad in Atlanta read: "If Macy's and Gimbels can do it, so can we," while stores in Baltimore, Newark, Chicago, Omaha, Oklahoma City, Albuquerque, and San Francisco were also among those slashing their prices. With Father's

Day two weeks away, men's goods were popular, but so were things like aspirin, which normally sold for 59 cents at Gimbels but fell first to 24 cents and then to 17 cents for a bottle of 100 tablets.

Of course, the mayhem could last only so long, and the crowds started thinning out about a month after the price war began. Still, the precedent had been set, and Congress moved to protect manufacturers by closing the "interstate commerce" loophole the following year. But that's not the end of the story.

When the Vietnam War sparked inflation in the late sixties that spilled over into the seventies with the help of the Arab oil embargo, a bipartisan coalition emerged to scrap fair-trade laws. Pro-business Republicans wanted to increase competition, while Democrats sought to ease the burden of rapidly rising costs on the poor and middle classes. In the winter of 1975, President Ford signed legislation repealing the fair-trade laws, with expectation of lowering prices in twenty-one states that still had them. Ford, who signed the bill as part of his "Whip Inflation Now" campaign, estimated that the laws were costing consumers $2 billion a year in prices over and above what they would be without the laws.

But department stores, which had fought against the laws for so long, weren't the big winners. In fact, the repeal paved the way for big-box discount retailers—which had been on the rise in recent years—to hasten their demise. These stores, like Kmart, Walmart, and Target, beat the department stores at what had been their own game by undercutting *their* prices, ultimately forcing the demise of many bargain basements and, by the mid-sixties, surpassing department stores as the most profitable form of retailer. By that time, the decline of downtown retailing was already well under way and had been since the advent of the suburban shopping mall decades earlier.

Coulter's Dry Goods of Los Angeles completed its Streamline Moderne flagship store in 1939 as part of an architectural shift in department store design. The Broadway operated a store there in the 1970s, but the building was demolished in 1980 while its nomination for a spot on the National Register of Historic Places was pending. Library of Congress, 1972.

Modern makeover

As retailers spread to the suburbs, downtowns tried to fight back by making themselves at least *look* relevant. Classical architecture was out; Art Deco was in. Columns, arches, and detailed stone carving looked increasingly outdated in a modern fast-paced world. A streamlined life required a streamlined look, and Main Street obliged.

Many storefronts had been created in the late nineteenth and early twentieth centuries. Two or three stories tall, with shared walls between them like townhomes, they appeared narrow from the front, but there was more to them than met the eye. Customers might have to walk a long way from the front door to reach the rear wall. The first Piggly Wiggly was three times as deep as it was wide. This kind of floor plan allowed more stores to share frontage (and exposure) on the street, while still giving each retailer enough space to stock a good-sized inventory. Often, the store owners lived in the second- and third-story apartments, which had windows overlooking the street below.

These shops were designed with a more leisurely pace in mind. There were more pedestrians and fewer cars (or carriages!) back then, so window shopping was the rule of the day, and window displays became a very big deal—especially as plate glass became widely available in the late 1800s. Downtown architects took advantage of this to create store windows that gave pedestrians a better look at what was inside, in hopes of enticing them to step through the front door.

The early twentieth century brought another innovation. Storefront designers began to set the front door back a few feet from the front of the building, creating a sheltered alcove that functioned as a neutral zone between the sidewalk and the store. Such alcoves had

This window-display alcove on Main Street in Danville, Virginia, shows just how far retailers would go to expose pedestrians to more of their merchandise. Stephen H. Provost, 2018.

several advantages. For customers, they created a place to open an umbrella before stepping out into the rain (or close it before stepping inside). For window-shoppers, they offered a middle ground where one could linger and avoid being jostled by passing pedestrians or accosted by overeager sales staffs.

For shop owners, meanwhile, they offered a way to display more goods through the windows on either side of the alcove. The advantages of this were so apparent that owners began remodeling their buildings to expand the alcoves, making them more like passageways or arcades that funneled patrons toward the front door. Many narrowed as they approached the doorway, and windows were arranged in a stair-step pattern on either side, providing even more display room outside the store itself.

As stores sought ways to attract new customers, storefronts continued to change in other ways as well.

"In many cases, the building was considered old and out of style, not in keeping with the retailer who wanted to present a fashion-forward look," said Joe Moore, an expert on the development of downtown Fresno, California. Stores often had "corporate design elements that unified their brand," he said, pointing to Zukor's, which sold elegant women's fashions in Fresno, as an example of this trend.

Benjamin Zukor had opened his first store in New York City back in 1916, and it became popular in the West, with stores in San Francisco, Los Angeles, and elsewhere. It didn't hurt that Zukor shared a name with Adolph Zukor, a movie mogul of some renown who was no relation.

The Fresno store that opened in 1936 was the fourteenth on the West Coast. The company invested $50,000 in creating an all-new front, with "various modernistic architectural and construction features" to the site, which had formerly housed a Moss women's store and, before that, an optometrist. The company boasted that its Fulton Street store would have "moderne" fixtures, figures, flowers, and a background. That was "moderne" with an *e*, as in Art Moderne, a style fast eclipsing the staid Main Street architecture that had been popular at the turn of the century. It was a streamlined approach, with flat, aerodynamic surfaces and rounded corners that stripped away the decorative flourishes of earlier eras.

As they refashioned their storefronts in this new style, businesses often covered those old second-floor windows with stucco, aluminum, or a thick layer of pigmented glass, creating a large, flat surface on which to write the store's name in bold or sweeping neon letters. That's what Zukor's did.

The store's outlets, Moore said, "had different variations on a theme, usually covering up the upper floors of a building with a new façade. . . . This provided the opportunity for larger-than-life neon signage. We often see them today and we don't get the full effect since the signage is gone. All we are seeing now is the blank billboard canvas, in essence."

J.J. Newberry, Woolworth's, and Berkeley's across from Gottschalks on Fresno's Fulton Street all followed the same template, spelling out their names in huge letters that stood out in contrast to stark plaster second-story backgrounds. Gottschalks itself adopted the Art Moderne look with a major 1948 overhaul, plastering over second-floor windows, archways, and stonework with a flat surface that jutted out over the sidewalk for the entire length of the building. On the corner, it added an Art Deco tower bearing the store's name to attract further attention.

"Many of these storefronts were also meant to be something that caught the eyes of drivers in moving vehicles—classic roadside architecture," Moore said. "Imagine the old Gottschalks building on Fulton when the moderne-era remodel was new, and the corner tower was lit up—it was a beacon—a temple of retail, of modernity, and fashion."

Some stores, like Sears, would adopt the same approach when they moved to the suburbs, building stores without any windows on the upper floors, where the company nameplate was scrawled in massive script letters across the front of the building. Sears had helped pioneer the idea of covering up windows. In 1934, it built one of its largest brick-and-mortar stores yet—a five-story structure in Chicago's Englewood neighborhood that had no windows at all above the first floor. The stark façade masked a modern interior that was equipped with escalators, air-conditioned and artificially lit.

The *Chicago Tribune* called it the "world's first windowless department store" and the "first application

Gottschalks redesigned its flagship store in downtown Fresno in Steamline Moderne style in 1948. Daniel A. Draper, 2019.

of modern functional design to department store architecture."

L.S. James, Sears's national director of display and store arrangement, explained the rationale behind the design: "One very practical factor will be the tremendous reduction in depreciation of merchandise through dirt, dust, and grime, nine-tenths of which enter a store through the windows," he said. The climate-controlled air would be "purer," and the store would be "much quieter, being sealed from the outside noise and hubbub of street traffic."

Ironically, the giant neon signs designed to attract passing motorists remained on Fresno's Fulton Street after it was converted into a pedestrian mall. The idea behind this transformation was, in part, an attempt to return to that era when window-shopping meant a leisurely stroll down Main Street. But by the time that experiment was under way, Sears had already abandoned its downtown location and fled to Fresno's first regional shopping center.

Its new store, which opened in 1955, had no windows, and the company name was spelled out in cursive above a massive asphalt parking lot—a parking lot that would still be there when Fresno opened Fulton back up to traffic in 2017.

Strip malls

Indeed, the suburbs beckoned: vast swaths of land with room for expansive new development and seemingly endless parking. Suburban shopping wasn't a new concept. Two variations emerged: the strip mall and the shopping center. One thing that came to distinguish the two was their "anchors"—larger stores meant to draw customers for the other tenants in the mall. The suburban shopping center would rely on branch department stores,

The Levy Jewelers building in Savannah, Georgia, shows the windowless approach retailers took to upper floors during the Art Deco period. Stephen H. Provost, 2019.

while strip malls would tap supermarkets and, to a lesser extent, drugstores as their major tenants.

The strip mall where I spent six years of my youth, in Calabasas, California, featured a Sav-on drugstore and a Vons supermarket as its anchors back in the seventies. It was a fairly common pairing in Southern California.

In fact, Southern California was one of the first places such malls began to appear, built around "drive-in" markets like the ones Ralphs founded. In 1928, the same year Ralphs opened its Westwood Village store, competitors were taking similar ideas and running with them. The Clock Market, named for its imposing clock-tower, opened that year on Wilshire Boulevard, with a dry-goods market, a pharmacy, and open-air produce booths. (It did have one thing in common with Main Street stores: The second story served as living quarters for the proprietor's family.) The building's L-shaped layout created a natural parking lot for cars out front, which would come in handy when it was later converted into a Porsche dealership. The Mandarin Market at Vina and La Mirada in Hollywood had a similar layout but a different theme: Chinese-style buildings that would have

fit in nicely in China's Forbidden City—or alongside Grauman's Chinese Theater, about a mile away.

By the end of the 1920s, there were about 250 mini-malls in California alone.

In 1931, a similar mall called Sam's Park & Shop opened in the Cleveland Park neighborhood, in northwest Washington, DC. More extensive than the Mandarin or Clock Market developments, it still featured the L-shaped design to provide customers with off-street parking. Early tenants included a Sanitary Food Store, Woodley Food & Liquors, a drugstore, a bakery, a restaurant/deli, and a barbershop. Its modest architecture—a slanted roof with three gabled windows on a portion of the structure, with a short country spire in the corner—had more in common with modern strip malls than with the elaborate Southern California structures that preceded them.

It may be surprising to some, more than eighty years later, that this red-brick structure with an awning that runs most of its length has been recognized as a histor-ical landmark. (It's still there. Tenants in 2014 included a coffee shop, a Petco, a fitness center, and a photo shop.) But when it arrived on the scene, it was the latest big thing. The May 1932 issue of the *Architectural Record* praised it as "a planned grouping of shops with parking space that does not interfere with traffic," contrasting it with downtown shopping districts "of Main Street character" where a hodgepodge of "unrelated 'Coney Island Architecture'" suggested "the need for cooperative and unified planning."

The magazine laid out a simple principle: "The more convenient and accessible the store is to the public, the better it is." To achieve this goal, a strip mall (which the journal calls a community shopping center) should meet three criteria:

- "The shopping center should be readily accessible to automobile shoppers in large numbers."
- "Parking space or garage facilities should be provided."

- "Filling stations, rest rooms, amusement and news centers and restaurants should be part of the development or adjacent thereto."

The Cleveland Park development fit this template pretty well. Even a theater was nearby (although a sign in the driveway warned theatergoers not to park in the Park & Shop lot).

A new surge in mini-mall construction took place in the seventies and early eighties, when some 2,000 popped up in the Los Angeles area. Many were built on sites abandoned when hundreds of gas stations went out of business during the oil embargo in the early seventies. Developers bought the land on the cheap and put up equally cheap, nondescript buildings to house tenants who couldn't afford the rent at Topanga Plaza or the Glendale Galleria.

Sam's Park & Shop in the Cleveland Park area of Washington, DC, featured a Piggly Wiggly among its tenants. The L-shaped parking lot was an innovation that allowed more cars to park closer to merchants than traditional street parking downtown. Library of Congress.

Vacant storefronts dominate the Central Plaza strip mall in Martinsville, Virginia. Stephen H. Provost, 2018.

In 1987, someone driving down Ventura Boulevard in the eastern San Fernando Valley would pass eleven strip malls and two more under construction, all in the space of just a mile and a half. The Los Angeles suburbs of West Hollywood and San Marino were so concerned that they passed ordinances banning them outright. Hollywood passed a two-month moratorium, and Eagle Rock halted new construction for a year. They were being built so fast—and the LA City Council was so slow adopting regulations—that council member Hal Bernson lamented, "By the time we get this thing passed, there won't be any ordinance yet to save."

Mini-malls were to regional shopping centers what motels were to hotels: a cheaper, easier, and more accessible alternative for shoppers. So, it's no surprise that they met the same fate as many motels. Just as you wouldn't find a Hilton in the red-light district, you wouldn't find a liquor shop, a donut shop, a laundromat, a payday lender, or an adult video store in a major shopping center. You could, however, find such businesses in some strip malls. Retailers such as these created a different sort of atmosphere, one that wasn't exactly family-friendly

and might not have seemed entirely safe. The "clientele" might include panhandlers, transients, and others who knew no one would bother them if they loitered while smoking a cigarette (or something else). Teenagers might be hanging out in the parking lot, cruising with their stereos blasting, and there would be plenty of discarded fast-food wrappers, beer cans, and other less savory items littered around the parking lot.

When the economy hit a downturn, many shops closed, leaving storefronts vacant and inviting further blight.

EARLY REGIONAL CENTERS

Sam's Park & Shop actually appeared a decade after what many recognize as America's first true regional shopping center to be built as an alternative to downtown. But no one would mistake Country Club Plaza for a strip mall. It was built just four miles south of downtown Kansas City, but back in 1922, that was far enough to make it the first shopping center ever designed to be reached by automobile (the original development included eight service stations!).

Dubbed "Nichols' Folly" by those who scoffed at developer Jesse Clyde Nichols's idea, it was modeled after Seville, Spain, and turned out to be an unqualified success. F.W. Woolworth was the original anchor, and a movie theater was added in 1928. The center even brought the tradition of the downtown Christmas decorations into the suburbs in 1925 by stringing upseventy-five miles of lights around the area, an annual display that continued as of this writing.

In the twenty-first century, the plaza was still going strong, anchored by Saks Fifth Avenue and Halls Department Store.

In 1928, another center shopping popped up—this one in Ardmore, about ten miles outside Philadelphia. Built along an important trolley route from the city, it came to be known as "The Downtown of the Lower Main Line." (The Main Line referred to both the trolley and the surrounding suburb, which was the most affluent in the Philadelphia area at the time.) By the time of its golden anniversary, the *Guinness Book of World Records* was calling it the world's oldest shopping center, perhaps because it had something Country Club Plaza didn't: a traditional department store. Strawbridge & Clothier of Philadelphia set up a suburban branch there in 1930.

"It was a risk at the time, and its success was a remarkable feat," Frank Veale, a former Strawbridge executive, told the *Philadelphia Inquirer*.

Strawbridge & Clothier was known for taking risks. A year after opening the Suburban Square store, it debuted a new thirteen-story downtown flagship location, built at a cost a whopping $10 million. Such an expenditure in the depths of the Depression put the company in a financial hole, but it eventually recovered and remained one of the oldest privately run department stores in the country. (Founded in 1868 by Quaker merchants Justus Strawbridge and Isaac Clothier, it remained in the Strawbridge family until its sale to May Co. 128 years later.)

While the new flagship store strained the company's finances, the Suburban Square outlet had the opposite effect.

"You never had anything like that before—a preplanned mix of nice stores," Veale said. It was a success from the outset, he said, for the same reason other suburban shopping centers would succeed decades later: "There were people, and they were people with money to spend."

The shops there reflected that clientele. The Dorothy R. Bullitt shop was among the original tenants and remained at Suburban Square for more than a half century before closing in 1990. When it did, it was the last place still selling the kind of long, white gloves generations of young women had worn to their debutante balls. The shop also had once had a millinery department, but that had closed in the sixties when ladies' hats went out of style. Other tenants over the years have included New York Fifth Avenue clothier Peck & Peck, which opened a store there in 1949, Helen Caro women's apparel, and, more recently, Kate Spade.

But the main attraction was Strawbridge & Clothier, which opened its 108,000-square-foot store in Suburban Square on May 12, 1930. The business wasn't done with exploring the suburbs either. A year later, it opened a four-story Art Deco store in Jenkintown north of Philly.

Despite these successes, projects like Country Club Park and Suburban Square remained anomalies. Department stores didn't immediately abandon downtown and invade the suburbs. In fact, little new development took place there over the next decade and a half as retailers were fortunate if they just made it through the Depression and then World War II.

As the war was winding down, however, developer Kemper Freeman bought a parcel of land twenty miles east of downtown Seattle and drew up plans for a shopping village with a "community feeling." That would include about forty stores and some 700 parking spots. Bellevue Shopping Square would be built in an unincorporated area and would feature trees and other greenery, distinguishing it from the concrete jungle downtown. There would be a 550-seat movie theater and restaurants and, yes, it *would* have a department store: Frederick & Nelson, a local retailer with a flagship store in downtown Seattle that had been purchased by Marshall Field in 1929.

The mall opened on August 20, 1946, announcing its debut with searchlights and an orchestra in an event covered live on radio. The Frederick & Nelson branch initially operated in a one-story building, selling only women's and children's clothing for its first three years

**This rendering of the distinctive Jordan Marsh "dome" at Shoppers' World
appeared in a 1951 ad for the innovative new shopping center.**

of operation, but the first regional shopping center in the Pacific Northwest was a huge success. Frederick & Nelson would later move into a much larger building, and a second anchor came on board with the arrival of J.C. Penney in 1955. Although Frederick & Nelson is no longer in business, the mall continued to grow and, as of 2018, included Macy's and Nordstrom as anchors among its 180 stores.

Bellevue Shopping Square was only the beginning. More regional shopping centers followed. In the early fall of 1951, a project called Shoppers' World opened in the Boston suburb of Framingham. Touted in the *Boston Globe* as "the world's largest suburban retail shopping center," it carried an $8 million price tag—eight times what it cost to build Bellevue Shopping Square. Jordan Marsh was the main anchor among fifty original tenants, which also included a small Sears branch and Gorin's Department Store, the second-largest shop in the mall at 30,000 square feet.

(Gorin's was a slightly more upscale outlet than, say, Woolworth's. The Shoppers' World branch occupied space on both stories and was the the twentieth in the regional chain, which had been founded just twenty-five miles away in Woburn at the turn of the century.)

Although the *Globe* described the design as "conservative, contemporary architecture," the distinctive 54-foot-high dome at one end made it look a little like a prototype for the Starship Enterprise. There was also a 100-foot smokestack on the west side of the mall, with "Sears" written on it. Extending from the dome were a pair of two-story rectangular wings on either side of a central green—landscaped with rhododendrons, yews, and English boxwood trees—where art exhibits were held. Covered walkways on both levels shielded window-shoppers from the elements, and a raised walkway between the two wings saved them from climbing stairs to get from one side to the other. The storefronts faced inward, offering visitors quite a contrast to the cars and fumes and sidewalk congestion they would have faced if they'd ventured downtown. An even starker contrast: In the era of parking meters and narrow downtown streets, visitors found a sea of free parking at Shoppers' World—6,000 spaces in all.

But it was the dome at one end, which housed the Jordan Marsh store, that really stood out. Extolled as the largest in the world, it had outer walls of glass and no interior dividing walls. It was clearly the crown jewel of Shoppers' World.

The stores themselves had something for everyone. The counters in one shop were shaped like miniature train cars to delight the kids, movie-lovers could attend a show at the cinema, and teens could use a walkie-talkie to request tunes at the record store. This must have seemed almost like magic, per the *Globe*: "The customer will sit comfortably in a den and merely request the number he wants; no clerks, no auditors, nobody else present. A microphone will pick up his request, and it will be played for him on a turntable he doesn't see."

But a headline that previewed the new center made the primary target audience clear: "Women Can Shop at 44 Different Types of Stores."

BALANCING ACT

None of this meant that downtown was dead. Far from it. Most chains continued to tout their downtown flagships as the place to be, home to larger selections and more opulent surroundings than their suburban counterparts could provide.

Leonard's in Fort Worth, Texas, tried to find a way around the problem of downtown traffic and scarce parking by building a rail system from its store to a 5,000-car parking lot nearly a mile away. Parking was free, and so was the air-conditioned train ride. The M&O Subway (named after store founders Marvin and Obie Leonard) operated on two tracks and could carry 100 customers in each car. It was only an actual subway for two-tenths of a mile, entering a tunnel as it approached the store and emerging at a terminal in Leonard's basement.

Shoppers didn't have to stay at Leonard's; they could exit the building for other retail and business destinations, but they had to pass through the department store to get there.

Some stores tried to strike a balance between downtown and the suburbs. When Rich's of Atlanta expanded into Knoxville, Tennessee, in the mid-fifties, it tried to have the best of both worlds, moving away from downtown's main thoroughfare, Gay Street, but settling on a new location just a couple of blocks away.

Gay Street showed how Main Street influenced the modern suburban mall, with a major department store anchor at either end of the retail district and smaller specialty shops in between that benefited from foot traffic between the two. One of those department stores, Miller's, opened in 1905 at the south end and the other, S.H. George, debuted six years later a mere two-minute stroll to the north. George's occupied a three-story building, while Miller's was larger at five stories, with a six-story Art Deco addition going up next door in 1935.

But when Rich's bought George's in 1952, it turned out to be the first stride in a two-step that ultimately left downtown Knoxville without a department store. Rich's acquisition was followed by an announcement that it would be closing the Gay Street shop and constructing a new store that would take up an entire city block about a quarter mile to the west. When that building opened three years later, it left Gay Street without one of its anchors.

It wasn't long before the other shoe dropped. In 1961, Rich's pulled out of the Knoxville market and sold its store to none other than Miller's. That store's Gay Street location remained open for twenty-two years before it finally closed, completing the migration of the city's major department stores away from its central district.

Truth be told, suburban shopping was great for chain department stores, because it gave them somewhere to expand in an era when downtown growth had hit a ceiling. Moreover, they had the wherewithal to do it, unlike their smaller competitors. This meant, simply, that the suburban retail boom helped fuel what would become an unending trend toward consolidation and uniformity in the industry.

Big department stores like Wards, Sears, Penney's, May Co., and, later, Macy's could afford to stake out claims in the hinterlands, because they had the capital to do so. Suburban developers, meanwhile, courted those chains because they were safe bets, financially speaking. Shoppers' World immediately snagged Jordan Marsh and Sears and also made a failed attempt to lure

Filene's. Other malls followed suit as they went up across America; by the seventies, a typical Los Angeles area mall included three of the following stores: The Broadway, May Co., Robinson's, Sears, and Penney's. Sometimes, a local department store would also be part of the mix, but many local merchants didn't have the money to make the transition and were forced to stay downtown (and, ultimately, close) as business dwindled there.

Miller's on Gay Street was a downtown anchor for years in Knoxville, Tennessee. Stephen H. Provost, 2018.

The result was a cookie-cutter approach to retailing, which sacrificed local character at the twin altars of convenience and familiarity.

The transformation was already well under way by 1964, when an article in the Journal of Marketing opened by declaring that "postwar migration to the suburbs, increasing traffic congestion in the cities, and new suburban shopping centers, have greatly reduced the popularity of downtown shopping." The article cited as evidence closures of major downtown department stores in cities such as Baltimore, Boston, Cleveland, Philadelphia, Pittsburgh, and even New York. Its authors set out to determine why customers chose to shop at three distinct kinds of department store: high-fashion houses,

discount (or "price-appeal") stores, and shops with broad appeal that fell between the two other categories.

The results were predictable. Stores in the *middle* were prospering in the suburbs because they were best suited to the emerging *middle* class that lived there. Downtown, meanwhile, was trending toward the extremes. High-fashion houses still attracted older women who were accustomed to shopping there, valued quality merchandise, and enjoyed the level of personal service such stores provided. Once that generation stopped coming downtown, those stores would be in trouble. But discounters faced a different problem. Unlike the aging glamour stores, which still drew a wealthier clientele in from the suburbs, they relied more heavily on those who lived nearby. As more people from the city relocated to the suburbs, the study warned, their customer base would decline.

In reality, this had already begun to happen. General downtown discounters such as S.S. Kresge and Sam Walton (who ran several Ben Franklin stores) were already opening big-box stores in the suburbs; over the next few years, those stores would grow to account for the bulk of their business, and the downtown stores would eventually disappear altogether. So would the high-fashion stores, as the older generation that patronized them was replaced by homemakers with baby boom children—young parents who had neither the time nor the inclination to drive downtown and when a regional shopping mall was at hand.

Over the course of the next two decades, downtown stores systematically closed, as both luxury stores and discounters found customers there too scarce. The in-betweens had already staked out their claim in the suburbs, and their higher- and lower-priced competitors had little choice but to follow. Downtown redevelopment projects provided little help. Some of them displaced the few residents still left downtown while others failed to provide housing for those who might have remained (or moved back). Downtowns became ghost towns.

$\boxed{\textbf{12}}$

MALLED

You can blame three people for the demise of the Main Street department store: Dwight Eisenhower, Bill Levitt, and Victor Gruen.

Of course, it's not that simple, but if you get down to brass tacks, the actions of those three men *were* instrumental in changing the face of retail in postwar America. Eisenhower, for his part, advocated for the interstate highway system, which was created by legislation he signed in 1956.

More than three decades earlier, the rise of the automobile had made it profitable for department stores to expand from the big cities into middle America. It had altered the dynamics of shopping by making Main Street a destination for the newly empowered, car-loving consumer. It was no longer necessary to order by catalog when you could hop in your car and drive five or ten minutes to a retail Shangri-La.

But by the mid-fifties, however, that Shangri-La was starting to show its age and getting a lot more crowded. The beginning of the postwar baby boom was adding to the population, and because downtown was a destination for shoppers and government workers alike, gridlock and bottlenecks were becoming typical. Before the interstate era, highways went through the heart of town, stopping for

The May Company store, undergoing renovation work, with Terminal Tower, right, on Cleveland's downtown public square. The fifty-two-story tower was the tallest building outside New York in North America from 1930 to 1964. Stephen H. Provost, 2019.

pedestrians, stop signs, and, later, traffic lights. As traffic increased, the congestion got so bad that commuters began to clamor for a way to bypass downtown.

Merchants, naturally, resisted the idea. They liked having a captive audience of drivers and passengers who had little else to do but look at storefront windows as their cars sat idling at an intersection. They feared that without this forced incentive, a portion of their customer base might dry up.

Eisenhower's priorities, however, dovetailed with those of the frustrated commuter. He wanted to build highways that could serve as supply routes in the event of a national crisis such as a foreign invasion. At the height of the Cold War, this seemed like a very real concern. Such highways would have to be wide enough to accommodate military vehicles, which couldn't afford to get bogged down navigating stoplights and pedestrian crossings. Thus, the Interstate Highway System was designed to skirt downtowns altogether, the happy result (for commuters) being a freer flow of traffic during peacetime.

TRACT-HOME REVOLUTION

As car production shifted from neutral into overdrive at the end of the war, postwar prosperity gave people the

means to hit the highway. It also gave them the ability to do something many of them had only dreamed of doing before: buy a house. That's where Bill Levitt came in. Before the war, city dwellers—many of them first- and second-generation immigrants—had been clustered together near city centers, living in apartment houses within walking distance of the big department stores. Levitt came along and changed the equation, adapting mass-production to the housing industry and creating what amounted to a Ford-style assembly line for the real estate industry.

Before the war, Levitt had focused on upscale housing in the Long Island area, but the emergence of a new middle class created a different sort of market. As the economy started to boom and GI loans began to kick in, young families had more money than they needed to keep renting that cramped downtown apartment but not enough to buy the kind of luxury homes Levitt's company had been producing. Not only were baby boomers being born, something else was being conceived: a new middle class. Suddenly, there were a lot of these young families, and a *lot* of homes would be needed to meet this new demand.

Levitt had a head start in doing so. He and his brother had worked on a government contract to build more than 2,300 war workers' homes in Virginia shortly after

Tract homes like these near Modesto, California, had started to create suburban sprawl before World War II, but the trend really took off after the war, specifically with the Levittown developments in New York and Pennsylvania. Dorothea Lange, 1940, public domain.

the attack on Pearl Harbor. Through trial and error, they had identified twenty-seven steps that were necessary to build a house, then created specialized teams to do the job.

The housing industry, like automotive production, had been comatose through World War II, having already been hit hard by the Depression. The number of new houses fell to one-tenth of what it had been during the Roaring Twenties, when a million a year were being built, but once the war was over, the trend abruptly reversed itself—and just kept going, hitting 1.7 million by 1950.

Levitt had maintained an option to buy some potato farmland out on Long Island, twenty-five miles east of Manhattan, since before the war. Now, he thought, the time was ripe to exercise that option. He envisioned it as the site of a massive new development, with homes that could be built quickly and inexpensively for the families of returning veterans and other newly employed young men with money to spend.

"Any damn fool can build homes," Levitt said. "What counts is how many you can sell for how little."

High volume plus low overhead. It was the same philosophy discount retailers would use to change the face of shopping. Levitt's company made its own nails and had its own sawmill to cut wood from its own privately owned forest. Levitt's specialized teams would go from one lot to the next, completing each step in the process of building the homes—as many as thirty-six a day. Trucks would deliver the materials to each home-site, and carpenters, tilers, painters, and roofers would do their thing in turn.

THE RESULT?

An ad in the *New York Journal American* laid it all out in glowing terms in the summer of 1948: "You're a lucky fellow, Mr. Veteran. Uncle Sam and the world's largest builders have made it possible for you to live in a charming house in a delightful community without having to pay for them with your eye teeth." You could choose from five exteriors on 6,000-square-foot lots, "unbelievably priced" $7,990—or just $58 a month with no down payment. "Practically everything" was included: a refrigerator, range, Bendix washing machine, Venetian blinds, GE oil burner—"the whole works." Some homes even had Admiral TVs built into the staircase. would

Even with all that, Levitt still made a profit of $1,000 on each home he sold.

Levitt & Sons built 17,000 of them in Levittown, and more than 80,000 people would live there. Not only that, it became the model for similar developments by the company and the template for the tract-home revolution that would sweep America in the fifties and sixties. The company built another 17,000 homes in Bucks County, Pennsylvania, in 1951, and a 11,000-home Levittown in New Jersey in 1958. Other Levitt developments not called Levittown popped up in sixteen states across the country, along with Puerto Rico and four foreign countries. Levitt-West built nearly two dozen developments in California alone, many of them in Orange County, which grew from 216,000 to 1.4 million people between 1950 and 1970.

Levitt was selling more than houses, though. The neighborhoods came equipped with community pools and playgrounds; new schools were built to serve them, and churches quickly appeared as well.

"Bill Levitt didn't just build a community here—he built a world," army veteran Hal Lefcourt told the *Trentonian* nearly five decades after moving into a Levitt home. "We were young, all of us who moved to Levittown, and we thought Bill Levitt was the greatest man in the world."

Lefcourt wasn't alone in that assessment. In July of 1950, Levitt appeared on the cover of Time magazine with the tagline "For sale: a new way of life."

That way of life was now open to thousands of families, but it remained out of reach for some—and not because of the price. Levitt refused to sell to black families, for fear that white families wouldn't buy his houses. He blamed the resulting discrimination on home buyers, not his policy: "As a Jew, I have no room in my mind or heart for racial prejudice," he said. "But, by various means, I have come to know that if we sell one house to a Negro family, then 90 to 95 percent of our white customers will not buy into the community. That is their attitude, not ours." It was the same attitude that kept department store staffs and customers largely segregated until the sixties. Levitt offered to build a separate housing tract for blacks but adamantly refused to integrate Levittown: "We can solve a housing problem or we can try to solve a racial problem," he said, "but we can't do both." The whites-only stipulation was built right into the homebuyer's contract. A Levittown house, Clause 25 stated, could not be "used or occupied by any person other than members of the Caucasian race."

Levitt wasn't the only one to segregate his neighborhoods. Racially restrictive covenants, as they were called, were commonplace in the United States during the first half of the century. The Supreme Court ruled such provisions were unenforceable shortly after Levittown was built on Long Island. But, oddly, the provisions themselves weren't ruled illegal until 1968, allowing de facto segregation to continue. Levittown evicted two residents for inviting black children from another neighborhood into their homes and branded those opposed to segregation as communists.

Levitt's second development opened north of Philadelphia in 1951, but it wasn't until 1957, when one family resold its house to a black family, that the color line was broken there. Mob violence, complete with rock throwing and a cross burning, followed.

Levitt continued to oppose integrated housing even after that, fighting a lawsuit by two blacks who wanted a home in his New Jersey development in 1960. Although the neighborhoods were eventually opened to nonwhite owners, most had to buy on resale, and other obstacles remained in place. Lenders for decades refused to approve loans for minority applicants, deeming them a poor risk and relegating them to poorer neighborhoods in industrial or blighted areas. Lending discrimination, combined with racially restrictive covenants cemented segregation long after it was no longer in effect. A 1996 survey found just 137 blacks among more than 53,286

Victor Gruen designed his first open-air shopping center, Northland near Detroit, which opened in 1954 as the first of four planned at various compass points around the city. Nikolai Nolan, 2015. Creative Commons 4.0 license: https://creativecommons.org/licenses/by-sa/4.0/deed.en.

residents of the first Levittown. And similar patterns persisted across the country, as mostly white and mostly black neighborhoods existed on "different sides of the tracks." In Fresno, a planning document from the seventies even referred to Shaw Avenue, a major east–west thoroughfare, as the city's Mason-Dixon Line: affluent, white suburbs to the north; poorer, often blighted minority neighborhoods closer to downtown.

Victor's vision

That image of downtown hurt the stores that remained there in the long term, not only in Fresno but across the country. The process of downtown decay was, however, a gradual one.

Thanks to the flight of downtown residents to the suburbs, department stores lost some of the foot traffic on Main Street. Fewer and fewer pedestrians saw the stores' expansive street windows, revealing professionally designed displays of mannequins decked out in the latest fashion. More and more people stayed away because they feared being mugged or panhandled. The new freeways gave them an escape route, and the new houses a suburban refuge. Thanks to the bypasses, downtown retailers lost much of their "drive-by" clientele, suffering alongside motels, juice stands, and other highway institutions. But they still had one thing in their favor: They were the only place in town that residents could go to shop—at least at the beginning.

Then came the regional shopping center, the indoor shopping mall, and Victor Gruen. Gruen was no stranger to retail. In the early forties, he had earned contracts with Joseph Magnin of San Francisco to design buildings for new branches in Reno and San Mateo, but those projects were mere warm-ups for Gruen's main act: changing the face of American shopping by steering consumers away from downtown and toward the vast new frontier of tract homes being built to accommodate the baby boom's fast-growing families.

Gruen's dream was bolstered by a new consciousness about just how precarious the nation's safety was in an age when atomic bombs were pointed at our shores. World War II and the nation's descent into a Cold War with the Soviet Union had changed people's thinking. On the one hand, they had spurred Eisenhower to propose building a network of streamlined highways for use in a national emergency. On the other, they also sparked Gruen's vision of suburban America. So much of the nation's wealth was concentrated in her cities, Gruen argued, that it was highly vulnerable in the event of an enemy bombing. He advocated for regional shopping centers, which could serve a dual purpose, just as the interstate highway system could: "merchandising areas, shelter areas, and large, paved parking areas" could easily be employed as bomb shelters.

But Gruen also had a personal agenda—an undisguised disdain for the automobile, describing its "threat to human life and health" as "just as great as the exposed sewer." It was the polar opposite of Eisenhower's approach, which created more room for more cars. Still, just as Eisenhower's interstate highway system had a profound impact on Main Street America, so did Gruen's vision of suburban shopping. Both created attractive detours away from city centers, unclogging gridlocked surface streets and, in the same stroke, forcing retailers to adapt.

One of the most notable features of department stores in the first half of the twentieth century had been their sheer size. They were behemoths, five, ten, or fifteen stories high, taking up entire city blocks. Woodward & Lothrop in Washington, DC, had started off as a modest dry-goods partnership in the Boston area between Samuel Woodward and Alvin Lothrop; seven years after starting up, they moved to the nation's capital.

Like other successful department stores of the era, the business expanded as it enjoyed greater success, eventually consuming almost an entire city block (400,000 square feet of retail space) and rising ten stories above street level. By 1904, annual sales were approaching $3 million. In the twenties, the store was a veritable city in miniature, including a restaurant, a theater, a travel agency, a merry-go-round, a hair salon, and art exhibits on top of nearly seventy retail departments.

Hudson's in downtown Detroit was even bigger. It had twenty-three floors aboveground in addition to two basements and six more stories for storage and mechanical support. Its 2.2 million square feet made it the second-largest department store in the world, surpassed only by Macy's in New York City.

Hudson's and "Woodies" (as it was affectionately called) were typical of the era. Everything you could possibly want was under a single roof. It was the ultimate in convenience—until, that is, cars became so numerous and traffic so snarled that it was an ordeal just to get there. When Shangri-La became off-limits, it tended to lose its appeal.

This was certainly true for Gruen, who held mega-retail stores like Woodies, Wanamaker's, and their ilk in low regard. Little better, he said, were the strip malls that started popping up in the aftermath of World War II. These new developments, he lamented, were merely "using the old formula" by arranging "stores along one side or two sides of a busy highway, like pearls of a necklace." The only progress he could see was that there was "more space for parking" to accommodate a public still "bothered by gas fumes and noise."

Gruen's solution to this problem was different from Eisenhower's. Instead of bypassing city centers with new roads, he proposed getting rid of the cars entirely and creating new malls geared to a different type of traffic: pedestrians. And rather than putting everything under a single roof in a department store, he called for an increase in the number of specialized retailers. Specialty stores, he said, "are offering their customers surroundings which, by making the customer feel comfortable and 'at home,' create an excellent shopping atmosphere."

Gruen set about making his dream into a reality, designing his first open-air shopping mall: Northland Center near Detroit, which opened in 1954. At the time, it was the world's largest shopping center and one of four planned to surround the city, each at a different suburban compass point (the others—Eastland in 1957, Westland in 1965, and Southland in 1970—were built later).

Victor Gruen's Southdale in the Minneapolis suburb of Edina, seen here in 2005, was the world's first indoor shopping mall when it was built in 1956. Public domain.

The key component to Gruen's plan was, ironically, a department store: Hudson's. It became the first "anchor" store at a regional shopping center, a role department stores would continue to fill for the remainder of the century. This Hudson's branch, however, was much smaller than its downtown flagship store—"only" four stories. It no longer needed to house everything under one roof, because the adjacent specialty stores would complement its selection of merchandise. Original tenants included the same sorts of retailers that would come to be staples of the suburban mall experience: shoe stores (seven), jewelers (three), women's clothiers (ten), men's clothiers (five), and restaurants (four). There were also four home-furnishing and appliance stores, a Kresge's five-and-dime, a record shop, a drugstore, a Kroger supermarket, a beauty parlor, a bank, and a post office. All the stores were air-conditioned, and the grounds featured thirteen sculptures by six artists.

For all that, however, Northland wasn't Gruen's defining moment. That would come two years later with the opening of Southdale Mall in Edina, a suburb of Minneapolis. Southdale was the next-best thing to an amusement park for the American consumer. As *Fortune* magazine put it, "The sparkling lights and bright colors provide a continuous invitation to look up ahead, to stroll on to the next store, and to buy."

The new creation had just about everything its predecessor had, but with a twist. It was all indoors. Entrances faced inward, toward a central corridor, rather than outward, while replicating a measure of open-air ambience thanks to fountains, sculpted trees, a skylight, and even an aviary in its central Garden Court. Delivery trucks were hidden from view thanks to an underground tunnel, where they entered and unloaded their goods, which were then taken to various stores through one of six elevators. Gruen's merchandising masterpiece was an aesthetic counterpoint to what he described as "avenues of horror . . . flanked by the greatest collection of vulgarity—billboards, motels, gas stations, shanties, car lots, miscellaneous industrial equipment, hot dog stands, wayside stores—ever collected by mankind."

Southdale, built around two big department stores—Dayton's and Donaldson's—was the first indoor shopping mall in America, and it was an immediate hit. To paraphrase New Yorker columnist Malcolm Gladwell, Gruen hadn't designed a building, he'd built an archetype.

And, some would argue, created a monster.

From then on, enclosed malls across America were built re-creating his vision, and their popularity soon began funneling shoppers from congested confines of Main Street to wide-open spaces of suburbs—soon to be even more accessible thanks to Eisenhower's system of interstate highways.

Taking the amusement park theme even further, some, like Fresno's Manchester Center and Parkway Plaza in San Diego County, installed carousels. Others had bounce houses, arcades, indoor miniature golf, and other attractions geared toward kids of all ages. As time went by, themed restaurants like the Rainforest Café took the concept even further. California's first enclosed mall, the Gruen-designed Topanga Plaza in the western San Fernando Valley, opened in 1964 with an ice rink and an artificial "rain fountain." It was the nascent mall culture's first footprint in the future land of the Valley Girl.

Other visionaries took the concept in a slightly different direction. Old Towne in Torrance opened in 1972 without any major anchors; it attracted shoppers using cobblestone walkways, vintage streetlamps, a row of artisans (woodcarvers, goldsmiths, potters, glassblowers, etc.), a merry-go-round, a gazebo, a "frog amphitheater" for puppet shows, and even a wax museum. In unveiling the $10 million concept, developer Robert Brindle told the *Los Angeles Times* that Old Town would "make shopping fun," using a concept he called "recreational retailing"—with a nineteenth-century theme.

"We're creating nostalgia, but not too authentic," Brindle told the Times. "We're all nostalgic for the old days, but it wasn't all pretty! We're staying true to the spirit, but it will all be bright and fresh—none of the dismal feeling of so much of the real yesterday, not a slum."

Brindle compared it to The Galleria in Houston, which had opened a couple of years earlier with a theme of its own, modeled after the world's oldest shopping mall, in Milan, Italy. The Galleria, which featured a glazed barrel-vaulted ceiling, chandeliers, and an ice rink, was paired with a hotel. It was an approach later used in Las

Vegas, where 100-degree summers made enclosed (air-conditioned!) malls a natural complement for the city's themed hotels. Caesars Palace had the Forum Shops, The Venetian had the Grand Canal Shoppes, and Planet Hollywood also had a mall of its own.

Bigger was better. After baseball's Twins and football's Vikings moved out of Metropolitan Stadium for a new domed stadium, they razed the Met and built the 2.5-million-square-foot Mall of America in its place (plaques in the floor mark the location of home plate for baseball and midfield on the gridiron). At the center of the mall was a full-fledged theme park called Nickelodeon Universe, complete with roller coasters. There was also a 300-foot aquarium tunnel from which visitors could see more than 4,500 marine creatures. You could even go snorkeling or scuba diving.

Even bigger were the Gruen-designed South Coast Plaza in Costa Mesa, California, which grew to 2.6 million square feet of retail space, Aventura Mall in Miami (2.8 million), and King of Prussia (2.9 million).

With Southdale, Gruen had unleashed his Frankenstein's monster on suburban America, and it had taken on a life of its own.

Developers, spurred on by new tax law passed in 1954, used Gruen's template as a cash cow for the next four decades, luring department and specialty stores alike away from downtown and toward this new frontier. Even flagship stores that had spent more than half a century serving clients at city centers turned their attention elsewhere, focusing on the suburbs or, in some cases, even shuttering their downtown stores entirely. Gottschalks,

The City of Fresno closed Fulton Street to traffic and created an outdoor pedestrian mall based on Victor Gruen's idea. But the initial flood of customers had slowed to a trickle by the new millennium, as most had followed retailers to the suburbs. Stephen H. Provost, 2015.

which had served downtown Fresno since 1904, closed its "home" store in 1988 and focused on branch locations that were bringing in far more money—several of them in the Fresno suburbs.

DOWNTOWN REIMAGINED

Ironically, the store's departure marked the ultimate failure of Gruen's other "big idea": using outdoor pedestrian malls to revitalize the very city centers his enclosed suburban malls were helping to destroy. In 1958, he designed the nation's first outdoor pedestrian mall in Kalamazoo, Michigan; seven years later, he created another in Fresno, California. In both cases, the malls were ultimately scrapped and the streets that had been closed to accommodate them were reopened to traffic. The primary reason? For all their amenities, they failed to stem the tide of consumers from inner cities toward the suburbs.

Gruen had never intended for the mall to be an end in itself. When he designed Southdale, he envisioned the mall as the cornerstone for a full-scale urban center, complete with schools, offices, and, most importantly, places for people to live. He wanted to re-create the European village in the United States, but he had to rely on developers to do it, and they wanted no part of this larger vision. The mall wasn't the carrot that enticed them to implement Gruen's full vision; it was the carrot cake they ate for dessert after skipping the main meal. They wanted a place to make a quick buck and attract as many paying customers as possible.

The mall did exactly that, and Gruen even got credit for creating the dynamic. In "The World in a Shopping Mall," Margaret Crawford described the "Gruen Transfer" as "that moment when a 'destination buyer,' with a specific purchase in mind, is transformed into an impulse shopper, a crucial point . . . in the shift from a determined stride to a meandering gait."

The pedestrian malls Gruen had hoped would revitalize urban downtowns failed, in part, for the same reason Southdale never lived up to his full vision: His plans called for a full-scale community, not just a retail smorgasbord. Apartments to support the refurbished urban hub were crucial to the plan, but those apartments never materialized. They were expendable in the suburbs, where mall-builders could substitute massive parking lots to accommodate visitors making their way to the hinterlands in the motorcars. They had seemingly limitless land at their disposal on which to build them. But downtown was a different story. The whole point of Gruen's plan was to de-emphasize the automobile; you could build a pedestrian mall downtown, but if you needed a car to get there, you weren't solving the problem. In some ways, you were making it worse by blocking off a city street. Meanwhile, you were presenting consumers with a psychological roadblock. You were asking them to invest time and gas money to drive downtown, hunt for a parking space and plop several coins into a meter—something you didn't have to do at a suburban mall. And for what? They were being asked to have faith that the old, rundown city core had, indeed, been transformed into a pristine crown jewel and that the blighted areas around it wouldn't impact their shopping experience.

It was, in the end, a bridge too far. If a large segment of the shoppers had lived within walking distance, as Gruen envisioned, they would have *seen* the transformation with their own eyes. It would have been right next door. They wouldn't have needed to hunt for a parking space. And they wouldn't have needed to feed the meter, then keep glancing nervously at their watches as they dashed from store to store, anxious to ensure that they returned to their cars before their time expired.

Still, Gruen's idea got off to a promising start. He pitched it first to Fort Worth, Texas, calling for a loop highway and parking structures to keep cars away from the central district, which would be reserved for pedestrians. The city ultimately passed on the idea, but Gruen pointed out that "similar plans, with variations to fit each individual case, could be developed for all our cities."

It wasn't long before other cities were stepping up to the plate. First in line was Kalamazoo, which didn't build the loop highway but did install a Gruen-designed pedestrian mall in 1959 at a cost of $60,000. Two blocks of Burdick Street were closed to vehicle traffic, and the asphalt replaced with tall trees, brick planters, reflecting pools, fountains, and grassy areas. Standing sentinel on either side of this oasis were stores like Woolworth's, W.T. Grant, J.C. Penney, and an upscale department store called Gilmore's. A third block was added the following year and a fourth several years later.

The initial results were encouraging. A year after the mall opened, retail sales had jumped 25 percent, pedestrian traffic rose by nearly one-third, and more than fifty other cities were planning pedestrian malls.

More than 200 were ultimately built, including one in Fresno with plenty of similarities to the Kalamazoo model. Central California's main highway, US 99, had long run directly through the heart of downtown, but that had changed with a new freeway bypass to the east. Sears had been lured away from the city center by a new regional mall to the north, and the area was in the midst of a downward spiral. Gruen's plan promised to not only halt that decline but reverse it, using the same formula he had proposed for Fort Worth and Kalamazoo.

Fulton Mall, designed by landscape architect Garrett Eckbo in consultation with Gruen, debuted in the fall of 1964 and was hailed as the turning point for downtown Fresno. Water sprang into the air from fountains installed along the mall; a series of sculptures greeted pedestrians as they went from shop to shop. There were benches, a children's play area, and wide-open spaces where the cars used to be.

"As I write this, I am sitting contentedly, a cool drink at my elbow, right in the middle of Fulton Street," Bernard Traper gushed in the October 1966 *Reader's Digest*. "Two and a half years ago, I would have been run over, arrested, or firmly led away to have my head examined. What I am doing now is simply part of the new pattern of life this bustling city has adopted; one starting from the premise that downtown is for people."

Fresno won a national award for Excellence in Community Architecture from the American Institute of Architects in 1965, and the US Department of Housing and Urban Development bestowed an award for "National Design Excellence" on the mall in 1968. That same year, a documentary touted Fresno as *A City Reborn*, thanks to its innovative downtown mall, telling the story of how Gruen's vision came to be implemented.

The narrator explains the problem the city was facing: "With the suburbs expanding and growing self-sufficient, downtown streets were clogged with traffic going *through* town, not *to* town."

"The solution? Separate cars and pedestrians for the benefit of both" using a one-way inner loop around a new superblock, which was to be reserved for pedestrians. It was a move right out of Gruen's playbook, but it turned out to be a Hail Mary pass. The excitement surrounding the new mall boosted pedestrian traffic by 115 percent in its first year, but the bustling crowds shown in the film wouldn't last, and the mall's heyday turned out to be all too brief.

Just six years after the mall opened, Montgomery Ward announced it was closing its downtown store and moving to north Fresno, the more affluent section of town where Fresno's first enclosed shopping mall opened that same year. The new, air-conditioned center, Fashion Fair, featured two branches of stores already on Fulton: J.C. Penney and Gottschalks. Both kept their downtown stores open—for the time being. But the move did cost Fulton Mall another major retailer: Cooper's Department Store, which had been purchased by Gottschalks some years earlier. Instead of keeping two stores open on Fulton, Gottschalks moved some of its Cooper's inventory to the new enclosed mall, which was to be run by former Cooper's manager Scotty Robertson. In effect, Fulton lost Cooper's to Fashion Fair. In a single year, Fulton Mall had surrendered two of its four anchor tenants.

It was the beginning of a slow decline from which Gruen's showpiece would never recover. Enthusiasm for the mall waned, and as shoppers left downtown for Fresno's regional malls, they were replaced by transients and residents of adjacent, less affluent neighborhoods. Rumors of crime and vagrancy ensured that the shoppers wouldn't return. In 1974, city leaders pulled back from fully implementing Gruen's plan, voting unanimously to keep Tulare and Fresno streets open to traffic rather than closing them in the "superblock," as originally intended.

Penney's kept its downtown store open until 1986 and Gottschalks for two more years after that before finally giving up the ghost, leaving the city center without a single department store. High-end specialty retailers—many of which had branches in competing centers to the north, Fashion Fair, and/or Manchester Center—closed on the mall as well, giving way to smaller, discount retailers and empty storefronts. One by one, they left: upscale men's clothier Roos/Atkins; women's fashion store Rodders; Walter Smith menswear; Edmond's Jewelers; and Leeds Shoes. Harry Coffee menswear had been in business since 1916 but closed on the mall in 1985.

Parking structures such as this one just off Fresno's Fulton Mall were designed to give shoppers easy access to downtown stores, public offices, and other destinations. Stephen H. Provost, 2015.

The elimination of paid parking for a time failed to spark a retail renaissance, as did the addition of a Triple-A baseball stadium adjacent to the mall in 2002. A cinema multiplex failed to materialize (one opened at Manchester instead), and hopes of luring a Bass Pro Shops store downtown also fell through. Meanwhile, a few scattered retailers hung on longer as the mall languished. But Luftenburg's Bridal, which had spent more than seventy years on Fulton, finally moved north in 2013 before going out of business three years later, while Procter's Jewelers, which predated the mall by two decades, soldiered on until it was gutted by fire in 2014.

A study of the area conducted at the time noted that the mall had become home to "vacant storefronts, empty office buildings, and a small collection of retailers."

"Today," it concluded, "Fulton Mall is characterized by relatively low levels of retail and other economic activity, it is devoid of substantial activity on weeknights after 5 p.m., when Downtown's more than 30,000 daytime workers leave Downtown. Vacancies are common among the storefronts and especially in spaces above the ground level along the Mall."

In the end, both Kalamazoo and Fresno gave up on the Gruen model, reopening the malled-up streets to vehicle traffic. Burdick Street in Kalamazoo reopened to cars in 1999; Fulton became a "through" street once again in the fall of 2017. The sculptures were moved to the sides to make way for the pavement, new signage was installed, and the area was rechristened the Fulton Entertainment District. The transformation brought new hope to the area, just as the mall itself had more than a half century earlier, but it also signaled the triumph of the soulless suburban amusement park over the heart of the city, at least for the time being. As of this writing, only a handful of pedestrian malls remain open, most of them in university towns.

Lost in San Diego

Even the most successful downtown shopping center on the West Coast was poised to call it quits as the twenty-first century approached its third decade. Horton Plaza had helped revive downtown San Diego when it opened in 1985 after being in the works for more than a decade. Designed like an indoor mall around a central corridor,

The design of Horton Plaza in downtown San Diego was based in part on an idea by author Ray Bradbury. Coolcaesar, 2018. Creative Commons 3.0 license: https://creativecommons.org/licenses/by-sa/3.0/deed.en.

it was open to the sky at the top, creating a courtyard feel that was somehow both open and cozy at the same time. Five stories vertical, it was an eclectic mix of boxy architecture, old-style streetlamps, escalators, and moving walkways.

There were sweeping curves, acute angles, archways, and vibrant colors in an array of patterns that created a sense of wonderment at what might be around the next bend. There was even a massive pendulum clock, dating all the way back to 1907, that was moved to the center from outside the Jessop and Sons jewelry store downtown. If the design seemed part historical and part whimsical, you can credit acclaimed science fiction author Ray Bradbury for that. His essay "The Aesthetics of Lostness" served as inspiration for Jon Jerde's design. In it, he lamented "blank facades" without mystery and texture; nothing to "draw the eye and attract the soul."

No way to lose yourself in the experience.

What if, Bradbury mused, a mall were to create an entire floor called The Attic? "Up there," he suggested, "stash all your antique shops, antiquarian booksellers, Victorian toy merchants, magic shops, Halloween card and decoration facilities, and little cinemas running Dracula fourteen hours a day, or name another half-dozen specialty stores that wouldn't mind being half lit and fully exciting."

The idea, he would later say, was to build a place "where people could spend an afternoon, getting safely lost, just wandering about."

Jerde took Bradbury's vision and ran with it. Before Horton Plaza even opened, it had earned him enough of a reputation to land a job as architect for the 1984 Los Angeles Olympic Games. He would also go on to design the CityWalk outdoor plaza in Hollywood, adjacent to Universal Studios.

Horton Plaza gave downtown San Diego an eclectic new vibe, a labyrinthine pair of parking structures and a new lease on life for the Gaslamp District, an area that had long been relegated to drugs, homelessness, and prostitution. (It also, incidentally, gave the area a few suicides. The year it opened, a man jumped to his death from a third-story walkway. He would not be the last.)

In a piece for the *New York Times*, architecture critic Paul Goldberger described it as "a conventional shopping mall on a stage set for an Italian hill town, a mix of turrets and colonnades and terraces and towers, all in tones of peach and apricot and rose and ochre. It is entered by a grand staircase, and its main walkway twists and turns to create constantly changing vistas."

"It is wildly exuberant, a kind of Southern California fantasy of a European street. It even has an abstract version of the cathedral in Siena as a focal point on the main plaza."

Over the years, however, its exuberance faded, and many of its shops closed. Founding tenant Nordstrom's, one of two major anchors along with Macy's, closed in 2016. Its only remaining full-service restaurant, Panda Inn, departed the following year. Already long gone were Planet Hollywood and a huge store in the now-defunct Sam Goody music chain, which together had moved into the space once occupied by Robinson's.

In 2018, shopping center operator Westfield sold the mall to a group that planned to remodel and convert it into an office/lifestyle center that would retain some retail elements.

If was a far cry from the days when Goldberger had lauded the then-new Horton Plaza's "freewheeling spirit," with its Art Moderne cinema and safari apparel store with a jungle-like ambience that made a visitor "feel as if he had stumbled into Disneyland's safari ride." Goldberger took the comparison one step further: "There is a bit of Disneyland inside every shopping mall struggling to get out," he wrote. "In Horton Plaza in the center of downtown San Diego, the struggle is over: Disneyland has burst through with a vengeance."

But this offshoot of Disneyland, as originally conceived by Ray Bradbury, was dead.

All of which brings us back to our friend Victor Gruen.

THE EPCOT DREAM

Although Bradbury's "aesthetics of lostness" became a reality, at least for a time, the most ambitious plan to bring Gruen's ideas to fruition never broke ground—a plan that took root during the sixties in the mind of Gruen's most famous admirer, none other than Walt Disney.

Like Gruen, Disney bemoaned the transformation of America's cities into cluttered, smog-filled centers beset by creeping urban decay. Disney's Tomorrowland attraction in Anaheim, with its elevated monorail, offered a glimpse of what he envisioned. But he wanted to create it on a far grander scale. What Disney had in mind was much more than just another amusement park, a "Disneyland East." It would be a full-fledged, self-contained city of some 20,000 people, who would live and work and move around there.

Disney put his money where his mouth was. In 1965, he spent $5.1 million to purchase a piece of Florida swampland twice the size of Manhattan, with an eye toward creating what he called an Experimental Prototype Community of Tomorrow, or EPCOT for short. In a 1966 promotional film, he described it as "a planned environment, demonstrating to the world what American communities can accomplish through proper control of planning and design."

Yes, there would be a theme park, but it wouldn't be the most important aspect of the project. Far from it. The theme park and other tourist facilities would fill just one small area of the vast ever-evolving development, Disney said. Plans included an "airport of the future," a 1,000-acre industrial park and a high-speed rapid-transit system. And that was just the beginning. EPCOT was meant to be experimental in a very real sense, offering American entrepreneurs a testing ground for a vast array of innovations.

Some of the words Disney used to describe the project could have just as easily come from Victor Gruen's mouth: "I don't believe there's a challenge anywhere in the world that's more important to people everywhere than finding solutions to the problems of our cities," he declared.

To meet that challenge, Disney borrowed several ideas from Gruen, including the shape of the city, which mirrored the design of Gruen's downtown revitalization projects: a central hub for commerce and entertainment, ringed by concentric circles of living space—apartments close to the center, followed by a greenbelt and, on at its edges, low-density residential housing.

The monorail was always part of EPCOT's design, but Walt Disney envisioned the project as much more than an amusement park. Leamericanos, 2007. Creative Commons 3.0 license: https://creativecommons.org/licenses/by-sa/3.0/deed.en.

Disney also shared Gruen's disdain for the automobile.

"Here, the pedestrian will be king," the film's narrator proclaimed, "free to walk and browse without fear of motorized vehicles." The primary modes of transportation would be a monorail and a WEDWay PeopleMover, the same system used in the Tomorrowland attraction at Anaheim's Disneyland. Automobiles and trucks would be consigned to an underground level, below the pedestrian sphere and out of sight, just as delivery trucks remained out of sight at Gruen's Southdale Mall.

Pedestrians wouldn't have to worry about going out in the rain or braving Florida's humid summer heat. Like one of Gruen's indoor malls, the entire community would be completely enclosed in what renderings depicted as a giant bubble. "In this climate-controlled environment," the film's narrator explained, "shoppers and theater-goers and people just out for a stroll will enjoy ideal weather conditions, protected day and night from rain, heat and cold, and humidity."

Disney even approached Ray Bradbury to help out, asking whether the author would contribute poetic metaphors to tell the history of mankind; his writings would be included in a building called Spaceship Earth. Bradbury produced a script in five acts, from a "Descent into the Past" in Act I to the "Future World" in Act V. A portion of his original script, from the fourth act, read:

We have gone deep down in Time
to see our Spaceship Earth

born in universal midnight
With new knowledge —
new technology
new <u>communications</u>
we built new Walls.
Walls that <u>Informed</u>—Changed Lives
<u>Changed Worlds</u>.
Now let us point up to Wall of Space!
Come up to Light
To Stars—to Worlds beyond.

But Disney never reached those "Worlds beyond" with his project, which—as originally envisioned—only got as far as the conceptual stage. He died the same year the short film was produced, long before he could even begin to develop his dream, and his successors did what developers had done to Gruen. They built the centerpiece of his plan but stopped there. EPCOT, in the end, didn't wind up being a community at all but merely another (albeit impressive) amusement park.

If Disney died with his dream unrealized, Gruen lamented how suburban developers—"fast-buck promoters and speculators"—had twisted his vision, for their own purposes, into something it was never meant to be. They had used his blueprint to create "selling machines" instead of the vibrant communities he had hoped would emerge. It's no surprise, therefore, that the divorce between Gruen and these builders who had betrayed him was a bitter one.

His commentary on their estrangement?

"I refuse to pay alimony for those bastard developments."

In a 1978 interview with the *Los Angeles Times*, two years before his death, he foresaw hard times in the future for the monster he'd created. Conventional shopping centers, he predicted, would soon be "a thing of the past."

It took a little longer than he might have expected, but thanks to the e-commerce revolution of the twenty-first century, he wasn't far wrong.

13

RUN OF THE MILL

Before Walmart and Target and Kmart and Woolco, a rag-tag group of entrepreneurs set up shop in old Northeast textile mills that were floundering after the World War II. They were a different breed of businessman than the immigrant peddlers who had cut their teeth as traveling salesmen before setting up a small dry-goods store on Main Street. These were home-grown capitalists who had spent their childhoods getting into trouble on

Brothers Sidney and Herbert Hubschman started the Two Guys from Harrison discount chain by selling lightly damaged TV sets in a vacant lot in 1946. Public domain.

that same Main Street and hanging out at the five-and-dimes their parents had founded.

Men like Max Coffman and Eugene Ferkauf didn't care much for the time-honored traditions revered by the previous generation. They cared about making a profit, and that's exactly what they set out to do.

Coffman, the son of Russian immigrants, found success after a childhood in which he worked as a grocery store delivery boy and engaged in sidewalk boxing matches to earn nickels from passersby. By the sixties, he had built a multimillion-dollar chain of discount stores called Mammoth Mart, and in 1967, he won the Horatio Alger Award for displaying initiative and perseverance in the face of major challenges.

"If you work hard, opportunity will come along and you'll be ready for it," Coffman said. "Be determined, work hard, run fast, fear nothing as you go up the ladder. Surround yourself with the best people you can find. Share responsibility, face reverses with determination, never give up. Keep fighting and you will succeed."

That fearless, never-take-no-for-an-answer attitude was the hallmark of the discount revolution. If something stood in your way, you plowed straight through it. Ferkauf, who founded the phenomenally successful E.J. Korvette chain, was bucking the system from the beginning. He started out working in his father's luggage business, where he slashed prices and went around the neighborhood dropping off business cards promoting big discounts. Other retailers in the area didn't take kindly to this and complained to his father, an old-school businessman who hadn't authorized the price cuts and didn't care for discounters. Discounted goods had a reputation for being low-quality merchandise: the product of shoddy workmanship and flimsy, second-rate material. The elder Ferkauf had built up a reputation for quality, and he had no interest in jeopardizing that for a few extra bucks. His attitude? The store was making a good profit anyway. Why mess with success?

Buffums' IS FORCED TO OPEN SUNDAYS BY COMPETITION

All Buffums' stores (except those located in Newport and San Diego) will be open the next two Sundays from 12 Noon to 5 P.M.

We don't want to open on Sunday—we have been forced to open by competition.

The great majority of stores competitive with Buffums' have been open the past 3 Sundays—frankly, the tremendous sales made by other stores on Sundays has hurt Buffums' business. We cannot permit this to happen any longer.

It is with great regret, and even some sense of guilt, that I have made this decision to open Sundays, but it was necessary to protect the interests of our stockholders a substantial number of whom are employees.

V. G. Young
Chairman of the Board & President

Buffums' took out a large ad in the Long Beach newspaper in December 1969 to explain why and apologize for the fact that it felt it necessary to open on Sundays, blaming "the competition."

But his son saw room for even more success, and it wasn't long before people started responding to those little cards he'd been spreading around. They worked so well that it wasn't long before he was pulling in ten times as much business as his father was. Having grown tired of the arguments between them, Eugene Ferkauf quit the business and struck out on his own. He would build the fastest-growing discount store of the fifties, and his father would be dead within a year.

Their divergent fortunes were a microcosm of what would happen in the world of retailing over the next four decades. Department stores would enter a slow decline, while discounters enjoyed a meteoric rise.

In a way, Ferkauf's father was right. Quality was secondary, even irrelevant for many discounters. They didn't worry about long-term results, focusing instead on customers in the here and now. That's where there was money to be made. If they could get customers to make a purchase in the moment, when they had money in their pockets, that wasn't half the battle, it was game, set, and match.

Instead of trying to have it all by catering to high-end patrons aboveground and cost-conscious customers in the basement, discounters were laser focused on the shoppers in search of a deal.

They weren't trying to put one over on customers, though; quite the opposite. Shoppers knew exactly what they were doing. They knew what they were getting at a discount store wasn't a high-fashion brand name with a ten-year warranty. They couldn't afford such things, and they were willing to live with the prospect that the goods they were buying wouldn't last more than a few years. Then they'd be able to afford a replacement. Sure, they could save up their pennies and buy something a little more durable from a department store a year or two down the line, but why wait when you could have it now? This kind of semi-disposable retailing could be a lot more profitable than the "old way of doing things," as Ferkauf's success proved.

The era of instant gratification had begun, supplanting the old Puritan work ethic of hard work, patience, thrift, and playing by the rules.

BLUE SUNDAY

To the new breed of discounters, rules were made to be broken: rules like closing up shop after dark, refusing to sell products like alcohol and playing cards, and "blue laws" that required shops to stay closed on Sundays.

Devout Presbyterian George Dayton, founder of Dayton's department store in Minneapolis, ran his business the way he ran his life; his devotion to punctuality,

prudence, and sobriety helped define the store's image. It didn't sell liquor on the premises, even after Prohibition was lifted. And the company wouldn't even run ads in any newspaper that accepted liquor ads. In Detroit, Hudson's didn't even allow references to the colors "burgundy" and "champagne" because of their associations with alcohol, and cocktail dresses were referred to as "after-five" apparel.

Not only did Dayton's keep its doors locked on Sundays; employees weren't allowed to travel on that day. But it wasn't just store policy that kept stores shuttered on Sundays, in many places, it was the law.

Blue laws had been in place since colonial times as a means of enforcing the Fourth Commandment in Exodus: "Remember the sabbath day, to keep it holy. Six days you shall labor and do all your work, but the seventh day is a sabbath to the Lord God; in it you shall not do any work, you, or your son, or your daughter, your manservant, or your maidservant, or your cattle, or the sojourner who is within your gates."

Blue laws weren't always universally popular. Indeed, the term itself appears to stem from sarcastic reference to rigid moral codes that were common in the eighteenth century. Sticklers about enforcing the laws were derided as "bluenoses." Nonetheless, they were widely accepted during the first part of the twentieth century. Sporting events weren't played on Sundays in Pennsylvania until 1931, when the Philadelphia Athletics baseball team was granted an exemption for baseball. It wasn't until two years later that the legislature passed a bill allowing football games on Sundays, paving the way for the Pittsburgh Steelers (then called the Pirates) and Philadelphia Eagles to join the National Football League.

But shopping was a different matter. Sporting events in the forties—even pro games—were still viewed more as leisure activities than big business. So were cinemas, most of which were showing movies by that time. Stores, on the other hand, were in the business of making money. There wasn't any ambiguity there, and although laws varied from state to state, stores generally stayed closed on Sundays. The fact was, there were other reasons to stay closed one day a week. Most owners and store managers liked the idea of having a regular day off, and so did unions, which supported the laws as friendly to labor. But more to the point, it didn't make business sense to keep the lights on and pay employees to show up when most people were in church anyway. (Even today, pro football games don't start until 1 p.m. on Sundays, giving devout fans enough time to attend morning worship service and make it back before kickoff.)

Discounters challenged this status quo, defying the laws and opening their doors for business seven days a week. Some department store owners—Orthodox Jews kept the sabbath on Saturday—didn't like the laws either because they lost too much business by staying closed all weekend. The majority, however, saw blue laws as a bulwark against the discounters. So, they tried to enforce them by taking violators to court. Macy's and Bamberger's sued New Jersey–based discounter Two Guys for staying open in 1959—and won. The Supreme Court affirmed the laws, too, agreeing with the department stores that there were nonreligious reasons for giving workers a set day off. But the discounters kept trying, and pretty soon, public demand became too much for the department stores.

"The discounters have been having a heyday by keeping open," one official with Nieman-Marcus told Women's Wear Daily. "If this becomes a way of life, it could affect the whole retail structure in the U.S."

His comments turned out to be prescient.

Sears and J.C. Penney both announced in 1969 that they would begin opening on Sunday, and others believed they had no choice but to follow suit. It was one thing to hold the line against discounters, but once the traditional retailers' unified front began to crack, it was clear the game was lost.

Buffums' in Southern California followed Sears's and Penney's examples just in time for the last two weeks of the Christmas shopping season. Buffums' chairman and president V.G. Young took out an ad in the *Long Beach Independent Press-Telegram* almost sheepishly lamenting the change while arguing that it was necessary.

"We don't want to open on Sunday—we have been forced to open by the competition," Young wrote in an ad that blamed "certain major discount stores" that had "burst upon the scene, seeking an advantage by opening on Sundays."

Young argued that since many of Buffums' stockholders were employees, they were being hurt by the Sunday closures, too. "It is with great regret, and even some sense of guilt, that I have made this decision to open Sundays, but it was necessary to protect the interests of our stockholders, a substantial number of whom are employees," he wrote, pledging that 10 percent of the money collected from customer purchases on December 14 would be donated to "the church of your choice." Perhaps it was an attempt to absolve himself of that guilt, or maybe it was just good PR.

Either way, the ad was clear in blaming discounters, not the store's direct competitors, for the move. It commended Sears and Penney's, "both of which bitterly fought Sunday openings in every legal way open to them" before they "had to capitulate their strong moral stand and announce opening for Sunday business." Three other Southern California heavyweights—The Broadway, Bullock's, and May Co.—had quickly followed suit. And while Young didn't blame them for doing so, he called on "all retail merchants to stop this Sunday opening nonsense. Now that nobody has an advantage, fair or unfair, because almost all stores are open on Sunday, nobody benefits. Let's everybody get back to doing business six days a week and give our employees their Sabbath—their days of rest."

It never happened. There were a few holdouts. When West Town Mall opened in Knoxville in 1972, it was closed on Sundays, and it stayed that way for a year. But as time passed, the holdouts were fewer and fewer. The discount stores' extended evening hours became, in some cases, twenty-four-hour working days. Walmart was open virtually all the time. It closed only one day a year, on Christmas Day.

THE OLD MILL REVENUE STREAM

Sunday hours weren't the discounters' only weapons in their battle with traditional department stores. Their biggest allies were high volume and low overhead. The more they sold—and the less they paid for things like rent, electricity, and fixtures—the more they could cut prices.

One way to keep costs down was to find a cheap place to rent out in the boondocks and set up shop there. Textile mills fit the bill perfectly. The abandoned Northeast mills and the discount stores that opened may not have been a marriage made in heaven, but it was a marriage of convenience that worked.

The move was reminiscent of Michael Cullen's decision to open the first King Kullen in an abandoned garage—but the mills were even bigger, and plenty of them were available. Dozens of them in the New England area had closed (many of the companies moved to the South), so new tenants were needed for the now-vacant buildings, and landlords were willing to lease them out for a song. Merchants looking to make a splash by loading a lot of merchandise into a cavernous space saw an opportunity, and a new type of store was born.

In the words of one operator, the philosophy was simple: "Pile it high, sell it cheap."

As with the Big Bear stores and other early supermarkets, these retailers would sign a lease, do some minimal remodeling, and then throw open their doors to let shoppers comb through racks of clothes and shelves of housewares, knickknacks, hardware, and so on. It wasn't just textile mills. Other industrial sites and old warehouses were fair game, too. An early Walmart even operated out of a shuttered Coca-Cola bottling plant.

CARTED AWAY

They had something else in common with supermarkets, too. Both followed the self-service model, and both had a relatively new weapon in their arsenal: the shopping cart.

Why was this innovation so important?

"First, the cart carries much more than one can carry by oneself," Paul Gilmore explained. "This is key to supermarkets—large orders are where the profit margins are. People without carts aren't going to purchase more than they can carry."

The shopping cart further streamlined the self-service process. It hadn't been around when Piggly Wiggly or King Kullen opened their doors. Shopping baskets back then were actual baskets—the wicker kind with a handle that you had to carry through the store. They could be heavy and cumbersome, so they made shopping less pleasant.

In 1936, a grocer named Sylvan Goldman decided he wanted to do something about that.

Goldman wasn't the only one to try. During the midthirties, Frank Packard noticed that some customers

The shopping cart was a boon to customers and businesses alike. Shoppers didn't have to wrench their backs lugging around heavy baskets, and they could fit more in the new wheeled contraptions—which meant more sales for retailers. Library of Congress.

The design for Sylvan Goldman's "folding chair" shopping cart, the forerunner of the modern cart. In Goldman's original design, baskets were separate from the frame and were carried on two platforms, one above the other.

Humpty Dumpty, and his family owned half of the Piggly Wiggly chain. He wanted a way to make shopping less cumbersome so people would enjoy it more and, as a result, buy more. "They had a tendency to stop shopping when the baskets became too full or too heavy," he explained. "I thought if there was some way we could give the customer two baskets to shop with and still have one hand free to shop, we could do considerably more business."

One possibility: The cashier could hold the basket up front for the customer and supply a second basket for another trip down the aisles, but that ate into the clerks' time. Goldman also considered hooking the baskets up to a track, like a trolley, but that didn't prove practical either. There wasn't really room for a railway inside a grocery store.

Then, one evening, he was working late when his glance happened to fall on a folding chair sitting in his office, and it occurred to him to use it as the basis for a new contraption. Enlisting the help of a mechanic, Goldman created his first cart out of a metal frame on wheels that held two wire baskets with handles—one up by the handle and the other below, just as they're positioned on modern carts—that could be removed and nested when the cart wasn't in use. The frame of the cart could then be folded for easy storage.

It *seemed* like a great idea, but some customers didn't want to use them. Men and senior citizens shied away from them because they didn't want to appear weak, while women didn't want people to think they were pushing a baby carriage. When Goldman visited his largest store, not a single customer was using one. "It was," he later observed, "a complete flop." Even other grocers weren't interested. They thought children would run off with the carts while their parents were shopping and make a mess of their stores.

were having a hard time getting all their groceries to their cars outside his New Jersey superstore, so he asked a blacksmith to weld baskets onto the chassis of an old baby carriage. It worked in a pinch, but it didn't catch on.

Goldman had better luck—and a better design. No stranger to the grocery business, he owned a store called

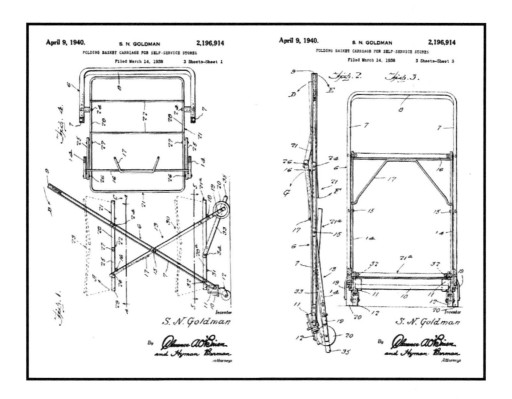

This early shopping cart design didn't become the standard. Library of Congress, 1942.

Undeterred, Goldman hired attractive women to stand at the store entrance, offering carts to customers as they arrived. He ran an ad that showed a weary woman struggling with an overloaded basket of groceries in one hand and her purse in another. Another ad asked shoppers, "Can you imagine winding your way through a spacious food market without having to carry a cumbersome shopping basket on your arm?" Still another proclaimed: "It's new. It's sensational. No more baskets to carry."

What finally did the trick was Goldman's variation on the old bandwagon principle. He hired actors to use his "Folding Basket Carriers," as he called them, smiling broadly as they moved through the aisles and deposited items in their carts. Once the shopping carts finally took off, Goldman had two successes for the price of one. He sold more groceries, and he also sold the carts to other grocers for $7 a pop.

A decade later, however, he found himself outdone when a machinist named Orla Watson designed and patented a shopping cart with a "rear swinging door" so that it could be stacked with other carts in a line "telescopically," the way carts are today. Goldman, however, had the audacity to copy Watson's idea and start selling his own version of the telescopic cart. He also had the deep pockets he needed to pay the legal fees that ensued after Watson sued him for patent infringement.

Watson, outgunned from a financial standpoint, settled for a measly $1 and the right to royalties from future sales of Goldman's carts. Child seats were added in the mid-fifties, and the modern design was pretty much set.

In future years, the invention would become ubiquitous, not only in supermarkets but in discount department stores, lineal descendants of those mill stores that started popping up in the late forties through the mid-fifties.

Outlaws on the outskirts of town

Unlike the shopping cart, mill stores weren't exactly convenient for consumers. Most were outside town, so you had to drive a good distance to get there. Obviously, too, the mills hadn't been *designed* as retail centers, and discounters didn't want to spend a lot of money on renovations. When William Palestine opened his first Rockdale store in 1953, he chose an old mill building out in the middle of nowhere—specifically, in Turner's Falls, Massachusetts, an unincorporated town of a few thousand people halfway between Boston and Albany (which were a two-hour drive in either direction).

After Palestine bought the place, he didn't do much to "transform" it. He slapped a coat of white paint on the outside and brought in some pipe racks and boards laid across wooden sawhorses to hold the merchandise. He cleaned up the parking lot and added fluorescent lighting inside, but he didn't bother to put in a ceiling. The bottom two floors of the three-floor mill were set aside for merchandise, but you couldn't take shopping carts between floors because the only way up or down inside was a staircase. (It was, however, possible to enter the second floor directly from outside via a ramp.)

Unlike some chains that moved into more conventional sites after opening their first stores in mills, Rockdale Stores stuck to the formula, opening its next three stores in two mills and a leased factory.

Palestine counted on his stores' low prices to lure customers out to the hinterlands, but he knew that added incentives never hurt, so he let customers spin a "wheel of fortune" to decide how much they'd have to pay for an item. He threw a balloon parade for kids during back-to-school season. He had celebrities make appearances once a month, put on vaudeville shows, and even showed sports films for the guys to watch while their wives shopped.

The chain never expanded beyond four stores, but it did manage to stay in business until 1972, when competitors like Mammoth Mart started to take their toll. Rockdale filed for bankruptcy that year and liquidated its assets.

Another early "mill" retailer was a store called Ann & Hope. Those weren't the names of its founders. Ann & Hope was the mill—which was named for a ship that was lost at sea off Rhode Island in the early nineteenth century. Hardly an auspicious name for a discount retailer, but since the mill was in Rhode Island, it at least made geographic sense. Plus, it had a sort of ring to it, kind of like Lord & Taylor or Forbes & Wallace.

Ann & Hope, however, was nothing like those places. It was the brainchild of Martin Chase, who had gotten his start managing a Rhode Island store that pioneered one-price men's clothing. Everything in the store was $23.50. A few years later, in 1938, he started his own discount clothier, which he ran on a shoestring out of a loft on the outskirts of Providence.

"At first, the manufacturers were so dubious about this new kind of operation that they were afraid to sell to me," Chase said in an interview for Robert Drew-Bear's book *Mass Merchandising*. "They said, 'You've got to go broke. How can you open a store in the outskirts of town in a manufacturing building and sell clothing?'"

He did well enough to stay in business for six years before things slowed down during the war, so he got out of the clothing business and bought a Connecticut factory that made ribbons for corsages in 1944. The next year, he bought the Ann & Hope mill and moved his ribbon operation on the third floor, renting out the remaining space to thirty-four other small manufacturers. But when he decided to retire in 1953, he had a lot of ribbon lying around—along with a huge supply of greeting cards he'd purchased from a company that had gone belly-up—so he decided to sell them to the building's other tenants and their employees.

The deals were so good, they asked if they could bring their friends, and pretty soon, people were walking up two long flights of stairs to get in on the deals; when a friend who made housedresses got wind of it, he persuaded Chase to add them to the inventory. The success spurred him to buy other kinds of merchandise and move the fledgling retail operation into the cellar, which was more accessible. As it prospered, the store grew, adding more products and more locations. In 1959, it added a grocery section in a new store, which was *not* in a mill. Other stores followed, and ten years later, Ann & Hope was a $40 million operation that served as an inspiration to both Walmart and Kmart.

The chain went out of business in 2001 but reemerged as Curtain & Bath Outlet with eleven stores in three New England states by 2018.

Mammoth success

Another Massachusetts-based mill store, Mammoth Mart, debuted in 1956 in Framingham (the same Boston suburb where Shoppers' World had opened five years earlier and where T.J. Maxx would start out a couple of decades later).

Founder Max Coffman worked for a local department store during college, then worked for New England grocer Stop & Shop before opening up an army-navy surplus store with his brother-in-law in 1941. It might not have been the best timing, because surplus military items weren't exactly easy to find during wartime. He kept things going by stocking up on work clothes and other apparel until the war ended and surplus items were, well, at a *surplus* again. After the end of the war, he opened up five more such stores before switching gears and opening his first Mammoth Mart in a 51,000-square-foot former foundry. Opening day should have been a nightmare. Snowdrifts piled up so high that they buried the searchlights Coffman had hooked up to draw people to the store. But the bad weather didn't keep customers away; they came in droves.

Mammoth Mart was so successful that Coffman closed down his military surplus stores to focus on the new venture. The snow hadn't stopped him, so he opened his next two stores about as far north as you can go in

Marty, the Mammoth Mart mascot, wasn't a mammoth at all but an elephant.

the US—Bangor (1959) and Lewiston (1961), Maine. He opened six of them in 1966.

By 1970, Mammoth Mart had grown into a chain with thirty-four outlets. Atop the entrance to many of the low-slung, single-story locations stood the chain's mascot: not a mammoth but a friendly, hairless elephant in a red blazer. The interiors were no more impressive. Like most discount department stores, Mammoth Mart was a bare-bones operation. One observer recalled the merchandise being housed in "stark, unfussy buildings," and another described the stores at "grimy, dark, and informal."

But despite the stores' underwhelming ambience, they made money—about $2 million a year at each location in 1969, about $100,000 of that in profits. Coffman sold all his own products directly, renting out space to the concession dealers who often operated jewelry counters and shoe departments at higher-end stores. Mammoth

Mart even had its own brand of nylons called Princess Anne.

Coffman's approach: "Don't use loss leaders, just sell every day at real low prices."

It worked until the mid-seventies, when Mammoth Mart ran into hard times. The company was forced to reorganize under Chapter 11 in 1974, when it closed a ten-store affiliated chain of children's stores called Boston Baby it had started a couple of years earlier. Then, three years later, Coffman sold all his stores to a "secret suitor."

That suitor was King's Department Stores, another Massachusetts-based chain that dated back even further than Mammoth Mart. A former department store night watchman named Murray Candib opened the first location in an old Indian Motorcycle plant circa 1949. It wasn't a textile mill, but, like the mill stores, it was nothing fancy.

J.M. Field's got its start in Massachusetts as Enterprise Stores, then expanded to areas as far afield as Chicago and Florida in the 1960s. This one was in the Jackson Heights neighborhood of New York. Library of Congress.

"In the beginning, it was just pipe racks and simple displays," said Candib's nephew, Edward Shore. "He built a lot of the displays himself in the beginning. They had a pet department, a men's department, a women's department, and a luncheonette" that served Kingburgers.

Candib and several other key people in management at King's had worked in the Enterprise/J.M. Fields chain, which wasn't unusual. Discounters often cut their teeth in another department store or discounter before striking out on their own. Coffman had spent four years with Enterprise two decades before he founded Mammoth Mart, and William Palestine had started a mill-store discounter called Arlan's with his two brothers before leaving to found Rockford Stores.

But King's was more successful than most such endeavors. It prospered by keeping prices low, vowing in one of its slogans to sell "everything for less" and by making its stores accessible. One way of doing this was staying open on Sundays, when many traditional department stores stayed closed, and extending their hours to stretch from 10 to 10 every day. Mammoth Mart had been open until 10 p.m. as well, providing a contrast to places like stores at the Shoppers' World center, which were open from 10 a.m. to 6 p.m. Monday, Tuesday, and Saturday, and from 12:15 to 9 p.m. on Wednesday through Friday. They were closed Sundays.

Advantage: Discounters. Longer hours. More customers. More sales.

By 1957, the King's chain had sixteen stores, a figure that eventually grew to more than 200 as far west as Denver and south down into Florida. King's remained in business until 1984, when it was absorbed by Ames, yet another discount department store chain with Massachusetts roots that started in 1958 and at one point operated 700 stores in twenty states. The first Ames store was in an old mill previously occupied by the Ames Worsted Textile Company (hence the store's name).

Ames began by opening stores in rural areas where it didn't face any significant competition. Then, in the seventies, it started acquiring smaller companies like King's that were facing financial difficulty and/or bankruptcy. The year after acquiring King's, it made an even bigger purchase by acquiring G.C. Murphy, a chain of variety stores that had emulated Kresge by starting a chain of big-box discount stores called Murphy's Marts.

The biggest purchase, however, came in 1988, when Ames bought the Zayre chain—purchasing nearly 400 stores.

HERE AND ZAYRE

Zayre, an early entry into the sweepstakes, had started off in 1919 as a wholesaler, supplying underwear and hosiery to department and specialty stores. A decade later, the company opened its own stores, Bell Shops, to sell its products, expanding to thirty stores by the end of World War II. In the mid-fifties, however, the sons of the original owners decided to take the company in a new direction. During a meeting with an advertising consultant, one of the owners paused to take a call, ending the conversation with "Zehr gut"—the Jewish phrase for "very good." The consultant latched onto the idea as a name for the new store, changing the spelling of *zehr* to Zayre.

The first Zayre store debuted in June of 1956, occupying a relatively modest, 5,000-square-foot space next to a new Stop & Shop supermarket in Hyannis, Massachusetts. The second, which opened three months later, was nearly eight times that size. Located in the brand-new Legion Shopping Center, it shared the strip mall with Woolworth's, an A&P market, a Sherbros appliance store, an Anderson-Little men's clothier, and liquor and drug stores.

In order to keep costs down, Zayre adopted a self-service approach that would become the standard in discount department stores. Instead of stationing clerks around the store to help customers find what they were looking for, Zayre patterned itself after supermarkets. Patrons were expected to do their own work, with the help of wheeled shopping carts, and check out at front-of-the-store registers. Grocers had been using this approach since 1917, when the Piggly Wiggly grocery store patented the idea and Woolworth took goods out from behind the counter, allowing customers access without having to ask a store employee.

"With our shopping carts, they will not be burdened down with bundles while they visit various departments in the store," company president Stanley Feldberg said, which helped the store provide "a policy of low prices on all merchandise, to give our customers more than a dollar's worth of value for every dollar they spend."

By 1966, Zayre was a major player in the large-scale discount marketplace later dominated by Kmart, Walmart, and Target. By that date, it had ninety-two stores in the eastern United States and had a near stranglehold on the Boston, Chicago and Miami markets. Joe Archie, 1976. Creative Commons 2.0 license: https://creativecommons.org/licenses/by-sa/2.0.

There were other advantages to this approach. Customers could shop at their own pace. On the one hand, they didn't have to wait around for a clerk to help them, and conversely, they didn't have to worry about one pressuring them. Kmart, Walmart, Target, and others would use the same approach in the years to come. In fact, Walton had done the same thing at his Bentonville five-and-dime.

"I read an article about these two Ben Franklin stores up in Minnesota that had gone to self-service—a brand-new concept at the time," Walton wrote in his book *Made in America*. "I rode the bus all night long to two little towns up there—Pipestone and Worthington. They had shelves on the side and two island counters all the way back. No clerks with cash registers around the store. Just checkout registers up front. I liked it. So I did that too."

Zayre just did it on a larger scale.

In 1966, *Barron's* described the typical Zayre store as "about 70,000 square feet and air-conditioned. All outlets are on well-traveled roads with ample parking space. While the stores are pleasant and neat, no attempt is made to create a high-fashion image." By then, there were ninety-two stores in the eastern United States, more than a third of them clustered in three markets: Boston (thirteen), Miami (ten), and Chicago (nine). In addition to clothing, the stores initially carried housewares, linens, cosmetics, toys, sporting goods, and stationery. The inventory later expanded to include such things as televisions, books, cameras, and records—a staple of discount stores before record retailers with names like Wherehouse, Camelot, and Licorice Pizza became widespread. A visitor to White Front in Fresno, California, would have felt right at home in one of Zayre's "Fabulous Department Stores" in Oak Lawn, Illinois.

Both stores would go out of business, but both would survive in different, if more specialized, big-box forms. White Front, a discount chain that took its name from the row of white appliances at the front of its store, opened its first store in 1929 in Los Angeles, and a second didn't follow until nearly three decades later, just north of LA in Van Nuys. Company president Harry Blackman called the 40,000-square-foot store "a colossus of discount merchandising," even though it was just one-third the size of some later stores. The Van Nuys store also lacked the distinctive arched entry that would become the chain's trademark within a few short years.

Razor-thin profit margins and plenty of merchandise ensured that "you never pay retail at White Front," which became the company's slogan.

Interstate Stores bought White Front in 1959 and opened a third store—much larger at 112,000 square feet—in Anaheim, the following year. Rapid expansion followed, and the chain moved into major cities up and down the West Coast and becoming, for a time, the nation's leading discount chain.

White Front announced in the summer of 1965 that it would be opening two new stores in San Diego, each with 120,000 square feet of floor space. Like many big-box discounters in the post-mill era, everything was on one floor. Products included apparel, sporting goods, toys, cosmetics, televisions, and "hi-fis" in departments marked by signs hung from overheard.

The following year, an ad in the San Francisco Examiner heralded "a rare opportunity for qualified management personnel to join the fastest growing, most aggressive

A typical White Front store, with its distinctive arch, in San Francisco's Mission District is seen in 1975. The parking lot is all but empty because the chain had gone out of business the previous year. Eric Fischer, 1975.
Creative Commons 2.0 license: https://creativecommons.org/licenses/by-sa/2.0.

discount department store chain." The ad boasted that "our expansion plans for this year and for future years have exceeded the capacity of our internal management training program."

White Fronts had pharmacies and sold groceries. Stores with as much as 150,000 square feet of floor space opened outside Southern California, and the chain expanded to Oakland in 1963, San Jose in 1964, and Fresno the following year. White Front invaded the Pacific Northwest by adding stores in Seattle (1967) and Portland (1970), and it opened downtown San Francisco's first new department store in more than two decades in 1968.

Playing off the chain's Hollywood roots, White Front invited celebrities to be on hand for the opening of its new stores. Rose Marie of *The Dick Van Dyke Show* and Emmy-winning comedian Pat Paulsen were special guests for the San Francisco store's debut. Allen Ludden of the popular *Password* game show helped preside over the Portland opening, and Troy Donohue, Jayne Mansfield, and Sebastian Cabot of TV's *Family Affair* appeared at various ribbon-cutting ceremonies. The governor of California and the mayor of San Francisco attended the opening of the Oakland store.

White Front's parent company, Interstate, filed for bankruptcy in 1974 and closed all ninety-nine of its White Front and Topps discount stores. The bankruptcy filing listed more than $195 million in debt, which at the time was the largest liability in retailing history. The only stores that remained open were a few conventional department stores and a chain of fifty-one specialty big-box outlets that Interstate had purchased in 1967 called Children's Bargain Town. Those stores were later rebranded as Toys "R" Us, which became the largest specialty toy chain in the country. It remained successful until the late nineties, when it came under siege from Walmart's toy department on one side and online sales on the other. It finally closed and liquidated its assets in the spring of 2018.

Zayre's demise also left a lasting legacy. It sold all of its stores (nearly 400 in all) to the competing Ames chain in 1988, a year after it decided to focus on a different aspect of its business. Impressed by the success of Marshalls, a discounter that focused on apparel and home fashions, Zayre tried unsuccessfully to purchase the chain

in the mid-seventies. Not to be deterred, the company hired a former Marshalls general manager to essentially copy that store's formula. The result was a store called T.J. Maxx, which opened its first location in 1976 in Framingham, Massachusetts. The store was such a success that Zayre sold its flagging discount department stores to Ames (the same company that had purchased King's) in 1988 and renamed itself TJX. Not only that, but the chain eventually succeeded where it had failed two decades earlier, buying Marshalls for a cool $550 million in 1996.

The new combined company had more than 1,000 stores and, by 2014, its revenue had surpassed that of Macy's.

Zehr gut, indeed.

OTHER DISCOUNTERS

Zayre should not be confused with Zody's, a West Coast big-box chain that opened its first store in June of 1960 in Garden Grove, with 67,000 square feet of retail space and more than 2,000 parking spots. The store would carry everything from fashion to furniture, televisions to typewriters, paints to patio accessories. A store in Redondo Beach opened later that year, but the store never grew beyond a regional force. At its peak in 1979, it operated thirty-seven locations in Arizona, California, Nevada, and New Mexico (for a brief period, there were also stores in Michigan). The last stores—in California—closed in 1986, some of them being converted into supermarkets.

Stores like these seemed to be popping up everywhere during the sixties. Shoppers Fair had thirty-five stores in a dozen states, mostly in the Midwest, by 1962, but it was out of business by 1975. Kuhn's Big K, not to be confused with the later Kmart enterprise, had 119 stores in the Southeast before Walmart acquired it in 1981. Texas-based Gulf Mart grew to forty stores in the South before calling it quits in 1975.

Caldor, which started as Walk-Up-&-Save on the second story of a building in Port Chester, New York, grew to a chain of 145 stores with 24,000 employees in 1998, but financial woes forced it to close completely the following year.

A former Caldor location, previously a Woolco, sits vacant in Willingboro, New Jersey. Tom Asher, 2003. Creative Commons 2.0 license: https://creativecommons.org/licenses/by-sa/2.0.

The store was the brainchild of Carl and Dorothy Bennett, who decided to open their own discount store after visiting an E.J. Korvette store in 1951. The newly married couple used their own first names as the inspiration for the name they chose, Caldor, and adopted the slogan "Where Shopping is Always a Pleasure." They expanded their initial location two years after it opened and added a 70,000-square-foot branch in Norwalk, Connecticut, in 1958—adding their own line of apparel the same year.

Caldor lasted longer than many discount competitors that sprang up during the postwar period, earning a reputation as "the Bloomingdale's of discounting" and taking over seven W.T. Grant locations when that chain folded in 1976. Nine years later, Caldor had reached $1 billion in sales and had been acquired by Associated Dry Goods, owner of Lord & Taylor.

The chain was liquidated in 1999, and many of its locations were snapped up by competitors such as Walmart, Target, Kmart, and Kohl's.

Another entry in the discount wars of the sixties and early seventies was Two Guys, founded in 1946 by a pair of brothers from Harrison, New Jersey. Herb and Sid Hubschman owned a snack bar in the RCA building there at a time when the new medium of television was in its infancy. During a tour of the plant, Herb noticed a number of TVs had been set aside in one area because of scratches on their cabinets. Dealers had said they couldn't sell them, but Herb thought he could. He and his brother struck a deal with RCA to buy the sets at a discount and keep them for a month; if they couldn't sell them in that time, they'd return them for a refund.

They marked them up at $5 more than what they'd paid for them and sold them in a vacant lot, printing up fliers and slipping them under windshield wipers around the neighborhood. It didn't take a month to sell all the sets they'd purchased; it took only a few hours, so the brothers bought more TVs and sold them just as quickly.

Soon, the Hubschman brothers had enough money to do some real advertising. Another retailer had referred to them sarcastically as "The Two Bastards from Harrison," so they decided to use that name as a way to thumb their nose at the competition. But newspapers refused to print ads from a company with a name like that, so the brothers changed it to the milder Two Guys from Harrison, and the moniker stuck (it was shortened to just Two Guys in 1958, after the company went public).

Two Guys adopted a sprawling single-story discount layout that would become standard for stores like Kmart and Walmart in future years. It carried most of the same products you'd find in those stores, and like them, it also had a food department, complete with dairy products, produce, and meat. Except for the fifties-style script lettering on the interior signs, you'd be hard-pressed to distinguish one of those stores from a Target today.

By 1965, it was the fifth-largest discount chain in the country, with twenty-five stores, and it continued to grow. Its biggest acquisition involved seventy Food Giant Markets on the West Coast, a deal that also included twenty Builder's Emporium do-it-yourself centers, 241 Foster's Freeze fast-food outlets, and a smaller discount chain called Unimart. The marriage, however, proved to be a poor fit. The original management team stayed on at Food Giant and adopted Two Guys' discounting system, because it had to adapt to tighter profit margins by shortening hours and ending its trading stamp program. Customers were not amused, so Two Guys took matters into its own hands and installed its own management. But efforts to introduce its own East Coast brand names out west fell flat, and the company had dumped its Food Giant stores by 1972.

The company still saw record profits that year, when it operated fifty-three Two Guys stores, but that turned out to be the high-water mark for the chain. When White Front collapsed, Two Guys bought three of those stores in California as part of a major expansion that peaked when it was operating twenty-two locations there by 1978. At that point, however, it quit the Golden State, selling all its properties there (including sixty Builder's Emporium stores). When a real estate investor took control of the company three years later, he closed the chain and disposed of its retail assets to capitalize on the growing value of the land on which the stores had been built.

E.J. Korvette was another example of a chain that burned brightly for a short time before eventually fading

away. For a brief period, it was one of the fastest growing in the country.

In 1966, Korvette's ranked second nationally with $612 million in sales, trailing only Kmart and just ahead of Interstate (White Front). By way of comparison, Woolco ranked fourteenth, Target was thirtieth, and Walmart didn't even make the top fifty.

Korvette's was something of a hybrid. On the one hand, it wasn't self-service. Cash registers were spread throughout the building, as in a department store, rather than up by the entrance. It also sold some high-end items, but it was still undeniably a discount store. In fact, it was owner Eugene Ferkauf's insistence on low prices that led him to break away from his father's luggage business and start his first store in 1948. It was an example of Ferkauf's insistence on doing things his own way. He hired high school buddies with nicknames like Lobster, Leaky, and Kuzzy to work in his stores. He made them work hard but rewarded them for the thing he valued most: their loyalty. When they complained their Brooklyn apartments were too cramped for them now that they were married and raising families, he took gave them $1.5 million to buy new houses.

Ridiculed by New York's retail establishment for his unconventional approach, Ferkauf responded by thumbing his nose at them and innovating all the more. In order to get around the fair-trade laws that were still in effect at the time, he made Korvette's a members-only store, but unlike club stores that catered only to government workers, membership was open to anyone. There wasn't even a nominal fee. Customers were "invited" to his warehouse, and membership cards were passed out at nearby office buildings and in front of its stores to anyone who wanted one.

Ferkauf's surname was appropriate to his profession. It was a variation on the Yiddish word for "sale." And that's what Ferkauf did. His philosophy: If you could make a dollar's worth of profit selling one refrigerator, you could make a million selling a million of them. One of his biggest sellers was a woman's dress he sold for $4.60. Korvette's would sell 2,500 of those dresses every couple of weeks, turning over its entire stock twenty-five times a year.

Ferkauf opened a second store in 1951, followed by two others, all in the New York area. It was the fifth store in the chain, however, that was the groundbreaker. At 90,000 square feet, it was one of the first true superstores when it opened three weeks before Christmas in 1953. Instead of taking over an old mill store, Ferkauf built the crown jewel in his chain from the ground up in a potato field on Long Island.

It was an immediate hit. So many customers turned out that first day that employees weren't allowed to leave the store at lunch, for fear they might not be able to get back in. More than a thousand patrons passed through the doors and spent $138,000 on that day alone, with sales rising to $2 million in just the short period before Christmas. It was an important milestone for a company that would catapult it to a place among the nation's leading retailers. From 1950 to '56, Korvette's sales increased by 2,650 percent.

The company went public at the end of 1955 and expanded rapidly, opening twenty-five stores in just three years, clustering them in major metropolitan areas along the Eastern Seaboard. By 1966, there were ten in the New York metroplex, five in greater Philadelphia, and four more in Washington-Baltimore. Expansion into the Midwest brought five stores to Chicago, three to Detroit, and two to St. Louis during the early sixties.

Korvette's had fifty-eight stores by the late sixties, but it couldn't keep up with its own rapid expansion, and success waned after that. The chain had dwindled to seventeen locations by late 1980, but Christmas never came for Korvette's that year. The chain that had made such a splash during the holiday season of 1953 shuttered the last of its stores on Christmas Eve.

One final bit of trivia: Somewhere along the way, someone started a rumor that E.J. Korvette was an acronym for "eight Jewish Korean War veterans" who supposedly started the company. In reality, though, there were only two founders: Eugene Ferkauf was the E, and his friend who founded the store with him, Joe Zwillenberg, was the J. The rest of the name was a variation on corvette—not the car, which didn't begin production until 1953, but a reference to a class of warship.

Another myth involved the name of a store called TG&Y, which started during the Depression in Oklahoma and expanded to more than 900 locations in twenty-nine states before going out of business in 2001. Creative young shoppers called it "Turtles, Girdles, and Yo-Yos" or "Toys, Games, and Yo-Yos," but it was really a combination of the founders' initials: Rawdon Tomlinson, Les Gosselin, and Raymond Young. Its original TG&Ys were typical five-and-dimes with about 7,000 square feet of floor space, but later locations included larger "Family Centers" that ranged from 20,000 to 80,000 square feet.

A surge of expansion in 1968 added forty-nine new units in sixteen states across the South and the Southwest, including two as far west as California. Among the attractions at the new Shreveport Family Center was a horticulture department (aka garden center) that earned the store yet another nickname in some quarters: "Tulsa Garden & Yard."

TG&Y wasn't exactly a five-and-dime, but it wasn't a dollar store either. It was something in between, as many of its signs indicated, advertising prices of 5¢ to $1.00 in big letters next to the store's name.

Because so many of the stores were located in "tornado alley," it was only a matter of time before they were hit by twisters. A Family Center in Tulsa was at ground zero for the worst tornado in that city's history, which struck in June of 1974. Photos of the aftermath show the letters T and G missing from the corner of the store, an area reduced to an open-air hodgepodge of broken and shattered building materials. Only the tile floor was largely intact.

In 2000, another tornado that touched down about sixty miles south-southwest of New Orleans tore the roof and one wall off a TG&Y store in a strip mall. Work began in January of the following year to rebuild the store, which was to be rebranded as McCrory, the old five-and-dime chain that had bought TG&Y back in 1986. Construction was due to be completed by March, but McCrory was hit by a disaster of its own eight months later when it filed for bankruptcy. All its stores eventually closed, the liquidation also spelling the end for the J.J. Newberry, G.C. Murphy, and Dollar Zone chains.

Paul Buxbaum, CEO of the liquidating agent, offered this epitaph: "Although McCrory had converted the vast majority of its locations to the 'dollar store' format last year, this sale nonetheless marks the final chapter in the history of the last of the major five-and-dime retailers in the United States."

14

BIG-BOX BONANZA

I'm not sure when I first heard the term "big box," but I do recall my initial reaction. I laughed. Was it supposed to describe the shape of the store, like a big box? Or did it refer to the fact that what you bought there *came in* a big box? Maybe both. Whatever the answer, I hadn't heard of the term before the nineties, when big-box stores started to pop up willy-nilly across the suburban retail landscape. Suddenly, they seemed to be everywhere.

S.S. Kresge had been a five-and-dime competitor with industry leader Woolworth for decades. But it turned the tables on its rival when the 1960s came along, refocusing on the big-box discount market and rebranding itself as Kmart. The new venture easily outpaced Woolworth's entry, Woolco. This Kresge store was in Washington, DC. Library of Congress.

But their appearance wasn't as sudden as it might appear. They began multiplying about the same time department stores and old-school five-and-dimes fell out of favor, but they were nothing new. In fact, they evolved out of those established retailers. The original big-box stores were born at the tail end of the baby boom, in an era when retailers were flush with success and eager to explore new frontiers.

As the new generation expanded out into the suburbs, so did they, adding stand-alone specialty stores that focused on a particular product or service, while also looking for bigger, better ways to package their brand. On the specialty end, Sears became all but ubiquitous in the seventies and eighties. It marketed brand names such as Kenmore appliances, DieHard car batteries, Toughskins (kids' clothes), Weatherbeater paints, and Craftsman tools, just to name a few. It opened portrait studios, a car-rental business, optical shops, and a travel service. It even launched a national credit card called Discover.

But it was the five-and-dime business that gave birth to the big-box concept. They'd seen what the mill scores had accomplished, and they wanted a piece of the action. They had one thing most of the mill discounters lacked—capital, and lots of it.

The big boom happened in the summer of 1961, when five-and-dime heavyweights Woolworth and S.S. Kresge started talking about plans to launch large-scale discount department store chains. By that time, Interstate Department Stores was already expanding rapidly. It operated fifty stores and was planning to add twenty-eight more in the next two years. Its 1959 purchase of Los Angeles–based White Front set the stage for that chain's rapid expansion and subsequent precipitous fall. King's Department Stores, which started the trend in 1949 in Massachusetts, was also growing quickly and would eventually cover a broad swath of territory east of the Rockies. Mammoth Mart was expanding up and down the East Coast.

"We foresee a day, five to 10 years from now, when 80 percent of the public will be relying on discount centers for the bulk of their purchases," Interstate president Sol Cantor enthused. "There is no practical limit on the amount of goods that can be purchased through discount centers, provided discount operators stick to their original and very basic philosophy, which is to keep markups low."

Woolworth and Kresge had been doing just that for years, but Woolworth president Robert Kirkwood said there would be "very little, if any, overlapping merchandise between our (Woolworth) variety stores and (Woolco) department stores," each of which would have at least 60,000 square feet of floor space. "Our goal," he said, "is to have the largest discount chain in America," adding, however, that he didn't expect sales at the new chain to surpass those at Woolworth's traditional variety stores.

One might have expected Woolworth to have a leg up in the discount store sweepstakes, yet it was rival Kresge that made the biggest initial impact. Many people today might not have heard of the Kresge chain, because it's no longer around. The last Kresge store, in the Canadian city of Hamilton, Ontario, closed in 1994, and most of the others called it quits long before that. The majority were in downtown areas, where fewer shoppers ventured during the baby boom years as they put down roots farther out in the suburbs. That's where the future of retailing lay on March 1, 1962, which is when Kresge opened its first large-scale discount store in Garden City, outside Detroit. For this new venture, the Kresge name was dropped in favor of one that was far easier to pronounce and remember: Kmart.

The chain was born about the same time Victor Gruen's enclosed malls were catching on, but Kmart shunned those developments in favor of stand-alone locations and outdoor malls with ample parking. Fresno's Southgate and Northgate centers were prime examples. The Southgate Kmart on Kings Canyon Road opened in 1963, just a year after the chain's first store made its debut. Plans for the second Fresno store, on Blackstone Avenue, were announced the following year. An ad in the *Fresno Bee* touted the store's arrival in Fresno by responding to two questions it expected to hear:

"WHAT is K-mart?" (The store later dropped the hyphen from its name.)

"The ultimate in super-size department store selections for family living at unheard of discount savings."

"WHO is K-mart?"

This full-page ad ran in the *Windsor Star* on May 6, 1963, touting the opening of Kmart in the Canadian city.

"A division of the S.S. Kresge Company, which operates over 840 stores in the United States, Canada, and Puerto Rico."

By the time it entered the Fresno market, Kmart was already growing fast. Just a year after the Garden City store opened, it boasted sixty-three locations, including fifty-one that offered auto repair. The new name—together with the rebranding of some Kresge locations as Jupiter Discount Stores—likely helped differentiate Kresge from Kress, a longtime rival with a similar name. But Kress stayed out of the big-box business, taking a different tack by relocating from downtowns to enclosed malls.

It turned out to be a bad decision. The chain was dead by 1980.

Woolworth, meanwhile, tried to go in both directions at once. It opened some stores in enclosed malls, where it also had a presence with a cafeteria chain called Harvest House. Barely three months after Kresge opened its first Kmart, Woolworth debuted its first Woolco at the Great Southern Shopping Center in suburban Columbus, Ohio. The company touted its move to the suburbs in the Columbus Dispatch by quoting the Bible: "Better is a neighbor that is near than a brother far off" (Proverbs 27:10). The message was clear: You might feel a kinship for your favorite downtown department store, but isn't it easier to drive up the street to find what you want than to go all the way into town?

Over the next few months, Woolco opened four stores in Ontario, Canada, one in Richmond, Virginia, and a second store in Columbus. The chain expanded to Britain in the mid-sixties, but growth was far slower than it was for Kmart. By the end of the decade, there were just 150 Woolcos, some of which contained Red Grille restaurants. By contrast, Kmart had more than 1,000 locations. The chain was so successful that, by 1976, it accounted for 95 percent of the company's sales. Kresge's downtown five-and-dime stores were fast becoming obsolete, and the company changed its name the following year to reflect this reality, becoming known as Kmart Corporation. By 1987, the company sold all seventy-six remaining Kresge and Jupiter stores to McCrory's—the same store Sebastian Kresge had worked for before he founded his own chain.

McCrory's itself, which at one point operated as many as 1,300 stores, would go out of business in 2002.

Those developments, however, were far in the future during the early days of the big-box era, when both Woolworth/Woolco and Kmart/Kresge were not only expanding but diversifying. Woolworth acquired Kinney Shoes in 1963, while Kmart made an abortive entry into the fast-food market by founding a small chain of burger joints called Kmart Chef. They failed to compete effectively

with chains like McDonald's and Burger King and closed in 1974 after opening just eleven outlets in seven years. Later efforts were more substantial, including acquisitions of the Builders Square home improvement chain, Waldenbooks, and PayLess Drugs in the mid-eighties.

Soon, Kmart was the nation's second-largest retailer, trailing only Sears. Woolworth—which still ranked fourth on that list—admitted defeat in 1983, closing all of its Woolco stores in a move that affected 25,000 workers. The $1 billion inventory liquidation was the largest in history at the time, surpassing W.T. Grant's $600,000 sell-off in 1975. Woolworth chairman and CEO Edward Gibbons put it succinctly: "We started about the same time as Kmart. We have 330 stores. They have about 2,000. Their commitment to the discount business was more complete than ours."

While Kresge and Woolworth moved from five-and-dime success into the discount department store arena, 1962's third big new entry arrived from the opposite direction. Dayton's, a chain founded in Minneapolis sixty years earlier, had been the cornerstone of Victor Gruen's first enclosed mall. (It would later acquire the prestigious Detroit-based department store Hudson's in 1969.) Now, it was venturing out in a different direction by opening a discount center.

The name Target was chosen from a list of more than 200 possible names. The archer's target logo featured three red rings, two white, and a white bull's-eye. (It would be simplified six years later to take its more familiar form: a red outer ring surrounding a white inner ring and a red bull's-eye.)

The chain announced it would open its first store on May 1 in Roseville, Minnesota, in a space formerly occupied by another store. That would be followed by three stores being built from the ground up. A mammoth 125,000-square-foot store that opened on September 1 in Minneapolis's Crystal Shopping Center would include a discount supermarket and parking space for more than 1,100 cars. Two other locations would follow in October: in the Minneapolis suburb of Saint Louis Park, with the same amount of retail space, and to the north in Duluth on the shores of Lake Superior.

The original Target logo. Runner1928, 2016. Creative Commons 2.0 license: https://creativecommons.org/licenses/by-sa/3.0/deed.en.

Dayton opened its first Target store outside Minnesota in 1966, expanding into Denver, and had grown to nearly 1,800 stores nationwide by 2018.

WALMART

But while Target, Woolco, and Kmart were grabbing much of the attention, a potential rival was gaining momentum almost under the radar, thanks to an army veteran named Sam Walton.

Walton had gotten his feet wet in retail straight out of college, when he took a $75-a-month job with J.C. Penney. He quit after eighteen months in 1942 and joined the army. After his discharge following World War II, he wanted to get back into the retail business, so he contacted Butler Brothers, the Chicago-based mail-order company. Like Sears and Wards, Butler Brothers had branched out into brick-and-mortar retail by the thirties, establishing about 100 of its own stores, branded as Scott and L.C. Burr. Its franchised stores, however, were far more widespread. By 1936, it had 2,600 five-and-dime Ben Franklin and 1,400 Federated chain stores (not to be confused with the Federated Department Stores holding company) across the country.

Walton, twenty-seven, used $5,000 of his own money and a $20,000 loan from his father-in-law to purchase a Ben Franklin franchise store in Newport, Arkansas. He'd considered a Federated franchise in St. Louis, but his wife had talked him out of it, saying she preferred to live in a smaller town. But the beginning of the idea that would rival and eventually eclipse Kmart—Walmart—happened across town, and almost by accident. A rival variety store was planning to expand into an adjacent space being vacated by a Kroger grocery store. Walton got wind of it and started to worry that the new, larger store would draw customers away from his Ben Franklin. So, he made a preemptive strike, persuading the landlord to lease him the space instead, and opening what he called the Eagle Store there.

Walton's brother, Bud Walton, said the Eagle "was really the beginning of where Walmart is today. We did everything. We would wash windows, sweep floors, trim windows. We did all the stockroom work, checked the freight in. Everything it took to run a store."

Walton did things a little differently at his Ben Franklin, reducing prices by purchasing 20 percent of his goods from suppliers other than Butler Brothers. Annual sales grew from $72,000 to $250,000 over the course of his five-year lease, making the store the region's top-performing Ben Franklin. Things were going well but perhaps too well: His landlord also happened to own a competing store in town, so when Walton's five-year lease was up, he simply refused to renew it. Walton was back to square one.

"It was really the low point in my business life," Walton would say later. "I felt sick to my stomach. I couldn't believe it was happening to me. It was really a nightmare. I had built the best variety store in the whole region and worked hard in the community—done everything right—and now I was being kicked out of town."

He sold the Eagle Store and all his inventory and quit town, moving about 240 miles west to Bentonville, Arkansas, just a few miles south of the Missouri state line. There, he and brother Bud opened another Ben Franklin store in 1951, but this time, he put his own name on it, calling it Walton's 5&10. The following year, they opened a second store thirty minutes down the road in Fayetteville. In 1954, they ventured outside Arkansas, opening a store in Kansas City, Missouri. That store was destroyed by a tornado three years later, but by the end of the decade, Walton had eight Ben Franklins (including four in northwest Arkansas) with annual sales of $1.4 million. It was still nothing to compared to Kresge or Woolworth, but it was a beginning.

Sam Walton opened his first Walmart-branded store in Rogers, Arkansas, on July 2, 1962, just four days before Woolworth opened its first Woolco store in Columbus. The latter event garnered headlines across the country; Walmart's debut went largely unnoticed, and no one would have guessed then that Walton's retail empire would outgrow and outlast that of Woolworth. It had already survived the demise of Walton's former boss, Butler Brothers, which sold all its retail properties (including Ben Franklin) in 1960. The Ben Franklin name survived—indeed, by 1966, Walton was the nation's largest Ben Franklin franchise holder with sixteen stores—but the Scott and Burr's Department Stores faded into history.

The original Walton's five-and-dime in Bentonville, Arkansas, now serves as a museum. Bobak Ha'Eri, 2006. Creative Commons 2.5 license: https://creativecommons.org/licenses/by-sa/2.5/deed.en.

Walmart's growth, meanwhile, was slow at first. It wasn't until 1966 that the fifth and sixth locations opened. A seventh store was added the following year, and six more debuted in '68, including the first locations outside Arkansas (two in Missouri and two more in Oklahoma). Wal-Mart stores incorporated on Halloween of 1969. Walton kept costs down by skimping on advertising. While other chains put out 50 to 100 ad circulars a year, Walmart ran just a dozen promotions.

It followed other chains by diversifying, adding pharmacies, auto centers, and jewelry in 1978, and by the end of the decade it was a $1.2 billion company with 276 stores in the central United States from Illinois south to Texas. By 1990, the year it expanded into California and Pennsylvania, it was the largest retailer in the country.

While Walmart was taking over the world (or at least the nation), the retail landscape was changing dramatically. W.T. Grant and White Front went out of business in the mid-seventies, and Woolco collapsed in 1983.

15

CLOSEOUTS AND OUTLETS

Big Lots was one of several "off-price" stores to find success in the second half of the twentieth century. Stephen H. Provost, 2019.

Marshalls and T.J. Maxx weren't the only stores of their kind to emerge from the ashes of the discount department store's golden age. These so-called off-price or closeout retailers created discounts by buying up overstocked goods and selling them at a cut rate.

There was a good deal of overlap between early big-box discounters, which tended to carry discontinued items and factory seconds as well.

One of the earliest and oddest examples of such a business was a Southern California–based chain called The Akron, which began in 1948 as an army surplus store on Sunset Boulevard called Akron Army & Navy. Its first ads included classifieds in *Popular Mechanics* that year advertising things like ID bracelets and two-way combat phones ("No batteries needed!"). By 1950, the inventory included tools, paints, camping equipment, watches, typewriters, and even a double-bunk bed for $1.99.

Indeed, according to cofounder Hy Fink, "you never knew what you were going to find" at The Akron, because the owners would grab whatever they thought they could sell. He said they'd drive around in a truck, scouting for what might work well in the store. One time, they came upon an orchid company in Pasadena that was being displaced by a new freeway. They paid 50 cents apiece for the orchids and put them up for sale at The Akron.

More conventional items for sale included cheap imports such as rattan chairs, similar to what was offered at Pier 1 or Cost Plus. But the store would also sell everything from houseplants to wine to more, shall we say, exotic fare. One former customer remembered buying canned kangaroo tail. Another ad promoted 3-, 4-, and 5-foot Hawaiian tiki gods; hand-carved from wood they were described as "primitive statue(s) to dominate your landscape," designed to "startle and amaze." Your choice, only $17.99. There were fire hydrants, motorcycles, and even live monkeys.

Fink later recalled one such simian who caught a cold and died shortly after a woman bought him. The Akron had a fourteen-day money-back guarantee, so the woman put the corpse in a paper bag and took it to the will-call. She was given credit, but a few hours later, the will-call secretary called the manager with a question: What should she do with the monkey. The answer: "Restock it."

Shopping at The Akron was, indeed, an adventure. A fire gutted the first store in 1952, but Fink and partner Bernard Field reopened and enlarged it by 25 percent the following year, to 13,000 square feet. The new store featured an exterior barbecue pit surrounded by a display of patio furniture and other items for outdoor living. Clearly, The Akron was expanding beyond its original army surplus identity, and it wasn't long before the owners dropped Army & Navy from its name in newspaper ads, adopting its familiar lowercase logo by 1954.

A year later, The Akron became a chain, opening a store in Burbank and others in West Los Angeles, West Covina, Torrance, and Anaheim over the next five years. Expansion continued beyond the LA area during the sixties and early seventies in San Francisco, Bakersfield, San Diego, and Santa Barbara. By the fall of 1974, there were twenty-three Akrons, all in California, along with a small chain of upscale stores outside the state that, coincidentally, shared the name of another Ohio city: Columbus. These stores were typically in smaller, specialty locations at indoor malls such as Houston's Galleria. They sold Akron-type items at higher prices to a more exclusive clientele; in Dallas, for example, the store was sandwiched between high-end retailers Lord & Taylor and Neiman Marcus.

The chain had five stores in all: two in Houston, the Dallas store, one in Phoenix, and one in Denver.

Thrifty Drugs bought the chain in the mid-seventies and subsequently sold it to a Hong Kong couple who owned one of the store's supply companies in 1982. They opened a new store in Anaheim the following year but quickly ran into financial problems and sold the leases on most of their remaining stores to Circuit City, which had previously operated electronic departments in Zody's discount stores. Circuit City took over a dozen former Akrons and opened them as stand-alone locations in November of 1985.

Several other "off-price" stores were more successful, if less colorful, than The Akron. Among them:

- Big Lots, a store featuring a wider variety of products beyond apparel and home goods (seasonal offerings, toys, furniture, patio products, etc.). It started off as Odd Lots, an offshoot of an auto parts store, in Ohio in the early eighties, growing to more than 1,400 stores by 2018. A bit of trivia: Big Lots' parent company owned a stake in the DeLorean Motor Company.

- Burlington Coat Factory, which started as a coat outlet store on Route 130, about fifteen miles southwest of Trenton, and grew to include more than 600 locations. In a bid to broaden its appeal, it dropped "Coat" from its name in 2017 to become just Burlington Stores. An ad campaign made the point that "it's not called 'coat factory' anymore—for a reason."

- Nordstrom Rack, which began in 1973 as a bargain-basement operation in Nordstrom's downtown Seattle store. As of 2015, it had more than 110 brick-and-mortar shops.

- Pic 'N' Save, a chain founded in Culver City, California, in 1950 that had grown to ninety outlets in seven western states by 1985. The store had a lot of quirky offerings, similar to what you might have found at Woolworth, with some discounted crafting products thrown in. It changed its name to MacFrugals in '91 and was absorbed by Big Lots near the turn of the millennium.

- Ross Dress for Less, a chain that grew to rival Marshalls and T.J. Maxx. By 2012 it had surpassed 1,000 stores, in addition to more than 100 affiliated dd's Discounts. It started in 1950 in San Bruno, California, and grew quickly during the eighties after it was purchased by an investment group led by Mervyn's founder Mervin Morris.

- Stein Mart, a discount department store featuring clothing and home accessories, which operated 260 stores in twenty-nine states as of 2013. The chain's history goes back further than most, to its founding in 1908 by a Russian Jewish immigrant named Sam Stein. The first store was in Mississippi, but the chain later came to be concentrated in the Southwest.

- Tuesday Morning, with a focus on closeout home goods and décor, including furniture, lamps, linens, luggage, small appliances, and crafts as well as bath and body products, and specialty food products (such as coffee, chocolate, and spices). As of 2018, it had more than 700 locations across the country.

Manufacturers got into the game as well. Originally, they sold their discontinued lines, overruns, and slightly damaged goods to their own employees at a discount, but somewhere along the way, they opened things up to the general public. Buyers still had to go out to the factory itself if they wanted a deal, which might mean a trip out of town to a dingy warehouse. But in 1936, men's clothier Anderson-Little changed that by opening up stand-alone outlets away from its factory grounds. And by the start of the seventies, women's lingerie maker and clothier Vanity Fair (not to be confused with the magazine by the same name) was becoming an especially popular destination.

As more manufacturers began to open their own off-price stores, it was only a matter of time before they started grouping them together in outlet malls. Pennsylvania, with a large number of clothing factories, was a natural place for this trend to start.

"It's a quick, easy way to get rid of overruns and discontinued styles," said Thomas Lucas, manager of the Vanity Fair outlet in Reading, Pennsylvania. "We sell both first-class merchandise and irregulars. Everything is 50 percent off retail."

Thomas made those comments in 1974, the year Vanity Fair established itself as the cornerstone of the world's first true outlet mall. Four years earlier, the company had opened a 5,000-square-foot outlet store in Reading, Pennsylvania, and before long, travel agents were making it a key destination for all-day bus tours. On a busy Saturday in the spring of '74, fifty buses pulled up in front of the store. By that time, Pennsylvania alone had sixty-eight factory outlets, and VF was attracting bus tours on a regular basis. A day trip from Philadelphia via Talmage Tours cost $14.50, including lunch, and stopped at five different outlets.

"It's going to get bigger," a Talmage consultant told the Associated Press. "It's popular because they get value for their money. If they do enough shopping, you save more than the fare."

By 1975, Reading was being billed as the factory outlet capital of the world. More bus tours were being offered. East Coast Parlor Car Tours was getting into the act with a $19.50 round-trip package that included a chicken dinner, cocktails, and six hours of shopping at more than a dozen outlet stores. Among them: London Fog coats and apparel, Mother Goose children's shoes, Misty Harbor raincoats, Lee sportswear, McGregor clothing, Schrafft's candy, and, of course, Vanity Fair.

Customers were sold on the idea of paying one-third to half of what they would have shelled out in a traditional store.

"I will never do any Christmas shopping in Washington again," DC resident J.D. Wooley enthused. "I think it's a steal. I spent $77, and in DC, it would have been $176."

Other outlet malls quickly followed, and by 2003, there were 260 of them across the country, generating $15 billion in revenue for their manufacturers. Typical outlet brands include Nike, Polo/Ralph Lauren, Tommy Hilfiger, Yankee Candle, Coach, Izod, and Williams-Sonoma. Apparel and shoes are among the most prominent products sold at the malls, which grew to be so popular that 37 percent of Americans in one survey said they visited one in 1997.

16

MEMBERS ONLY

What if you tried to shop at a department store, but they wouldn't let you in? Maybe they even asked to see your ID or (imagine this!) made you *pay* to shop there.

That's exactly what happened in the latter half of the twentieth century, when membership and bulk stores began emerging on the West Coast as a viable alternative to traditional department stores. Some originally targeted workers in specific fields, the way credit unions served teachers or law enforcement officers, then gradually opened up to the general public for a small fee. Others focused on discount warehouse sales to businesses that couldn't afford their own warehouses.

Sol Price founded FedMart in San Diego and expanded it as far east as San Antonio, where this store was located. Price would later start another membership department store, Price Club. Costaricky, 1979. Creative Commons 4.0 license: https://creativecommons.org/licenses/by-sa/4.0/deed.en.

Eventually, the trend resulted in huge membership stores such as Costco and the Walmart offshoot Sam's Club with a presence from coast to coast.

Among the first of this new breed of store was Fedco, short for Federal Employees' Distributing Company, which ran a chain of stores in Southern California from 1948 until just before the turn of the century. Unlike other department stores, Fedco wasn't created to make

money. It was a nonprofit retailer set up by several hundred US postal workers who were suffering from a wage freeze and wanted a way to buy products directly from wholesalers. The key to Fedco was a membership card that originally cost you $5, a new concept when it debuted in '48. (The membership fee had doubled to $10 by the time the store went out of business.)

Fedco's nonprofit status was challenged in the late fifties, but the Federal Trade Commission dismissed the case, and the chain prospered. A look inside a Los Angeles location on La Cienega Boulevard in the mid-eighties revealed a bustling store that looked not too different from a Kmart, with a grab bag of products ranging from cameras to televisions, groceries to luggage to greeting cards. There was even a pharmacy. At its height, the Fedco chain consisted of ten regular outlets at various times—nine in the Los Angeles area and one in San Diego—along with three others that only sold appliances.

Fedco offered a credit card called Fedcharge and sent a catalog/magazine called the Reporter to its members every other month; it touted the latest deals and also contained articles on California history and federal policy. One page featured a membership application with the invitation to "give this to a friend." By 1957, membership was open to all federal, state, county, or city employees—military or civilian; active or retired—along with employees of educational, scientific, or nonprofit religious institutions; and anyone receiving regular disability, pension, Social Security, or railroad retirement annuities from the US government. It was almost more difficult not to qualify than it was to meet the standard.

There were already 240,000 members by 1957, the same year Fedco ventured outside the Los Angeles metro area for the first time. Late that year it opened its fifth location, featuring "60,000 square feet of self-service shopping all under one roof" at 54th and Euclid in San Diego. In 1984, the store would move to a location more than twice that size down the road in National City.

Only two more Fedco stores would open after that: a second San Diego–area store in 1986, at a former Sears store in Escondido; and a Buena Park Mall store at an old May Co. in 1993. A year earlier, however, the business had suffered a major blow when the La Cienega store was looted and its auto center set ablaze during the Rodney King riots, causing more than $14 million in damage. The store reopened two weeks later, and all 750 employees returned to work, but by some measures, it was the beginning of the end for the chain.

By 1999, Fedco had filed for bankruptcy, and most of its properties were sold to Target, which opened its own branches in former Fedco locations in Cerritos, Los Angeles, Pasadena, San Bernardino, and Van Nuys. Barry J. Stone of Culver City wrote a short but fitting epitaph for the store in a Los Angeles Times letter to the editor in August: "When I got my lifetime membership at Fedco, I never dreamed it would expire before I do."

It wasn't the first time Target had taken over a struggling membership department store. Back in 1983, it had purchased the similarly named FedMart, and three years later, it had bought out Gemco.

The latter chain opened its doors in the fall of 1959, establishing a 70,000-square-foot, fully air-conditioned store on Lincoln Avenue, west of Brookhurst in Anaheim. Contrary to urban legend, Gemco wasn't an acronym; it didn't stand for "Government Employees' Membership Company" or anything like that. It was the brainchild of David and Frank Grand, owners of the Le Gran Corp., which operated a Long Beach store known as (fittingly) Gem Jewelers. That business had been around since 1923, but by the fifties, it was selling much more than jewelry. A 1957 article in the Long Beach Press-Telegram named Le Gran Corp. and Gem Jewelers as a suppliers of Hamilton Beach small kitchen appliances. Other Gem ads from the same era touted wool blankets, cameras, Sunbeam shavers, televisions (rented for $6 a month with no credit check), and Revere Ware for sale. Such a diverse inventory created the perfect foundation for opening a new discount department store, and that's exactly what the Grands did.

The store opened on October 29, 1959, announced by a nearly half-page ad in the Los Angeles Times that described it as a "new star in the sky" and encouraged readers to come out for a "four-day preview of G*E*M*C*O, Orange County's newest department store buying organization."

Residents were invited to tour the store, but in order to make any purchases, they'd have to buy a lifetime membership—covering the entire family—for the astronomical sum of one whole dollar. If they didn't like it, they could withdraw within ninety days and get that dollar back, no questions asked. Those eligible for membership belonged to most of the same categories as those who were members of Fedco: government employees, veterans, nonprofit workers, and so on. The membership fee was more an incentive to revisit the store than a way of raising revenue; a later article described "most" of the fee as being used for charitable donations and college scholarships.

Gemco ran a 1959 ad announcing its arrival as "a new star in the sky."

The Grands didn't last long as owners of Gemco. A year after they opened the store, they sold it to Lucky Stores, one of the first supermarket chains to dive into the department store business. In doing so, they created an early hypermarket, adding a complete grocery section, a pharmacy, and a snack bar to the Anaheim location, which they expanded by 20,000 square feet. The hypermarket concept was later emulated by Target, Walmart, and Kmart, among others, but Lucky president Gerald Awes said he'd seen it work effectively in the eastern United States: "Lucky is taking this advanced step because this type of marketing is becoming an important factor in the East," he said. "The trend is moving West, and Lucky management feels it imperative to meet competition of this type with prompt and aggressive action."

Although Lucky owned the entire business, it would focus on operating the supermarket. The Grands stayed on as company vice presidents to oversee the rest of the store's operations, with an eye toward expansion to other locations. By November of 1963, three more Gemcos had opened: one east of Los Angeles in La Puente and two others in Cupertino and San Jose, both

closer to Lucky's home turf in the Bay Area. A fifth store, a 103,000-square-foot unit on Valley Boulevard in San Gabriel, was targeted to open in April of 1964.

Rapid expansion continued, and David Grand was supplying jewelry and other concessions—radios, tape recorders, record players, cameras, typewriters, and luggage—to some twenty Gemco locations in 1969. The same year, the chain moved eastward, opening 100,000-square-foot stores in the Washington suburbs of Annandale, Virginia, and Camp Springs, Maryland. Those stores (and eleven other stores built in that area) weren't called Gemco, though. Instead, they were branded as Memco to avoid confusion with GEM stores, a chain already operating in the area.

Unlike Gemco/Memco, GEM was a Fedco-style closed operation. It stood for Government Employees Mutual (or Government Employees Mart). The electronics and home appliance section of the store was run by Wards Company—which was unrelated to Montgomery Ward and later moved out on its own to become Circuit City. The first GEM store opened in Denver in 1957, and the company merged with Parkview Drugs of Kansas City

The first Price Club operated out of this building in San Diego. It was later converted into a Costco. RightCowLeftCoast, 2018. Creative Commons 4.0 license: https://creativecommons.org/licenses/by-sa/4.0/deed.en.

nine years later, expanding to thirty-eight stores by 1970 but going out of business three years later as government membership model faltered.

Gemco, meanwhile, lasted a bit longer and continued to thrive. In 1970, the company announced plans to build a $4 million store and freestanding auto center in Fresno, California, which spurred the installation of a stoplight at the intersection of First and Shields avenues. It was almost fully stocked ten days before its scheduled November 5 opening and was poised to undergo its final inspection when a fire started over the coffee shop. The flames spread from there, fueled by cardboard boxes that were strewn along the aisles. The blaze destroyed almost the entire structure, along with merchandise and furnishings. One firefighter died of a heart attack battling the blaze, and two others were injured.

The auto center was undamaged.

"It was like an inverted tornado that created winds up to 50 and 60 miles an hour," sending flames and smoke 2,000 feet into the air, Deputy Fire Chief Jack Huneke told the *Fresno Bee*. "In my 30 years on the fire department, I have never seen this phenomenon."

The company immediately pledged to rebuild, taking out a full-page newspaper ad proclaiming that "Gemco in Fresno is down . . . but not out!" and pledging that reconstruction would begin immediately. It made good on its word, opening the new store (its twenty-seventh) in March.

And it continued to grow. By 1986, it had eighty locations, including seven in its original home base of Orange County. But a three-month strike by union workers in 1984 and an eight-week supermarket strike the following year had eaten into profits, even as the store contended with the advent of big-box membership rivals like Sam's

Club and Costco. The final straw was a New York investor's takeover bid, which spurred Lucky to divest itself of everything except its core grocery store business. That included its Gemco locations, fifty-four of which were sold to Target. The Fresno location that was rebuilt from the ground up following that 1970 fire continues to operate as a Target today.

FedMart and Price Club

The other membership chain absorbed by Target, FedMart, was the brainchild of Sol Price, a former lawyer whose father had manufactured women's apparel. He was still practicing law when, at the age of thirty-nine, he found himself with a new project. His father-in-law had died in 1947, leaving his wife a piece of property on the western edge of San Diego's Balboa Park. Price persuaded his mother-in-law to trade it for a warehouse on Main Street to the south, along the coast.

Then, he had to figure out what to do with it.

The answer came in 1953, when one of Price's clients, a jeweler named Mandell Weiss, invited him to visit the Fedco store in Los Angeles. Weiss's company was supplying more jewelry to Fedco than to any other retailer, and the pair began talking about the idea of bringing Fedco to San Diego, with a new location in the Main Street warehouse. At the time, however, Fedco "didn't want anything to do with us," Weiss later recalled. That would change in a few years, when Fedco did, in fact, expand into San Diego, but Price and Weiss had no intention of waiting that long. Instead, they decided to start their own business in the warehouse, modeled after Fedco. Like Fedco, it would be a membership department store open to federal employees and veterans—of whom there were plenty in the San Diego area, with its heavy concentration of military sites. The US Navy depot, for one, was less than a mile away, on 32nd Street. A lifetime membership would be $2, and hours would be skewed toward late afternoons and evenings (except on Saturdays), when more military families were able to shop. Initially a nonprofit like Fedco, it was reorganized a few months later as a profit-making business.

When FedMart opened, Price recalled, "it was an immediate and spectacular success. We had anticipated we might do $1 million the first year, but it ended up approximately three times more than we expected. It was the hottest thing to hit San Diego in a long time." It was so successful, in fact, that Price quit his legal practice to become a full-time retailer. Within the next few years, he'd opened stores in Phoenix and San Antonio, along with more in Southern California. FedMart even established its own FM brand, applying it to everything from cola to bleach to detergent, which was sold in 20-pound tubs. The bulk pricing was a hint of things to come.

FedMart ended its membership requirement in 1963, and the chain continued for two decades after that, expanding to seventy stores in four states (Arizona, California, New Mexico, and Texas) before hard times hit. It closed all forty-six of its remaining stores in 1983, selling most of them to Target. The company had gone public in 1969, and a German investor had loaded up on stock in the mid-seventies to take majority control.

Just as Fedco inspired the FedMart name, it in turn inspired another retailer: "I learned a lot from Sol Price," Sam Walton would later say. "I guess I've stolen—I actually prefer the word 'borrowed'—as many ideas from Sol Price as from anybody else in the business. . . . I really liked Sol's FedMart name, so I latched right on to WalMart."

Walton might also have been inspired by Price's next big venture: Sam's Club, which appeared in 1983. Walton formed the store's moniker using his own name and the word "club," just as Price had done with his own Price Club seven years earlier. Both were membership stores that kept prices low through bulk purchases.

Price founded his new venture just one year after being ousted by FedMart's new owners in 1975. Price Club started off as an exclusive store open only to local businesses, who were invited to buy in bulk. Price Club would store items in a 102,000-square-foot warehouse and sell them at discounts of 6 to 20 percent. This not only gave merchants a break on their supply costs, it allowed them to avoid the cost of storing items in their own warehouses.

Price explained the concept: "The small businessman needs a break. The Price Club gives him at least two. First, what he buys for resale to his customers or for use in his own business will be purchased cheaper and in desired quantity. Second, the substantial inventory . . . makes it possible for the small businessman to sell products and services he cannot presently offer without expanding his own inventory or without a [significant] cash investment."

Price later expanded membership opportunities to other groups, charging $25 a year for access to his warehouse stores. By 1985, he and son Robert—the company president—had twenty-four of them in Arizona, California, Maryland, and Virginia, with annual sales approaching $2 billion.

Walton wasn't the only one to emulate Price's formula. A *Los Angeles Times* article in the spring of 1985 noted that it had been "copied by competitors right down to the green paint selected for the shopping carts." Sixty-four warehouse membership stores, operated by eight companies, had opened in cities from Anchorage to Tampa, the article said, with the number pegged to reach 111 by year's end.

Price Club had expanded to ninety-four stores by 1993, but some of the other chains had grown more quickly: notably, Costco and Sam's Club.

Costco was the brainchild of Jim Sinegal, who had started his retail career as a grocery bagger at the first FedMart store just after it opened and had eventually risen to become the chain's vice president of merchandising and operations. Sinegal and partner Jeffrey Brotman, an attorney like Price, opened the first Costco in Seattle in 1983. The company was so successful it became the first company to reach $3 billion in sales in under six years.

Walton, feeling the heat from Costco, suggested a merger of Sam's Club and Price Club, but the Prices rebuffed him. Sol Price explained: "We were good at innovating, but when it came to expanding and controlling, we weren't so good."

Instead, Price Club chose to merge with Costco, creating a company of 206 stores in 1993. A quarter century later, Costco had grown to a company of 759 warehouses in eleven countries. On its website, Costco traces its own roots back to the first Price Club store on Morena Boulevard in San Diego.

All this competition took its toll on the venerable Kmart brand, which found itself squeezed by Walmart on one side and Target on the other. Walmart, which had grown to a massive 11,000 stores in twenty-seven countries by 2015, had beaten Kmart at its own game: selling

essential products as cheaply as possible. Target, meanwhile, had claimed a slightly higher end of the discount marketplace, focusing on so-called cheap chic products. Kmart had tried to push its way into this marketplace in the nineties by offering exclusive product lines associated with the likes of former *Charlie's Angels* star Jaclyn Smith and lifestyle guru/chef/TV host Martha Stewart, but Target had still come out on top.

Kmart attempted to diversify its image with a couple of associated brands. The first, Super Kmart, incorporated a grocery section in addition to Kmart's regular merchandise (something Target had done in its first store and a practice it continues today, as does Walmart in its Super Walmart stores). Other features of these mega-stores included a video rental store, a bank branch, an arcade, a portrait studio, a pharmacy, and a deli café. The first one opened in 1991, and the last one closed in 2018. Then there were the confusingly similar-sounding Big Kmart stores, which weren't as big as a Super Kmart but offered many of the same products.

Kmart even made an abortive attempt to compete with Sam's Club and Costco/Price Club in the membership warehouse category, purchasing PACE Membership Warehouse stores, a company that had grown to forty-one locations in just six years by 1989. PACE, which founder Henry Haimson admitted was modeled after Price Club, had opened its first store in Denver and—charging a $25 annual fee—had quickly built a membership of 135,000 at the store. A year later, he was planning a store in Tampa and three outlets in Atlanta.

PACE's growth to become the nation's fourth-largest warehouse club chain enticed Kmart to purchase the company for $322 million in 1989, adding it to six Makro warehouse stores it had purchased a year earlier. It later added seventeen Price Savers outlets, converting them to the PACE nameplate.

But by 1993, Kmart had given up on the project and sold ninety-one of its 113 warehouse sites to Walmart. The rest were closed, remodeled, or sold to other buyers.

Meanwhile, Kmart's core business declined and it sold off many of the specialty stores it had acquired, including its Walden/Borders bookstores, Sports Authority, and Builders Square, all of which subsequently went out of business. PayLess Drugs was absorbed by Thrifty, and OfficeMax became part of the similarly named

A former PACE site in St. Louis. Kmart purchased PACE as its ultimately failed entry into the membership warehouse market. Mike Kalasnik, 2016. Creative Commons 2.0 license: https://creativecommons.org/licenses/by-sa/2.0.

Office Depot chain. But Kmart's biggest move came in 2004, when it acquired struggling retail giant Sears for $11 billion. The marriage of two former kingpins was expected to create a worthy rival to Walmart, but the new company never found its identity.

The two brands began their union with 3,500 stores between them, but five years after the merger, store closings started to become routine. Fresno, for example, lost all its Kmart locations and, in 2017, the last Kmart in Alabama closed. Kmart pulled out of Hawaii, Arkansas, and Kansas the following year, leaving it without any presence in eight states, and by October, the two brands had fewer than 700 stores between them—one-fifth of their total at the time of the merger. The company warned more closures were coming, and that same month, it filed for bankruptcy.

17

INDOOR IMPLOSION

The indoor mall hit its heyday in the eighties, when it was celebrated in pop culture and a host of teen-oriented movies. Want evidence? Check out *Fast Times at Ridgemont High, Weird Science, Clueless,* or *Bill and Ted's Excellent Adventure.* Then, of course, there's *Mallrats,* which was set in, yes, a mall, not to mention the more recent *Paul Blart: Mall Cop.*

But that Kevin Smith comedy hit the screen toward the tail end of the era of big indoor malls. At least one new shopping mall was built in the United States every year from the fifties through 2006, and nineteen were built in 1990 alone. But in 2007, something strange happened: No new malls were built. Growth stopped on a dime, and dollars stopped rolling in. By the time *Paul Blart:*

The entrance to an abandoned Kmart stands guard over the cracked asphalt of an empty parking lot at a North Carolina shopping mall that's seen better days. Stephen H. Provost, 2018.

Mall Cop hit theaters in 2009, the trend was unmistakable. Over the previous two years, the Great Recession had forced the closure of 400 malls—20 percent of the nation's total. Malls, like newspapers, just kept dying off, taking a piece of our childhood with them.

Want to take a step back in time and visit the Sherman Oaks Galleria, where *Fast Times*, Arnold Schwarzenegger's action film *Commando,* and a handful of other eighties movies were filmed? Sorry, but you're out of luck. The Galleria is still there or, rather, something *called* the Galleria. But the original mall was torn down in 1999 and replaced by an open-air center that looks nothing like its namesake, the skylit, three-story teen playground mentioned in Moon Zappa's hit single "Valley Girl." Gone were the Swensen's Ice Cream, Florsheim Shoes, B. Dalton Books, and Licorice Pizza record store. In their place: a collection heavy on fast-casual food chains, and fewer than half a dozen retailers sprinkled in for good measure. And no department stores.

The demise of the quintessential San Fernando Valley shopping mall is typical of the fate that befell hundreds of enclosed malls across the country at the dawn of the new millennium.

What happened?

For starters, US tax laws had long encouraged developers to build new malls, not to maintain them. A 1954 change in the tax code allowed builders to take accelerated depreciation on their assets, which would save them money on taxes. Put simply, they were making a real-world profit but losing money on paper. Those phantom losses, chalked up to depreciation, offset their actual profits and meant they'd have a small (if any) tax bill. As profits went up, taxes went down. It was a win-win situation in which developers had two slices of cake, ate them too and got fat in the process.

Developers didn't need any other reason to build new malls. They didn't even need a clientele. They could build a mall on the outskirts of nowhere in the knowledge that it would drive growth (if you build it, they will come), and write it all off with the IRS. In 1953, the year before the tax law changed, just one shopping center was built in the United States. Three years later, twenty-five were built. In Scranton, Pennsylvania, the population fell by 73,000 between 1950 and 1970, but the area got three

sparkling-new indoor malls and thirty-one shopping centers in all.

But a couple of things happened in the mid-nineties to change all that.

First, the bill came due. When they were built, shopping centers were assumed to have a lifespan of about forty years; after that, owners could no longer take depreciation. The tax incentive to hold on to these assets went away, and there was certainly no incentive to maintain or improve them. If you did *that*, their value would rise—and so would your tax bill. The obvious choice would be to build a new mall instead, but so many people had already built malls that the landscape was saturated.

Second, a new obstacle was appearing on the horizon. It wouldn't be long before online shopping would start eating into profits, then gobbling them up wholesale, helping to kill off malls the same way online news would begin making printed newspapers obsolete.

Still, the demise of the indoor mall also parallels the decline of the American department store that, in fact, predated the internet age. As Macy's and May devoured their competitors, and then Macy's absorbed May, the time-tested strategy of building malls around anchor tenants began to fail. With fewer department stores to serve as anchors, malls across the country had a hard time adapting. The anchor tenants had been the glue holding the American shopping mall together, and without them, the malls themselves started coming apart at the seams.

Case in point: East Hills mall in Bakersfield, which had opened in 1986 with three anchor tenants—Mervyn's, Gottschalks, and Harris. The choices couldn't have been worse for the mall's long-term viability. First, Gottschalks bought Harris in 1998, eventually leaving that spot vacant. Then Mervyn's went out of business in late 2008, and Gottschalks' demise was hot on its heels. Suddenly, East Hills had zero anchors. A decade later, it was being torn down to make way for a "lifestyle center," a return to outdoor retail shopping that had begun picking up steam in the late nineties.

As department stores folded, consolidated or fled to these new locales, indoor malls were faced with the task of finding new tenants for their largest retail spaces. Some of those spaces were abandoned as chains scaled back or went out of business. Others were walled off as the stores that used to occupy them were absorbed by Macy's—which already had a store in many of the malls and no incentive to occupy two sites in the same location.

TRANSFORMATIONS

Various malls tried different strategies to make things work.

Fresno's first indoor mall, Fashion Fair, opened in 1970 with three anchor tenants (Weinstock's, Gottschalks, and J.C. Penney) and added a fourth when Macy's came aboard in 1983. But when Macy's bought out Weinstock's parent company, it closed that store. Gottschalks took advantage of the opportunity to move from the central anchor into the larger eastern spot, while Macy's converted the old Gottschalks site into its own branded men's store.

Unfortunately for the mall, Gottschalks went out of business in 2009, forcing the center to find yet another eastern anchor. It settled on Forever 21, a youth-oriented clothing store that had previously occupied a much smaller, specialty store site inside the mall. The move was part of the chain's strategy to transition into larger store sites by taking over fourteen old Mervyn's stores and fifteen Gottschalks sites.

But that transition didn't always go as planned. Forever 21 found some of the stores simply too big for its catalog—and for the number of customers who shopped there. It left the former Riverside Gottschalks in 2013 and moved into a former Borders Bookstore. The former Gottschalks in San Luis Obispo closed three years later, followed swiftly by the Hanford site (all in California). The Fresno store, however, remained open.

Across town, Manchester Center also turned to a specialty retailer when it lost its first anchor. After Liberty House closed, Manchester brought in linen/housewares retailer Home Express on the first floor and devoted the second to a Gottschalks clearance center. But

J.C. Penney was the only original anchor tenant remaining at Fresno's Fashion Fair shopping center when this photo was taken. Stephen H. Provost, 2013.

Home Express went out of business in the mid-nineties, and Manchester couldn't find another retailer willing to take a chance on the site after that. Instead, it converted the former Liberty House space into a huge office for the state's department of transportation.

That left two other anchors—original tenant Sears at the north end and Gottschalks in the middle. Smaller tenants at the south end of the mall began pulling out, creating two cavernous corridors, one on top of the other, lined with few or no destinations. Next, the mall failed to find a replacement when Gottschalks went belly-up in 2009, and that space sat empty for years. A plan unveiled in the summer of 2018 called for the space to become a food court, housing eleven different eateries. Most of the customers, however, wouldn't be shoppers. They'd be the 2,000 transportation and police employees who worked in a mall that was, increasingly, devoted to office space.

(This wouldn't be the first time Manchester had tried to reinvent itself. Built as an open-air shopping center in 1955, it was renovated to become an enclosed two-story mall in 1978, and ambitious plans in 1994 called for adding a third story. That proposal, however, never got off the drawing board, and vacancy rates had risen to 60 percent by the turn of the century.)

In a reversal of fortune, indoor malls seemed to fall out of favor, and outdoor "power centers" or "stretch malls"—dominated by big-box tenants rather than traditional department stores—were replacing them. This was true even in Fresno, where summer temperatures routinely top 100 degrees and outdoor shopping can result in equal parts perspiration and frustration. As Manchester Center and (to a lesser extent) Fashion Fair struggled, a new outdoor center on the city's more affluent northside called River Park thrived. Big-box retailers like Best Buy, Bath & Body Works, and Dick's Sporting Goods stood alongside traditional department stores (Macy's, Kohl's), smaller specialty retailers, and a movie multiplex. Palm trees and fountains added to the ambience of a center that, in many ways, brought Victor Gruen's vision of a pedestrian mall to life even as the city paved over his downtown work with asphalt, opening the old Fulton Mall to traffic once again.

Meanwhile, Fashion Fair and Sequoia Mall in nearby Clovis repackaged themselves as hybrids by adding outdoor walkways and courtyards to their designs, mimicking the success of River Park.

Other malls abandoned the indoor model altogether and reinvented themselves as open-air centers. Owners of the San Jacinto Mall in Baytown, Texas, favored that approach. Plans called for the center, which opened in 1981 as a massive indoor mall with eight anchor spaces, to be demolished in favor of an outdoor center by 2019.

Sheta Kaey of Baytown worked in the mall when it was enclosed—and thriving.

"When I wasn't working, I hung out at the mall a lot," she said. "I got to know other shopkeepers. And there were fountains you could sit around [on the retaining walls], and music stores still existed; VHS was still just a glimmer in someone's eye.

"It still exists, in a much less interesting way. The rent is high, and the mall limits what sizes you can sell if you're a clothing store. Everyone used to shop there for Christmas, and now no one does. All my favorite places are gone. . . . It is now almost solely big-box stores, the food court, and the cinema.

"I miss malls. I really *liked* malls as a centralized shopping experience. So much variety, and you only had to park once. You could browse and see a huge variety of offerings. From Spencer's to the Discovery Store to Build-a-bear to Macy's. I thoroughly enjoyed even holiday shopping, and the impulse buys were almost never reason for regret—at least until the pushy seasonal kiosks became ubiquitous."

In Martinsville, the owners of Liberty Fair Mall converted it from an indoor mall to an open-air center, too. It had opened in 1989 with three traditional department stores as anchors: J.C. Penney, Sears, and Leggett, along with discount retailer Walmart. But Walmart had moved up the road in 1997, while J.C. Penney converted its site to an outlet store two years later and ultimately abandoned the site altogether. Sears closed in 2012, leaving Belk (formerly Leggett) as the only traditional anchor for the center.

New owners demolished the indoor mall and rebranded its open-air successor as Village of Martinsville. Instead of department stores, its focal points now included a sporting goods store, a big-box office supply retailer (which closed in the fall of 2020), and a Kroger

The Liberty Fair opened as an indoor mall in Martinsville, Virginia, in 1989 but had lost three of its four main anchors by the time Sears closed in 2012. So it reinvented itself as an outdoor center, rechristened the Village of Martinsville. Stephen H. Provost, 2019.

supermarket alongside Belk. The J.C. Penney building was torn down.

Ironically, Liberty Fair had lured Penney's away from the city's first major shopping center when it opened in 1989. Penney's had anchored the Patrick Henry Mall when the 60,000-square-foot location opened just about a mile east of downtown, in 1966. Miss Virginia was on hand to welcome the store and the 200 jobs that came with it. Actually, the center wasn't really that big. It fell somewhere between a strip mall and a full-fledged outdoor center. The buildings were set up in a typical L shape around the parking lot, but there was also an open-air concourse behind two of the smaller structures that provided access to a second anchor: A Rose's discount department store. Other primary tenants were a Peoples Drug and a Colonial Stores market.

The arrival of Liberty Fair—and the departure of Penney's—relegated the mall to the status of a glorified strip mall. The three other main tenants eventually pulled out, and the mall became a jumble of small specialty stores, cut-rate retailers, and vacant spaces. As of 2018, a Family Dollar store occupied the former drugstore space, while a Goodwill-type thrift store called REA had set up shop in the former J.C. Penney. The Rose's building remained vacant.

Ariel's Clothing, a women's apparel shop founded in 1980, was a throwback to the more traditional shopping center tenants, and CVS—the successor company to Peoples Drug—occupied a space in the parking lot.

The former J.C. Penney building at the Patrick Henry Mall in Martinsville has gone through several tenants since its original occupant departed. Stephen H. Provost, 2019.

ON LIFE SUPPORT

While some malls managed to reinvent themselves as big-box centers and office space, others struggled to hang on.

Sequoia Mall in Visalia had become a virtual ghost town as of 2018, even though it stood at one of the city's busiest intersections, Mooney and Caldwell. With a larger enclosed center, Visalia Mall, less than half a mile away, the city of fewer than 140,000 people in California's San Joaquin Valley may simply not have been big enough for both of them. Whatever the reason, Sequoia Mall seemed on the verge of failing completely.

During the mid-seventies, when it opened, it had been home to such shops as Harry Coffee's menswear, General Nutrition Centers, Leeds Shoes, and Waldenbooks. In 2004, the center suffered a big blow when its large Borders bookstore (a sister chain to the smaller Waldenbooks) closed as the entire company went out of business. The same year, Men's Wearhouse pulled up stakes and moved up the street to Visalia Mall. Then, in 2008, the mall lost one of its anchors when Mervyn's went out of business;

the mall did get a boost when big-box craft store Hobby Lobby moved into that space two years later but that failed to stop the bleeding.

In April of 2017, the mall was down to sixteen businesses. By November of 2018, just nine were listed on the mallsinamerica.com website—and that's if you included a bank branch in the parking lot and the Sears Auto Center in addition to the main Sears store. Only four of the twenty-six smaller spaces inside the mall were filled. As for Sears, it was facing bankruptcy and looking to lease half its space to another tenant. The biggest tenant, apart from Hobby Lobby, was a twelve-screen Regal Cinema.

Sequoia Mall was on life support, but it wasn't quite dead.

Even worse off was the Eden Mall in North Carolina. In its heyday, it featured three strong anchors in Belk-Cline (later just Belk), Globman's, and Kmart, along with smaller tenants like Kay Jewelers, Waldenbooks, a Hallmark shop, and Lerner Shoes. Opened in 1980 in the midst of the mall boom, it rode in on the coattails of a new Miller brewery that had opened two years earlier.

"I'm glad the brewery's here," the mayor, James Norman, said in an interview a year after the single-story retail complex opened. "The mall wouldn't be here if the brewery wasn't here."

Norman also happened to work for Fieldcrest Mills, the town's biggest employer at the time. But Fieldcrest pulled out of town in 2003, and the Miller plant closed in 2017. By that time, the mall was already in dire straits. Globman's had been replaced by Peebles, a Houston-based chain, but that store later closed, too, moving down the road to a strip mall in 2008. Kmart had been gone since the mid-nineties, and in 2010, Belk had closed off its interior entrance, requiring patrons to enter from the parking lot.

Even well-intended improvements came to naught. In 2010, someone decided to build a go-kart track in the parking lot behind the abandoned Kmart. The developer of the track said he spent $200,000 putting the project together, but fire codes prevented him from ever opening. As of this writing, what's left of the track—a few makeshift light standards, a couple of aluminum canopies, and the disconnected outlines of the track—lay abandoned in the back parking lot, never used and not yet disposed of years later.

A new owner tried to resuscitate the mall in 2014, spending tens of thousands of dollars on improvements and renting the spaces once filled by chain stores to local businesses. Ironically, the same approach had been used decades earlier by downtown districts to fill empty spaces after businesses fled Main Street for enclosed malls. Downtown Fresno, for example, had replaced chain stores like Newberry and Gottschalks with locally owned businesses catering to the Latino community and by converting a former department store into a thrift "mall" featuring a variety of small concessionaires.

The Eden Mall's strategy was similar. The new owner got rid of the moldy smell, fixed the leaks in the roof, and succeeded in getting the roster of tenants up to twenty-nine. He even started an innovative program allowing people to rent a table for a Friday-Saturday flea market. But the renaissance proved to be short-lived. Belk pulled out altogether a couple of years later, leaving the mall without a single anchor, and things went downhill again from there. By the fall of 2018, occupancy was listed on a chamber of commerce website as consisting of just half a dozen businesses—two of which were run by an upholsterer doing double duty as the mall's new manager.

Eden Mall (in Eden, North Carolina) was still operating in 2018, but former anchors Kmart, Belk, and Globman's were all long gone. An antique mall in the former Belk space appeared to be the busiest tenant. Stephen H. Provost, 2019.

Still, the mall remained open. Wide open. One visitor filmed a video in which the doors to the former Globman's/Peebles behind the mall were wired open, so anyone could get in twenty-four hours a day. It wasn't as if there was much to steal. No guards patrolled the center; the only "security" consisted of a placard nailed to one of the doors inside, offering a $200 reward for the arrest and conviction of anyone damaging the property, signed simply "The Management."

The doors were subsequently locked, and the chamber of commerce site promised that "good things are happening," offering spaces available for rent starting at $80 a month. But it was hard to see many of those good things on a visit to the mall. A thrift center operated in the old Belk store, while Kmart and Peebles remained empty. Looking through the Peebles backdoor revealed a dark and cavernous expanse, punctuated oddly by an old chandelier that remained hanging from the ceiling. The adjacent parking lot was strewn with junk across asphalt that was so badly cracked it seemed almost like it had been hit by an earthquake. The remains of the old

go-kart track added to the eerie atmosphere that one blogger compared to something out of *The Twilight Zone*.

"It's pretty much like an apocalyptic wasteland out here," a video commentator said while touring the mall in the fall of 2018. "This place should not even exist. . . . It really honestly looks like I'm on the scene of *The Walking Dead*."

Eden Mall and Liberty Fair were among many malls in the North Carolina-Virginia region that found themselves struggling amid a difficult economy and shifting retail habits. One of them, Oak Hollow Mall in High Point, North Carolina, opened in 1995. In contrast to some of the smaller malls in the region, Oak Hollow was a major undertaking hailed as the largest economic development project in the city's history. It covered a million square feet and showcased four anchors, two of which—Penney's and Belk—had deserted the smaller Westchester Mall in what proved to be a death blow for that site.

Westchester wound up being converted into a community center with church offices and a sanctuary in one of

The huge Oak Hollow Mall in High Point, North Carolina, was indeed hollow by 2018. The only remaining tenant was Dillard's, which had closed the second floor of its two-story building and converted the ground floor to a clearance outlet that was closed off from the rest of the shuttered mall. Stephen H. Provost, 2018.

Roses, seen here, and Belk remained as tenants of the Pennrose Mall in Reidsville, North Carolina, as of 2018. But Belk's entrance to the rest of the mall had been shuttered, and the store could be accessed only from the parking lot. Inside, only a couple of specialty stores remained. Stephen H. Provost, 2018.

the former anchor spots. At the other end is a senior care center. Some of the smaller store sites are occupied by health care and other facilities. Much of the activity these days, however, involves mall walkers who use the mostly deserted main corridor for exercise rather than braving the cold in wintertime.

Westchester went by the wayside when Oak Hollow was built. But the new mall didn't last, either. One of its other anchors, Goody's, closed in 2008 and eventually became a Sears customer service center. Another, Dillard's, downgraded its presence to a "clearance store" the following year. Meanwhile, smaller tenants were leaving the mall, which was sold to a local university in 2011. Penney's pulled out that same year, and Belk departed in 2014. The mall had just eleven stores left by the time it closed three years later. In 2018, the entire mall was walled off, with the exception of the first floor at the Dillard's clearance store, which was still operating. Otherwise, its massive size made it look very much like a proverbial white elephant, sprawled out across a deserted deathbed of asphalt. It was, true to its name, hollow, having been built too close to other malls in the Triad area (High Point, Greensboro, and Winston-Salem) and having come along at precisely the wrong time.

Many other malls were in decline by the start of the new millennium. One observer suggested the Eden

Mall might have been a nonstarter from the beginning, posting on the Sky City website: "I remember when the mall was first built. They had the most stores there the first year, then it was downhill from there, as they lost a few every year, until now there is almost nothing there."

It didn't help that the Eden Mall was less than a half hour from both Liberty Fair in Martinsville and Pennrose Mall in the small town of Reidsville to the south. The two-story Piedmont Mall in the slightly larger city of Danville was just a little farther away, to the northeast.

The Piedmont Mall, which changed its name to the Danville Mall as part of a 2013 renovation, had been through some struggles of its own but still had several popular chains on its roster five years later. Two of its five anchor spaces sat vacant following the 2018 closure of its Sears, and a former Boscov's remained empty for a decade after closing just three years after it opened.

For Eden residents, though, it still had a lot more to offer than their comatose hometown mall or the Pennrose in nearby Reidsville, just twelve miles to the south. Pennrose was faring only slightly better than Eden at the end of the 2010s. Anchor stores Roses and Belk (which seems to hang on longer than most in dying malls) were still open, but the rest of the mall was a virtual ghost town. According to the mall's website, active tenants included a sports shop, gift shops, a florist,

The mall entrance to the old J.C. Penney at the Pennrose Mall in Reidsville, North Carolina, is no longer accessible. Yellow caution tape separates it from the rest of the mall, and water damage is visible on the ceiling. Stephen H. Provost, 2018.

a cellular provider, and a couple of shoe stores. But a visit to the mall revealed the truth of the matter: Only two of those stores were still operating. Signs out front advertised several businesses—Cato Fashions, a Hallmark store, a Beltone hearing center, and Lemon's Jeweler's—in faded or chipped letters, but they were nowhere in evidence inside. Hibbett Sports, a de facto anchor near the center of the mall, was vacant, too.

"They won't even take the signs down when the businesses are gone," said Scott Adams of Bob Adams Florist, one of the two specialty stores still doing business inside the mall. "Hibbett Sports has been gone three or four years."

Adams's store seemed like an oasis inside the largely forgotten mall during the most recent holiday season. Colorful floral displays and cheery Christmas décor greeted the customer upon entering the brightly lit store. It was almost as though you were stepping out of a dystopian world into a vibrant alternative dimension.

Adams' father, who started the store that bears his name, first rented a space in the mall back in 1970, when the center was just two years old. "A local businessman

built it, and it was kind of cutting edge then," Adams said. "Frank Penn is who owned it. His roots were in the tobacco industry; that's where his fortune was made."

Penn's father perfected the blend for Lucky Strike cigarettes, which became the nation's best-selling brand during the Great Depression and coined the brand's slogan: "It's toasted." The Lucky Strike name can still be seen, painted in large white letters on a large smokestack as you drive into town.

Penn eventually sold the mall, which at one time included a J.C. Penney store and a Winn-Dixie. Adams remembered Eckerd Drug as a longtime tenant, lasting about twenty-five years in the mall. All of those stores are gone now. The Winn-Dixie, which occupied a separate building behind the mall, stood vacant and boarded up in 2018, its signage gone and the interior littered with garbage. It had been closed, at that point, for thirteen years. The J.C. Penney space had been vacant even longer—since 2001—and a line of yellow tape was stretched across the width of the mall just north of Rose's, keeping mallgoers from venturing into that area.

"They've made some repairs," Scott said of the current owners. "We used to have leaky roofs. We used to have fifty buckets out there catching water." But, he added, "The J.C. Penney store, I'd be scared to walk in there."

As it had been in Eden, Belk's main entrance—onto the mall—was locked and papered over; customers could access the store only from the side parking lot via a small, secondary door.

"That's been closed off for years," a Belk sales associate said. "There's just not a whole lot of activity in the mall."

Adams suggested that shoplifting was a concern.

Although the mall has gone downhill "the last five to ten years—the last five years, really a lot," Scott said the flower shop continues to do well. Much of that, he said, has to do with the nature of his business: "Seventy-five to 80 percent of our customers are call-in. When people come in, they come to see us. They're not just passing by." As a result, there's really no need for him to relocate. "I'm fifty-six years old," he said, "and I don't want to spend $300,000 on another piece of property."

Dead and gone

The Bristol Mall at the Virginia-Tennessee state line suffered a slow and painful death, its occupancy dwindling to a single tenant before the mall finally closed for good. It was a far cry from the optimism that greeted the mall when it opened in 1975 in the midst of a growth spurt for the city, which increased in population by 28 percent during that decade. Sears, Belk, and Miller's (later Proffitt's) were the original anchors, and a J.C. Penney was built as an addition in the mid-nineties. Meanwhile, however, growth in the area stalled, providing few new customers from a now-stagnant population. A country music museum provided an added attraction when it opened in the mall in 1998, but the museum pulled up stakes and moved across the state

The Bristol Mall near the Virginia-Tennessee state line was closed in 2018, but banners extolling customers to "love where you shop" still hung in the deserted parking lot. Stephen H. Provost, 2018.

line to Tennessee amid declining mall traffic fifteen years later.

The downhill spiral, however, had begun in 2005, when Belk bought Proffitt's and converted it into a second Belk store focusing on products for men, children, and the home. Penney's closed in 2014, and a year later, Belk announced it would be moving to a new site. Sears dropped out in 2017, leaving the mall with no anchor tenants and only a few specialty stores such as Kay Jewelers and GNC hanging on for dear life. The last tenant, an instructional aid company, closed in 2017.

The shell of the mall remained as of this writing. The parking and loading docks were empty, and the Sears and J.C. Penney signs have long since gone from the exterior. Pennants depicting fashionably dressed young people and exhorting visitors to "love where you shop!" still hung from light standards outside, one of them partially detached by the wind. Inside, vacant storefronts and fixtures largely untouched since the mall's closure remained, along with a banner proclaiming the mall's planned future use: CASINO. The electronic signboard out front was still working, displaying the message, "We're betting on Bristol."

As the mall culture declined and Americans turned to the internet or big-box stores, more and more enclosed shopping centers were shuttered, abandoned, or converted into something else. They continued to hold such a fascination for some, however, that internet sites popped up, complete with videos devoted to exploring their empty shells and chronicling their continued existence. One site, deadmalls.com, listed something like 450 dead malls in North America as of this writing.

The decline of some, like the Tarrytown Mall and Cloverleaf Mall, was hastened by outside forces. Cloverleaf was the first major indoor mall in Richmond, Virginia, when it opened in 1972, but access issues and tragedy helped keep shoppers away. For years, Richmond buses wouldn't take residents there because it was just outside the city limits. Then, in 1996, two women were found stabbed to death at the All for One Dollar Store. The murders were never solved, and shoppers were afraid to come back to the mall after that. Sears closed down its second floor and Penney's left altogether; the mall closed for good in 2008.

At Tarrytown, the culprit wasn't crime but Mother Nature. It was just the nation's twenty-sixth enclosed mall in 1962 when it opened in the unlikely town of Rocky Mount, North Carolina, a city of just 32,000. Local resident Bob Gorham had returned to North Carolina after receiving his MBA from Harvard and wanted to create something special for the community, so he pooled his savings and took out a $94,000 loan to build the mall. It wasn't just a shopping center but a town meeting place.

It had a teen center and hosted talent shows, job fairs, and various civic events. But the mall's location was a problem in more ways than one. Not only was it in a small town, it was built on low-lying swampland that was vulnerable to a 500-year flood, which would have been no problem the 499 other years, but when just such a flood hit Rocky Mount in 1999, the mall was under water. The flood rendered the mall unusable, and it was torn down in 2006 to make way for a Sam's Club.

Both malls were already facing economic pressures when disaster struck. Thalhimer's had closed at Cloverleaf; at Tarrytown, Montgomery Ward had gone out of business and a charter school had moved in to replace the departed J.C. Penney store. The changing economic climate hit other malls across the nation, too. Some went under when factories closed, as in Eden, leaving towns without their largest employer. Others were victims of a shift toward big-box power malls such as River Park in affluent north Fresno and the Highlands shopping center in western Virginia, which opened in 2007 less than ten miles from the Bristol Mall. Its tenants in 2019 included Target, Books-A-Million, Ross, Best Buy, and T.J. Maxx, and its location just off Interstate 81 draws travelers as well as local residents. A Walmart Supercenter, Home Depot, Office Depot, and a multiplex cinema add to the mix, all less than a mile away. Clearly, the retail nexus of the area had shifted westward, leaving the Bristol Mall high and dry on an abandoned beachhead.

Even high-end malls weren't immune to the terminal illness infecting. The Promenade in Woodland Hills opened a year after I moved there with my family in 1973, just down the street from Topanga Plaza. Its design was a triangle rather than a strip, and three corridors lined with shops radiated out from the center toward its anchors: Saks Fifth Avenue, Bullock's Wilshire, and Robinson's. It was one of my grandmother's favorite shopping destinations, because it featured "exclusive" stores like Saks and Bullock's. It had *three* bookstores (Pickwick, Walden, and Brentano's), jewelry shops, a luggage store, and a shop just for neckties. The Magic Pan, a restaurant with a menu built around crepes, was one of my grandmother's favorite stops—and mine, too, for the pea soup.

Saks closed in 1994 after the building was damaged in the Northridge earthquake, and the store never

Sears at the Salem Mall sits abandoned in Dayton, Ohio. Nicholas Echart, 2014.
Creative Commons 2.0 license: https://creativecommons.org/licenses/by-sa/2.0.

reopened. Instead, the building was torn down to make way for a sixteen-screen multiplex. Both Robinson's and Bullock's Wilshire were rebranded as Macy's in the early 2000s and then closed in 2015. The next year, the owner of the center announced plans to demolish it and replace it with a mixed-use complex of 1,500 apartments, a park, a 15,000-seat concert and sports arena, and two hotels.

As of 2019, however, the mall remained standing. And vacant. Concerns over traffic were among the issues holding up the proposed transformation.

Another upscale mall that went by the wayside was White Flint Mall in Bethesda, Maryland, a few miles north of the nation's capital. Initially anchored by Bloomingdale's, Lord & Taylor, and the only I. Magnin on the Eastern Seaboard, the three-level center featured extensive skylights and a central glass elevator shaped like a time-release capsule.

As time passed, the mall tried to switch gears and cater to a younger, hipper crowd. Borders Books replaced I. Magnin in 1992, and Dave & Buster's opened a "funhouse for 'big kids'" there four years later in a 60,000-square-foot space. The business combined a sports bar and a restaurant with a midway-style collection of amusements ranging from billiards to video games "created especially to meet the needs of today's 'pressure-cooked' adults." But such businesses weren't exactly a good fit with the upscale stores that had originally signed on to the center.

When the property owner decided to tear it down, it spawned a pair of lawsuits. Lord & Taylor successfully

claimed developers had violated an agreement to maintain the mall as a "first-class shopping center" until 2042. Dave & Buster's, meanwhile, lost its fight to defy an eviction notice. The mall owners, who needed the business to close so they could demolish the building, argued (successfully) that the business had violated its lease by opening another location too close to the White Flint site.

The mall was eventually torn down, except for the Lord & Taylor store, which remained open as the only reminder of what had once been there. Landowners unveiled ambitious mixed-use plans similar to those for the Promenade property, but as of 2018, nothing had come of them. Instead, the owners remained bogged down in legal challenges to the $31 million in damages they were ordered to pay Lord & Taylor.

Also demolished was the Salem Mall in suburban Dayton, Ohio. It opened in 1966, three years after local department store Rike's (later Lazarus) set up shop on the site. Sears was the second anchor, and J.C. Penney joined the mall in 1981 with the addition of a food court and a second story. At its peak, the mall included ninety-one stores and employed just shy of 2,000 people.

But a major highway on the drawing boards for the area when the mall was conceived never got built. That wouldn't have mattered in the boom years of the fifties, but when hard times hit in the nineties, it took its toll. As sales languished, both Lazarus and Penney's shut their doors in 1998, as did a cinema. Home Depot came on

**Forever 21 at Fresno's Fashion Fair took over for Gottschalks, which in turn
had replaced original tenant Weinstock's. Stephen H. Provost, 2013.**

board in a separate building in 2003, in preparation for the mall's planned conversion to an open-air "lifestyle center" complete with a multiplex, housing, and a public library. Salem Mall fell to wrecking crews in 2005 and 2006, four decades after its opening. But the open-air project meant to replace it never got off the ground. Only Sears remained open on the site, and it closed its doors two years later.

Even the Northland Center, Victor Gruen's open-air playground that started it all, is no more. The suburban Detroit shopping hub lost first one anchor (Wards in 1998), then another (Penney's in 2000), and still another (Target in 2015). By the time everything was said and done, only the former Hudson's store—now a Macy's—remained. It closed in 2015, and the rest of the mall was demolished two years later.

An entire book would be needed to cover the history of malls that have failed in an American landscape littered with empty buildings, reconditioned "lifestyle centers," and vacant lots where shopping centers once stood. The once-invincible indoor mall, which strode out boldly onto the retail battlefield and slew the goliath of the downtown department store, now lies mortally wounded itself.

Oh, how the mighty have fallen.

18

CONVENIENCE IS KING

When I walked up to stand in line at the front of the store, the clerk was engaged in a leisurely discussion with the customer ahead of me about what seemed like nothing in particular. I scowled. I had a schedule to keep, and clerks are paid to ring you up, not *chat* you up, right? I waited as patiently as I could until the customer finally finished her story, pulled out a debit card, and inserted it in the keypad.

Rejected.

"Try again," the clerk said, but the result was the same. "Do you have a checkbook, hon?"

The customer smiled, raised an index finger, then started rummaged around, looking for the checkbook in the bottom of her purse. Once she'd finally retrieved it, she took it out, asked the clerk for a pen, then paused to impart another nugget of sudden inspiration before taking it and scrawling her name and filling out the check.

A farmer takes a load off in the Lamoille, Iowa, general store. The days of hanging around the stove and shooting the breeze at the local emporium are long gone, though. Today's hustle and bustle demand more self-service and less human interaction. Arthur Rothstein, 1939, Library of Congress.

"I'll need to see some ID."

"Of course."

Back to the purse.

How long was this going to take? I didn't want to get a speeding ticket heading to my next stop. I'd allotted only a certain amount of time for this, and . . .

I finally got through the line, made my own purchases as quickly and with as little conversation as possible. How was my day? Fine. Did I find everything I was looking for? Yes. Cash at the ready, change accepted. Groceries bagged.

"Have a nice day."

"You, too." To myself: I'm outta here!

I got out to the parking lot only to discover that, in my haste, I'd forgotten something. I'd have to go back! Ugh. I didn't bother grabbing a cart this time; I just dashed back inside, retrieved the item from the shelf, and speed-walked up to the checkstand. The express lane was closed, and I was behind a couple with a heaping cart full of groceries that looked like two weeks' worth of shopping. Served me right. I had resigned myself to being there for the next ten minutes, my eyes glazing over and calluses forming on my feet, when the woman turned to me and said, "Is that all you have? Please, go ahead!"

My eyes opened a little wider and I smiled, "Are you sure?"

"Of course! We don't want to hold you up with all this." She stepped backward behind the cart to let me pass. The man smiled at me, too. "Great shirt," he said.

I looked down and noticed I was wearing a concert T-shirt. "Thanks. I saw them in Irvine maybe five years ago."

"Really? We were at that same concert."

"Seriously? Small world!"

"Yeah, they're great. My favorite band back in high school."

"Mine, too."

"Well, nice meeting you . . . ?"

"Steve."

"Rob." He gestured toward the woman beside him. "Karen."

Shopping used to be like that all the time. It wasn't just a chore to be checked off the list so we could get on to the next thing; it was an opportunity to catch up with people we knew and get acquainted with some we didn't. Once upon a time, couples really did meet each other for the first time while shopping for groceries. Probably not as much anymore. Most of us (myself included) are in too much of a hurry to actually interact with anyone during a trip to the store. We've been conditioned not to.

Over the course of the past century or so, retailers and customers have conspired to take the personal touch out of shopping and replace it with convenience. Because convenience equals more sales for the business and less hassle for the customer. Innovation has been the name of the game, the goal always to get more customers' eyes on more merchandise in less time and to create more sales.

That meant more automation and fewer, well, *people*.

Clarence Saunders' philosophy of cutting staff so he could cut prices didn't stop with Piggly Wiggly. His fully automated Keedoozle supermarket might not have worked, but not because it was out of step with retailing trends; if anything, it was ahead of its time. Self-service checkstands at today's Walmart operate under the same principle. Little by little, over the course of the 20th century and into the 21st, retailers have been chipping away at shopping as a human experience and reshaping it as purely a matter of the bottom line.

Harry Selfridge's vision of shopping as a pastime meant for enjoyment, rather than a mere necessity, has long since gone by the wayside, along with the doormen who greeted you at the downtown department store, the tailor who fitted your clothes, and other staffers who knew your name from memory because it was part of their job.

"Shopping used to be like an outing, a change of pace from the kitchen and the kids," marketing executive Kurt Barnard told the New York Times. "But the American woman has stopped being a hausfrau, and become a working woman. She doesn't have time for leisurely trips."

Barnard was commenting on the demise of Garfinckel's, a venerable Washington, DC, department store known for its upscale selection and service that went out of business in 1990.

This view looking east on F Street in Washington, DC, shows Garfinckel's
on the left. Harris & Ewing, 1931, Library of Congress.

MIDDLE-CLASS MELTDOWN

Ruth Kehler of Fresno remembers the days when "the
outside elevator doors didn't close completely" at J.C.
Penney on the downtown Fulton Mall. "When I was
little, I used to watch the elevator cars go up and down.
When the doors opened on my floor, there was an
elevator operator asking which floor I wanted."

Not only is the elevator operator gone, the store is
gone, too. It closed more than thirty years ago.

In rural areas, the general store was once a social
center where community members took calls on the
town's only telephone or picked up their mail. Residents
would congregate to hear the latest town gossip, talk
politics or simply connect with neighbors who lived a
few miles down the road, people they might never see
otherwise. They'd set up a table for a game of checkers or
head upstairs for a grange or town council meeting. With

the advent of rural free delivery and parcel post, there
was a little less need to head into town; neighbors got
to know each other a little less   and catalog companies
sold a lot *more*.

Saunders's Piggly Wiggly herded customers through a
one-way labyrinth that ensured that they focused on the
products, not each other, and that they got in and out as
quickly as possible. Supermarkets like Big Bear were so
massive that customers weren't likely to find anyone they
knew there, even if they managed to take their eyes off
the impressive displays of cans and cereal boxes piled in
pyramids worthy of Giza.

Shopping carts made it easier to move quickly
through stores—and put up barriers between customers.
Conveyor belts at the cash register moved items through
at a rapid clip, as shopping became less interactive and
more like an assembly line. Department stores dispensed
with personal service, following grocery stores and

discounters in emphasizing convenience. Some, like Kohl's, even put their cash registers in rows at the front of their stores, dispensing with the age-old practice of scattering them throughout the building, one in each department.

As the population grew, it became harder to know everyone on a first-name basis. Shoppers moved to the suburbs and commuted to do their shopping downtown, then stayed away from Main Street altogether when retailers came to them, opening branch stores in modern, air-conditioned regional malls. Those malls became the new social center for teens from the seventies through the nineties, spawning the kind of subculture their parents had largely abandoned with the advent of two-income households and increasing time constraints. The more time people saved, the more commitments they ended up making, so that in the end, they were busier than ever and actually had *less* time on their hands instead of more.

Gone were the warm and elaborate store window displays at Christmastime, replaced by the cold calculation of how to get the best place in line before daybreak on Black Friday. Gone, too, was the sense of a unique shopping experience downtown at Filene's or Bullock's or Globman's or Sibley's.

"I remember there was a ladies clothing floor, a gentlemen's floor, furniture, households; children's clothes were in there somewhere," Connie Hansen said of Sibley's. "There was also a cafeteria, but Mom didn't like to eat there. She would rather go to a regular restaurant. (Mom was a bit stuffy.) When I became older, I would ride the bus downtown with my girlfriends and sometimes shop at Sibley's to buy a pair of shoes or something. In the fifties, it was natural for kids to go off on the bus and come back hours later. I think I was about eleven when I was allowed to ride the bus by myself.

"This past summer, I returned to Rochester to see my grandson play his trumpet at the Eastman School of Music. The school is close to the old Sibley's building. I was so disappointed to see it had closed."

Each store's distinct character was part of what made shopping excursions fun and memorable. But as time passed, that distinctiveness faded, a casualty of economic conditions and the quest for convenience. As branch

stores began to open in the suburbs during the fifties, the merchandise became standardized—along with the stores themselves. Busy adults didn't have time to spend browsing or window-shopping; they wanted to know they could get what they'd come for before even setting foot inside a store. Chain stores (like fast-food chains) were known quantities, but shopping at an independent shop you'd never visited before? That was a risk, and a potential waste of time.

Gradually, the independents and small chains sold out to larger concerns, which in turn sold out to still larger operations. Underperforming locations were sold, and others were rebranded with the new owner's name. After a while, Marshall Field's was gone. So were Foley's and Burdines and Filene's and Gottschalks. Before you knew it, almost everything was a Macy's.

The middle class, which burst onto the scene with the flood of growth and prosperity following the World War II, was disappearing, too—or at least shrinking. A survey of 229 metro areas from 2000 to 2014 documented the trend in stark terms. The share of lower-income residents rose in seven of ten of those areas, while the share of upper-income individuals rose in three out of four. The number of middle-income residents, meanwhile, fell in 89 percent of the areas surveyed.

Those figures played out like a movie reel on the suburban streets and in the neighborhoods that had formed the middle-class heartland. For decades, new homes had been built in the suburbs. Tracts like Levittown and its imitators had helped redefine the American landscape. There had, of course, been ups and downs. Surges in home building during the early seventies and eighties had been followed by reversals, but nothing like what occurred when the housing bubble burst in 2006. Housing starts hit nearly 2.3 million that January, then plunged to 478,000 in just over three years—a remarkable 320,000 fewer than the *smallest number* recorded at any time in the four previous decades.

Not only were fewer new suburbs being built, but the older ones weren't what they used to be. The San Fernando Valley, that once-verdant playground in Hollywood's backyard, had been paved over and neglected. Gone were the heady days when it was a hippie haven, rock

The Dillard's clearance store at Oak Hollow Mall in High Point, North Carolina. Dillard's, along with Belk and Macy's, are among the few surviving department store chains. Stephen H. Provost, 2018.

star retreat, and an investor's paradise where property values went nowhere but up. Not so long ago, it had been the center of the universe for Valley Girls and mall rats; now malls like the Sherman Oaks Galleria, Fallbrook Mall, and Woodland Hills Promenade had died or been repurposed.

Of the "big three" stores that once catered to the middle class, Montgomery Ward was gone and Sears was in bankruptcy, a shell of its former self. Only Penney's remained, along with a few other holdovers like Belk and Dillard's. Brick-and-mortar stores that survived, increasingly, did so either at the high end (Neiman Marcus, Nordstrom, Saks) or, more frequently, on the discount side (Walmart, Target, Ross, T.J. Maxx, Dollar General). And they all needed to have websites, because those suburbanites who remained liked to shop from home. They browsed online. They paid online. They had their goods delivered to their doorstep.

COMMUNITY PARTNERS

The online revolution did more than bring change America's way of shopping; it put another nail in the coffin of a means we had of connecting with one another, dating back to the Selfridge's, Marshall Field's, and the old country store.

Department stores did more than provide a *place* to connect; their owners reached out to help forge those connections. The sponsored fashion shows, holiday parades, and contests both drew people to the stores and drew them together. The stores often took the lead in civic involvement, giving to charities, sponsoring Little League teams, and supporting the community's youth.

"Gottschalks downtown had a high deb [debutante] board, which was [to honor] one girl from all of the high schools, and it was special to be selected," said Marilyn Madrid of Fresno. "We modeled new bathing suits for summer, and one spring we got to select the fall clothes to be put in the Junior Department for fall. They even gave us a credit card with a 20 percent discount. We did so many fun things for the store. Just before graduation, we got to select the next deb girl from our school."

Salvation Army bell-ringers have long stationed their kettles outside major department stores, and Toys for Tots bins have been placed inside. In Atlanta, notable Southern chef and author Nathalie Dupree opened a cooking school at Rich's that continued there for a decade. At the time, it was just the latest example of community involvement at the Atlanta mainstay.

When the cotton market collapsed in 1914, Rich's agreed to accept cotton as payment from farmers in lieu of cash. After a major fire three years later, the store set up an on-site collection center for clothing that could be donated to "those who lost all they had" in the blaze. Customers who wanted to help out but who couldn't make it to the store were asked to hang a white flag in front of their home, and Rich's delivery drivers would come by and pick up their donation.

When the city issued its own scrip in the Depression as part of its relief efforts, Rich's stepped in to help make the system work. In general, people receiving scrip could convert it into cash, but only at less than face value; it wasn't considered the equivalent of cash because it wasn't universally accepted. Rich's, however, helped bolster the value of the scrip by cashing it at full value with no proviso that it be spent in-store. Its willingness to accept worthless government checks when the city couldn't pay its teachers helped keep the schools up and running.

Thalhimers, a regional chain based in Richmond, Virginia, issued a mission statement in 1950 that epitomized the community-minded approach:

> "We have always believed that a store should be a part of the lives and hopes, part of the growth and future of the people who share its fortunes. For that reason, we have always endeavored to contribute more than our function of supplying goods and services. We have built, and we intend to keep on building, a store that will make the vast area we serve a better place in which to live by our earnest effort to add to the pleasures, the accomplishments, the cultural achievements, the education, the higher standards of living of every person who crosses our threshold."

The outlook was similar at Globman's.

Abe Globman's money helped build a synagogue in Martinsville—in a roundabout way. In a story related by his grandson, Barry Greene, Globman explained: "I decided to move all of the store's basement housewares to a temporary location for a few months. For years I had been playing cards with one of my best friends, Mike Schottland, who owned a vacant place next to City Hall. So, in the morning I went to see him. We dickered for a little about the rent. I told him, 'Mike, what do you care? You'll never see a penny of it because we are building a new synagogue. . . . Mike Schottland shook his head in mock despair, and five months later he endorsed a sizeable rent check back to the synagogue's building fund."

When new Jewish neighbors moved to town, Pam Globman added, Abe and Masha Globman "often took in the newcomers, sharing their home with them—literally—and provided employment at the store until they got on their feet."

In Fresno, Gottschalks chairman Joe Levy was active in the Boys Club, two museums, and the business school at California State University, Fresno. A former chamber of commerce president, he won the chamber's Leon S. Peters Award in 1989 for service to the community.

Foley's in Texas had an auditorium that hosted rehearsals for the Houston symphony.

In Washington, DC, Woodward & Lothrop supported such community stalwarts as the Kennedy Center and the National Symphony Orchestra. Its final president was a Boys Club trustee who also served on the Salvation Army Advisory Board. Its four-story branch at the Seven Corners shopping center in Falls Church, Virginia, opened in 1956 and included a 300-seat auditorium. The company hailed it as more than just a store but a place "where friends and neighbors meet" to attend such events as "flower shows, art and historical exhibits, benefit card parties, and other worthwhile activities."

Why?

"Because we believe in being part of the community."

GRADUAL DRIFT

Ironically, however, as chains such as Woodward & Lothrop expanded away from downtown and into the suburbs, they became *less* a part of the communities

The Seven Corners Shopping Center, the first in suburban Washington, DC, is seen in 1965 (Library of Congress/Warren K. Leffler) and in its current incarnation (Stephen H. Provost, 2018).

they served. Connections between staff and customers, and among customers themselves, became less frequent and less personal. The personal service found at a downtown store like Woodward & Lothrop was replaced by a cookie-cutter approach to big-box commerce, with chain store clones supplanting the distinctive shops of yesteryear.

The Seven Corners center was a prime example. It had opened with two Washington-based stores (Woodward & Lothrop and Garfinckel's) as its primary anchors, along with Woolworth's and a handful of other stores. Garfinckel's closed in 1990, and by the middle of the decade, Woodie's had shut its doors and the mall had begun a massive demolition/overhaul that left it looking nothing like its previous incarnation. It was reborn as a big-box power mall showcasing national chain tenants such as Barnes & Noble, Home Depot, Burlington Coat Factory, Best Buy, and Ross.

Seven Corners had been the first shopping center in suburban DC, but it wasn't the only one for long. A pair of enclosed malls—Landmark Center and Tyson's Corner, both within a five-mile radius—opened in the mid- to late sixties. Seven Corners enclosed its north and south concourses in 1977, but it was fighting a losing battle. By 1988, it was competing with twenty regional shopping centers in the area. Seven Corners was no longer "where friends and neighbors meet" but a place where business was done, pure and simple.

The arrival of the internet, meanwhile, gave adults a new way of socializing—albeit in two dimensions—without the need to get in their cars and drive anywhere. And it wasn't long before online retailers began to lure them away from brick-and-mortar stores by giving them the ability to shop from home. The most successful of these businesses, Amazon, started out selling books and quickly became the undoing of bookstores across the country. Borders, Waldenbooks, Brentano's, and B. Dalton went out of business, as did a number of smaller bookstores. The days when an enclosed mall might offer three bookstores, as the Promenade had in Woodland Hills during the seventies, were at an end, and it wasn't long before the malls themselves began to close. Again, Amazon and other online retailers had a hand in this.

Just as Sears had branched out after starting as a watch company, Amazon diversified from books into virtually every segment of retail.

Some stores, such as Walmart, managed to stay in business by making the successful transition to online sales; many others were not as fortunate. Malls were converted into other purposes, and the era of the great downtown department store began to fade in many people's minds.

When Pam Globman married Barry Greene's brother Dicky Globman, the family's eponymous store was already history. Dicky Globman had been the company's executive vice president, but he didn't say anything to her about his role there.

"I married into this colorful family, and I didn't grow up in this community," Pam Globman said. "My living in Alabama meant that ours was a long-distance courtship, and Dicky was a business consultant by that time. That's all I knew; he never mentioned a family business.

"Indeed, my daughter and I arrived in Martinsville almost a decade after the Globman's stores had closed. She and I were driving around to familiarize ourselves with the area when we happened across the uptown Martinsville building with 'Globman's' still boldly engraved in the stone storefront.

"Wait, what? As it happened, there was work going on inside, so we sneaked in, rode the escalators, noticed the still-installed signs denoting every imaginable department and service, and marveled at the few remaining interior fixtures. Then we raced home and demanded to know why a building housing such a very complete and comprehensive department store had his family name on it. That was the first I ever heard about this community cornerstone.

"Since then, upon hearing my married name, people volunteer their memories of the store. Without fail, they tell me, 'If you couldn't find it at Globman's, you didn't need it.' A close second to that is, 'I still have the (insert purchased item—most often a coat or collectible coin) that I got at Globman's.' Right up there, too, is, 'My first job was at Globman's' (most often, as a teen in the gift-wrapping department) or, 'My (insert relative) worked at Globman's.' Whatever story they tell, it's always followed by, 'Be sure to tell your husband we miss that store.'"

19

PROS AND CONSOLIDATIONS

As the era of the American department store came crashing down, stores that had become institutions in their communities faced one of two fates: They closed their doors forever, or they were gobbled up by one of the few survivors. In most cases, the store that did the gobbling was Macy's—which wasn't really Macy's anymore but rather the Federated Department Stores group, which had *purchased* Macy's in 1994 and taken that name.

Federated was a group of stores that had joined forces in 1929 to form a holding company—an umbrella group that would "hold" enough stock in the stores to exercise

Macy's has grown from a dominant New York store on Herald Square, seen here in 1942, into a huge chain with stores across the country. Marjory Collins, 1942, Library of Congress.

ultimate ownership rights, while leaving the nuts-and-bolts operations to the companies themselves. This strength-in-numbers approach helped Federated stores weather the Great Depression while leaving local and regional operators free to do what they did best—assess and meet the needs of the specific communities they served.

The Federated group originally consisted of Abraham & Straus in New York; Filene's in Boston; and two Ohio-based stores, Shillito's in Cincinnati and F.R. Lazarus & Co. in Columbus. Bloomingdale's of New York joined a year later. Over time, the group gobbled up a number of other stores and chains before running into trouble and filing for bankruptcy protection in 1992. It not only survived but purchased Macy's in 1994, creating the nation's largest retail corporation.

The history here can get a little complicated. As mentioned earlier, the Straus brothers at one time owned both Macy's and Abraham & Straus but did so separately. A&S became part of Federated initially, but Macy's didn't until Federated purchased it in 1994.

Federated itself ran into trouble in 1988, when Canadian entrepreneur Robert Campeau took out a big loan to purchase the company. It turned out to be *too* big, and Campeau was forced to sell off a couple of major assets (Filene's of Boston and Houston-based Foley's) in order to stay afloat. Even that wasn't enough, and four years later, Federated was in bankruptcy and Campeau was forced to sell.

A quick point of clarification: Those who grew up in the Los Angeles area might remember a chain of sixty electronics stores called the Federated Group, which also operated in Arizona and Texas in the eighties. The regional chain featured a TV spokesman named "Fred Rated" and was, at one time, owned by Atari, creator of the old *Pong* video game. It was, however, never owned by Federated Department Stores, which was an entirely different entity.

However, those who grew up in the Los Angeles area are also likely to remember the May Co. and Robinson's department stores—both of which *do* in fact have integral parts to play in our story.

Like so many other department store founders, David May was a Jewish immigrant-turned-entrepreneur who built a successful business stateside. Born in Bavaria in 1848, he came to America six years later and eventually wound up in Cincinnati, where he attended night school and worked in a clothing factory for $5 a week. May soon left that job to become a salesman, connecting with a German Jewish businessman who offered him a job at his Indiana clothing store. Not only did he excel at the job, he did so well that the owner eventually gave him a one-quarter share of the business.

May stayed there for nine years before a fire and a cold spring day conspired to alter the course of his future.

The May Co. building on Wilshire Boulevard in Los Angeles, early 1970s. Library of Congress.

When the store caught fire, he braved the chill to salvage what he could of its merchandise. In the process, however, he contracted bronchitis, a health condition that led him to sell his share of the business and move to Leadville, Colorado, in the hopes of improving his health.

There, he opened his first store in 1878. The Great Western Auction House and Clothing Store sold overalls and wool underwear to the miners who worked in the area. (May obtained the overalls from another Jewish immigrant who shipped them in from San Francisco: Levi Strauss.) Over the next decade, he added women's clothing to his stock and opened two other stores in Colorado, eventually moving to Denver and expanding outside the state by purchasing stores in St. Louis and Cleveland before the turn of the century. The company incorporated in 1910 as May Department Stores and made a significant move in 1923, when May—now age seventy-five—paid $4.2 million for a Los Angeles store named A. Hamburger & Sons, rebranding it as the May Company.

May died in 1927, but more acquisitions followed for the company he had founded. Among them:

- Kaufmann's of Pittsburgh in 1946
- Associated Dry Goods (including Loehmann's and Lord & Taylor) in 1986
- Los Angeles competitor J.W. Robinson in 1993
- Wanamaker's in 1995
- Marshall Field's in 2004

A year after acquiring Marshall Field's, however, May Department Stores ceased to exist. The company agreed to an $11 billion acquisition offer from Macy's/Federated.

Holding companies

It wasn't the first time the department store landscape had changed. Around the turn of the twentieth century, department stores had proliferated so fast that some of them were bound to fail—and 40 percent of them did between 1905 and 1915. It wasn't long before some of the survivors responded by banding together in holding companies, seeking to maximize their buying power while insulating themselves against economic downturns and the consequences of failed risks.

Associated Dry Goods was formed in 1916 by five stores: Lord & Taylor of New York, Stewart's of Baltimore, Hahne's (pronounced like the underwear company) of Newark, and two Buffalo stores, J.N. Adam and William Hengerer. Over the years, it added stores such as Sibley's of Rochester and J.W. Robinson of Los Angeles, both in 1957; Goldwater's of Phoenix in 1963; The Denver Store of Colorado and Stix, Baer & Fuller of St. Louis, both in 1966; and Caldor in 1981. Stix, Baer & Fuller was sold to Dillard's in 1984, and the entire business was swallowed up by May Department Stores two years later.

At that point, only Lord & Taylor retained its own identity. Goldwater's was rebranded as J.W. Robinson, which was in turn merged with former rival May Co. of California to form Robinsons-May; Sibley's locations became Kauffman's; and Hahne's stores were rebranded as Lord & Taylor.

Another holding company, City Stores, formed in 1923 as an alliance of three southern stores: Loveman's in Birmingham, Lowenstein's in Memphis, and Maison Blanche in New Orleans. It expanded outside the region by adding major stores such as Lit Brothers of Philadelphia in 1928, whose owner ran the company for two decades after it went into receivership during the Depression. Another major acquisition was R.H. White of Boston; City Stores kept the brand intact but closed the downtown flagship store in 1957.

Lit Brothers folded in 1977, and City Stores filed for Chapter 11 bankruptcy two years later.

Hahn's Department Stores (not to be confused with Hahne's) formed a holding company of its own in 1928, a year before Federated got its start. Hahn's early lineup also included Jordan Marsh of Boston, Maas Brothers of Tampa, and The Bon Marché of Seattle; the chain morphed into Allied Stores in 1935.

But it was Federated that expanded over the years to become the 800-pound gorilla of the industry, taking over Macy's in 1994 and adopting the store's iconic name as its own. And it was the rebranding of stores across the country as Macy's that ended an era in which department stores served as reflections of the communities they served. That concept may have been strained as chains ventured away from their original hometowns, planting branches in other cities, but it remained intact, at least to some extent, through the traditions they'd nurtured and the reputations they had built.

"We must keep the Texas-ish-ness in Neiman Marcus," Nan Tillson Birmingham wrote in her book *Store*. "Saks anywhere must be Very Fifth Avenue. It's unconscionable for some foreign company that probably doesn't even know Chicago to run Field's. When CHH (Carter Hawley Hale) approached Marshall Field & Co. in 1977, a Christmas Day article quoted one Chicagoan as saying the takeover would be received 'as warmly as might be a bid by New Jersey to take over New York City's Broadway or an effort by the Grinch to steal Christmas.'"

With the Macy's revolution, what was once unconscionable became reality, even in Chicago and even for Marshall Field's.

Before long, Macy's was everywhere. In the mid-nineties and again after its takeover of May Department Stores in 2005, the company went about attaching the Macy's name to virtually all its assets. In some cases, it eased the transition by slapping hybrid names on acquisitions: The Bon Marché became Bon-Macy's, Rich's became Rich's-Macy's, Burdines became Burdines-Macy's, and so forth. But such changes were only temporary. In 2006, the company eliminated almost all the old regional nameplates altogether, even as hyphenated prefixes, and branded the stores simply as Macy's.

Macy's bought Lord & Taylor but turned around and resold it. Library of Congress.

Even Marshall Field's became history. As Birmingham had predicted, fans of the venerable retailer lamented its passing with reminiscences and protests, launching a website dedicated to bringing the store back that remained active thirteen years after the deal was done. Every Christmas, they'd look forward to giving and receiving gifts in the distinctive green boxes adorned with the Marshall Field's name. On the Fields Fans Chicago website, a visitor named Sylvia posted that "Macy's simply is not Fields. . . . My grandmother sent me a doll from there when I was little, and everything that came in a Field's box was sure to be special."

Marshall Field's fans weren't alone, as shoppers across the country lamented the loss of their beloved brands. A list of companies converted to the Macy's nameplate reads like a department store hall of fame: Abraham & Straus, L.S. Ayers, The Bon Marché, Bullock's, Burdines, The Emporium, Famous-Barr, Filene's, Foley's, Goldsmith's, Hecht's, I. Magnin, The Jones Store, Jordan Marsh, Kaufmann's, Lazarus, Marshall Field's, Meier & Frank, Rich's, Robinsons-May, Strawbridge's, and Stern's.

Macy's also bought Lord & Taylor, but turned right around and resold it. Of the stores it maintained, only Bloomingdale's kept its own separate identity.

The idea was to create a singular entity that could be recognized—and advertised—nationally, but the conversion came at a price. A study by Scarborough Research tracked shoppers at five established stores that had been converted into Macy's: The Bon Marché in Seattle, Burdines in Miami, Goldsmith's in Memphis, Lazarus in Columbus, and Rich's in Atlanta. Between 2002 and 2006, the number of customers who shopped at the Seattle store fell 10 percentage points. In Columbus, the figure dropped 9 percentage points, and in Memphis, it slipped 8 percentage points. The survey also found Rich's had a substantially larger clientele in Atlanta than Macy's did; the only place where habits were unchanged was in Miami.

The results shouldn't have been surprising.

"Stores are born and take on life. They pulse with the energy of their management, employees, and customers. They develop personalities," Birmingham wrote in *Store*. For this reason, she said, "the death of a store is painful, for it takes with it bits and pieces of our lives."

When my hometown, Fresno, lost its homegrown department store, Gottschalks, in 2009, I remember feeling very much that way. I was forty-six years old at the time, and the store had been around my whole life, indeed, more than twice as long as I had. It had outlived my grandmother, an inveterate shopper, and my mother, who'd held a charge card there. Now, it was dying, too. As I walked through the Fashion Fair branch one last time—many of the racks half-empty beneath blazing red-and-yellow closeout signs proclaiming 30, 50, and 70 percent off—the finality of it all sunk in. It wasn't just the end of an era for my hometown, but personally for me as well.

Gottschalks

As the retail landscape changed, some stores battled to the bitter end, and Gottschalks was among them.

The chain had endured for 105 years when the end came. It had grown slowly at first, operating a single store downtown for fifty-seven years before opening its first branch. A chain of smaller, junior apparel stores called Bobbie West followed in the sixties to appeal to the teen crowd, and the company launched the first of its twenty-five Village East women's specialty stores for plus-size apparel in 1970. (Bobbie West was rebranded as Petites West in the eighties.)

Still, by 1980, the primary department store chain remained compact with just six locations, avoiding the competitive Bay Area and LA markets to focus on small to midsize cities in California's San Joaquin Valley, which the company called "the other California." Often, Gottschalks was the only department store in town, enjoying a virtual monopoly and a head start in building brand identification as those towns grew. It also featured name brands, something few local retailers could boast. The cosmetics counter, with its selection of Clinique, Lancôme, and other popular brands, was particularly successful. A bonus: Wages were lower in rural areas, so labor was cheaper. So was the rent at new malls going up farther away from city centers.

Gottschalks was the first air-conditioned store in Fresno and, in 1976, became the first in the nation to automate sales transactions. It monitored inventory using point-of-sale wands to read barcodes and credit cards. By 1991, the system was so accurate it was tracking sales and inventory on an hourly basis, and chairman Joe Levy boasted that "with our computer system, we can plunk down a new store on the moon if we want."

An article in *Chain Store Age Executive* suggested one reason for Gottschalks success: "There's no doubt that as an independently held company, Gottschalks enjoys certain freedoms to experiment with more entrepreneurial concepts that often elude publicly held companies that must constantly justify actions to shareholders," Susan Warner wrote.

But that was about to change. Gottschalks went public in 1986, selling roughly half its equity on the New York Stock Exchange. This ushered in an era of growth for the chain, which had already expanded to eighteen stores. That growth was piecemeal at first, through the acquisition of various stores. The J.M. McDonald company went out of business in 1983, and Gottschalks took over that chain's store at Fig Garden Village in Fresno. (J.M. McDonald had been there since the mall's early days, the sole department store in an upscale "village" that was among the city's first suburban shopping centers.)

Gottschalks grew some more over the next two years with the acquisition of two small family-owned chains

Gottschalks flagship store on Fresno's Fulton Street. Daniel A. Draper, 2019.

in 1987 and '88: Brock's of Bakersfield with two locations and Leask's of Santa Clara with three. The company branched out beyond California for the first time in 1992, opening stores in Washington and Oregon, then entering the Nevada market three years later.

It then went on a buying binge at the end of the twentieth century, adding the nine-store Harris chain in 1995 and expanding into the Pacific Northwest when it bought Seattle-based Lamont's five years later. But the Lamont's stores never did well enough to justify that purchase, and Gottschalks wound up closing most of the thirty-four locations it acquired. The Great Recession compounded the chain's problems. The chain reported its final profitable quarter in the final three months of 2007, and it was downhill from there.

Still, the company fought tooth and nail to stay open amid declining sales, weathering $19.7 million in losses through the first three months of 2008. It filed for Chapter 11 bankruptcy protection early the following year, citing "persistent challenges in the economy" and "tightening credit markets," while looking for a cash infusion to stay afloat. It was able to strike a $30 million deal with Everbright, a Chinese firm that would have allowed it to boost profit margins by importing low-cost merchandise from Asia. But that deal fell through, leaving the chain no other choice but to liquidate.

Many of the spaces vacated by Gottschalks were taken over by Macy's and clothing retailer Forever 21. Former chairman Joe Levy—seventy-eight-year-old grand-nephew of the store's founder—tried to revive the brand as "Gottschalk by Joe Levy" in 2010, with stores in Clovis, Oakhurst, and Auburn, but the plan was pushed back to 2011 and ultimately never came to fruition.

Levy died three years later.

GLOBMAN'S

While some chains went out of business and others succumbed to mergers, a few owners saw the handwriting on the wall and got out of the retail business before disaster hit.

Globman's fell into this category. The store in southern Virginia had added a couple of branches in the early 1920s, opening a store in tiny Chatham forty miles to the northeast of its flagship Martinsville location and another in Leaksville (now Eden) seventeen miles to the south. Both closed after brief runs, but two other new stores—an hour and a half west in Galax and a second try in Leaksville—followed in 1929. Both made it through the Depression and remained open until the chain closed in 1991.

Globman's opened branches in the Eden Mall in 1980 and the Piedmont (Danville) Mall five years after that. At its peak, the company owned four department stores along with ten smaller off-price apparel stores in North Carolina branded as Lots of Labels. Through it all, Globman's was an anomaly. It remained a family-owned business even as corporate takeovers started coming fast and furious.

The front entrance of Globman's on Church Street in Martinsville, Virginia. Stephen H. Provost, 2019.

"Having worked with a family business myself, I must say that given the number of relatives and their strong and colorful characters, the fact that this business not only succeeded but thrived for so many years is truly a great feat," Pam Globman said.

The business was truly all in the family. Abe Globman's sister and her husband opened the Galax store, and Masha Globman's sister and husband started the Leaksville branch in the late 1920s. The next two generations remained at the heart of the family business as well. Son Leon would serve as chairman of the board, and his wife, Minnie had worked at Thalhimers, in Richmond.

"I've heard that she had no qualms about voicing her dissatisfaction about how things were being done and, if they weren't changed to meet her standards, she would intone, 'That's not how they would do it at Thalhimers,'" Pam Globman said. As for Leon, she said, he "invented the power nap: He kept a cot in his office, where he lay down each day for about fifteen minutes, then awoke refreshed and carried on with business."

Grandson Barry Green would serve as president and CEO during Globman's final decade in business, and even the extended family got into the act at Thanksgiving:

> "For many years, Minnie's numerous relatives from Richmond and Miami came to share the long Thanksgiving weekend in Martinsville. Among the many family activities that became tradition, one of the highlights was their trip to Globman's to make use of the discount coupons they all received. From the stories I've been told, it seems pretty clear that they basically swarmed the place; they took over. For example, it was quite common to hear cousin Janie on the store intercom paging Rosie Kahn to the Junior Department, an announcement requesting that Mr. Nathan Cantor meet his wife in Better Dresses, followed by another asking Esther Seldes to go immediately to meet Donna in Shoes, etc."

Within a span of six years, however, beginning in 1979, four family members—including founders Abe and Masha—passed away.

The company continued to operate for a few years after that, but it was paying a considerable sum in rent for the mall space in Danville. Meanwhile, the new Liberty Fair Mall in Martinsville opened in 1989, siphoning business away from the flagship store. Although the store was still doing better than forecasts it had provided its creditor, the bank decided to pull its loan the following year. Some local businessmen stepped forward with an offer to replace the loan, but the company decided to call it a day.

"We looked at our declining sales, the impact of the mall, and the deteriorating economic positions of family-owned department stores throughout the United States, and finally concluded that we needed to close down the seventy-six-year-old business while we could still pay our bills in full," Barry Greene recalled. "It was one of the saddest days ever for our family, and for the community."

20
WHAT EVER HAPPENED TO . . .

The list of department stores that have come and gone through the years could take up an entire volume by itself. What follows is a selection of retailers, ranging from downtown stalwarts to large chains, that operated in large, medium-size, and small markets across the country. It's not an exhaustive list, nor is it intended to be. Scores of downtown department stores have come

and gone over the years, and this volume has covered some of them—such as Gimbels and Gottschalks—in earlier chapters.

A complete list would doubtless include such stalwarts as Carson's of Chicago, Goldsmith's of Memphis, Grand Leader (Stix, Baer & Fuller) of St. Louis, Hess's of Allentown, Higbee's of Cleveland, Horne's of Pittsburgh,

The Miller & Rhoads sign still hangs proudly on a building on Broad Street in downtown Richmond, Virginia, although the building now houses apartments and a restaurant. The company, founded in 1885, went out of business in 1990. Stephen H. Provost, 2019.

Lazarus of Columbus, Maison Blanche of New Orleans, Miller's of Tennessee, Miller & Rhoads of Richmond, Proffitt's of Tennessee, Rike's of Dayton, Shillito's of Cincinnati, Stern's of New Jersey, and R.H. White of Boston.

Instead of attempting an exhaustive list, I've assembled what I consider a representative sample of once-iconic stores that fell by the wayside in the late twentieth and early twenty-first centuries.

THE BON MARCHÉ

Founded: 1890

Closed: 2005

Headquarters: Seattle

Locations: 42

A German immigrant's stop in Paris on his way to the United States inspired the name of this Seattle-based department store. Edward Nordhoff was just seventeen when he began working in the Louvre store there, but he was more impressed by Maison a Boucicaut au Bon Marché (House of Boucicaut of the Good Deal).

The Boucicaut in the store's title was a hatmaker's son named Aristide Boucicaut, who had become the driving force behind the fourteen-year-old business in 1852. He revamped it to become what's often recognized as the first department store, adopting fixed prices, offering home deliveries, and accepting exchanges and a "big shop" format that became the blueprint for the industry.

More than one American department store would pay homage to Boucicaut's store by taking its name, but Nordhoff's was the most successful. From Paris, Nordhoff moved on to the United States and eventually found his way to Seattle, where he set up a store called The Bon Marché in 1890. The city, driven by the lumber industry, was in the midst of a huge boom, having grown from just 3,500 residents to nearly 43,000 over the previous decade.

The Bon Marché grew quickly as well, and it moved to a larger store sixteen years after it opened. One important innovation Nordhoff introduced involved pricing. He brought a sack of pennies back from the East Coast and started charging prices such as 29 and 49 cents,

instead of rounding to the nearest nickel, as local stores had been doing prior to that.

Nordhoff died in 1899, and the store was eventually sold to the New York–based Hahn chain in 1928, a holding company similar to Federated that would be renamed Allied Stores seven years later. It eventually merged with Federated in 1988. As for The Bon Marché, it expanded over the years into areas like Spokane, Boise, and Missoula establishing a presence in five Northwestern states: Washington, Oregon, Idaho, Montana, and Wyoming.

Its stores became Macy's as part of that store's rebranding efforts in 2005.

THE BROADWAY

Founded: 1896

Closed: 1996

Headquarters: Los Angeles, California

Locations: 82

Slogan: "The Broadway is Southern California"

If you grew up in Southern California in the latter half of the twentieth century, chances are you remember The Broadway. British immigrant Arthur Letts founded the company in 1896 with a store at Fourth and Broadway in Los Angeles; it made him so wealthy that he was able to pay $2 million for a ranch he dubbed Holmby Hills (his son later built what would become the Playboy Mansion there).

The Broadway was one of the four major department store chains (along with Bullock's, Robinson's, and May Co.) that dominated the regional scene. Its iconic neon sign, The Broadway-Hollywood, shone down from atop the company's nine-story building, which overlooks the Walk of Fame.

Over the years, The Broadway expanded into Arizona, Colorado, and New Mexico, purchasing Weinstock's of Sacramento in 1949.

As the sixties drew to a close, The Broadway's growth accelerated. In 1968, it gobbled up retail bookseller Waldenbooks and ritzy Dallas-based Neiman Marcus; two years later it added Capwell's in Oakland and The Emporium in San Francisco. The Broadway's parent company, Carter Hawley Hale, failed in a bid for

The Broadway store at Huntington Center in Huntington Beach, California, seen in 1965. Courtesy Orange County Archives.

years later, the company was sold to Federated, which also repackaged Broadway stores with former Bullock's and I. Magnin locations to form Macy's West. Some of these locations reopened under the Bloomingdale's nameplate, but The Broadway name was history.

BUFFUMS'

Founded: 1904
Closed: 1990
Headquarters: Long Beach, California
Locations: 16
Slogan: "I've been to Buffums'!"

This high-end chain had stores between Glendale and San Diego but never expanded beyond Southern California. Charles and Edwin Buffum moved west from Illinois and purchased a Long Beach mercantile in 1904 and marketed their store to older, more conservative patrons. By 1925, the original store had expanded to include a six-story addition that had entire floors dedicated to children's clothing, designer clothing and lingerie, and bed

Marshall Field's in 1977, but the following year bought Wanamaker's for $60 million in cash. The decade saw The Broadway's parent company rise to become the nation's sixth-largest retailer.

But The Broadway soon became a takeover target itself. During the eighties, it sold off Waldenbooks to Kmart and shed Wanamaker's and Neiman Marcus, as well, ultimately filing for Chapter 11 bankruptcy in 1991. Four

A rendering shows the Buffums' store at Fashion Island in Newport Beach, California. Courtesy Orange County Archives.

and bath. Customers could dine on the top-floor terrace at the Four Seasons Restaurant.

The store was known for its advertising slogans "I've been to Buffums'!" and "Southern California's most gifted store."

Ronald Reagan, described in the Long Beach Independent as an "actor-turned-author," appeared at Buffums' in the summer of 1965 to sign copies of his autobiography, *Where's the Rest of Me?* According to one writer's recollection, other celebrities also made appearances: Elizabeth Taylor took time out from filming scenes from *The Sandpiper* in San Dimas to pop in and purchase travel tickets, and Groucho Marx's wife bought children's clothes there.

Buffums' went out of business in 1991, but a family member's name still graces a famous Southern California building: the Dorothy Chandler Pavilion in Los Angeles, host to many Academy Awards ceremonies, is named for Edwin Buffum's daughter, Dorothy Buffum Chandler (wife of former *Los Angeles Times* publisher Norman Chandler).

Note: Because there were two Buffum brothers, the apostrophe appeared after the *s*.

BULLOCK'S

Founded: 1907
Closed: 1996
Headquarters: Los Angeles, California
Locations: 22
Slogan: "Suprema Regnat Qualitas" (Latin for Quality Reigns Supreme)

The Bullock's chain bought San Francisco–based I. Magnin & Co. in 1944 and was itself acquired by Federated Department Stores twenty years later—three decades before the group took over Macy's. Federated took the chain into the Bay Area under the Bullock's North nameplate, opening six stores there between 1972 and 1982, but abandoned the project the following year and sold all six locations (three of them to Nordstrom). The chain also entered the Arizona market.

The original Bullock's Wilshire store, seen from the rear. Public domain.

Bullock's, like Buffums', was known for its high-end merchandise and high-class clientele, epitomized, of course, by the marquis Bullock's Wilshire store.

Bullock's had an interesting role to play in the formation of the modern-day Macy's chain. When Federated ran into cash problems in the late eighties, it sold Bullock's and I. Magnin to Macy's for $1 billion. The new owners closed the company's Los Angeles offices and folded the two stores into their own business framework, but the gambit proved a poor one. The stores didn't perform well enough to justify the massive debt, and the resulting money woes contributed to Macy's bankruptcy filing in 1992. Bullock's Wilshire was rebranded as I. Magnin, which itself was shut down in 1995. A year later, a leaner Federated group turned the tables by buying Macy's—and the remaining Bullock's stores, which were promptly rebranded as Macy's.

(Note: I. Magnin, founded by Isaac and Mary Ann Magnin in 1876, is easily confused with Joseph Magnin, a store run by one of their four sons. The Joseph Magnin chain grew to thirty-two stores but eventually filed for bankruptcy and closed up shop in 1984.)

Cohen's

Founded: 1867

Closed: 1987

Headquarters: Jacksonville, Florida

Slogan: "The Big Store"

Cohen's in downtown Jacksonville was called "The Big Store" for good reason. The St. James Building, in which it was housed, was four stories tall and covered an entire city block when it opened in 1912. Total square footage: 300,000 square feet.

The building was not only big, it was bright. Fourteen 3,000-candlepower streetlamps allowed Jacob Cohen to claim that it was the brightest illuminated city block in the country. Cohen's brothers had started the business as the Cohen Brothers Dry Goods House in 1867; Jacob, who became known as "The Wanamaker of the South," took over in the 1880s, when his brothers left town to pursue other ventures.

He suffered a major setback in 1901, when his store was destroyed in a major fire, but he responded by building the St. James Building. At the time of its construction,

The former Cohen's in downtown Jacksonville, Florida, now serves as City Hall. Stephen H. Provost, 2019.

it was the ninth-largest department store in the country and Jacksonville's third-largest building. From 1935 to 1958, it housed radio station WMBR. Escalators were added in 1947.

May Department Stores purchased Cohen's in 1958, making it the forty-seventh store in the chain and rebranding it as May Cohens.

The downtown store closed in 1987, and the St. James Building now houses Jacksonville's City Hall.

DAYTON'S

Founded: 1878

Closed: 2001 (converted to Marshall Field's)

Headquarters: Minneapolis, Minnesota

Locations: 19

The history of Dayton's can be told in two parts: first as a successful department store chain and second as an even more successful discounter. It was originally known as Goodfellow's after its founder, but Reuben Goodfellow retired shortly after moving into a new six-story building owned by George Dayton in 1902.

Dayton didn't have any experience as a retailer. In fact. He had purchased the property as an act of faith. The Presbyterian church he attended had burned down and had no way of raising money to build a new place of worship. Its only source of income was an unsalable piece of property next door, and Dayton purchased the lot, ultimately building his six-story structure there. He bought Goodfellow's business shortly after it moved in, renaming it Dayton's Dry Goods.

Dayton's was the impetus behind the first enclosed shopping mall, Southdale Center, where it was an original anchor along with local rival Donaldson's, Walgreens drugs, and Woolworth's. The mall was built indoors as a means of insulating shoppers from the harsh Minnesota climate, which yielded just 113 good shopping days a year.

In 1969, Dayton's made what must have seemed at the time the most significant move in its history, acquiring Detroit's mammoth J.L. Hudson downtown store and the branches in that chain. The result was a new company called Dayton-Hudson. But the truly pivotal move in Dayton's history had come seven years earlier, when it got into the discounting business by establishing Target Stores.

Target became so successful that Dayton-Hudson eventually divested itself of its department stores, changed its name to Target Corporation, and focused on that brand. Dayton's and Hudson's were both rebranded as Marshall Field's in 2001, and all the stores together were sold to May Department Stores three years later. The following year, Macy's bought the May group, and you know the rest of that story.

THE DENVER

Founded: 1879

Closed: 1987

Headquarters: Denver, Colorado

Locations: 12

Slogan: "Where Colorado Shops With Confidence"

The Denver Dry Goods Company kept "Dry Goods" as part of its name, though it was generally known as just The Denver. Like other stores, it was originally named after its founder, Michael J. McNamara, who built "the finest department store building west of St. Louis" in 1889 but then ran out of money and had to auction off the business during a financial crisis in 1893. The new owners initially kept him on as manager, then ousted him and renamed the business The Denver Dry Goods Company.

Like other department stores, it grew to occupy a massive structure that rose six stories and occupied a full city block. Declaring itself the largest department store west of Chicago, it claimed to have 1,200 employees $2.5 million worth of stock spread out over seven acres of floor area. The tea room on the fifth floor seated almost 800 people, making it the largest food-service venue outside the hotel industry in Denver.

The Denver chain eventually expanded to include a dozen stores, including one in Billings, Montana. It joined Associated Dry Goods and was the holding company's no. 2 moneymaker behind Lord & Taylor. Nevertheless, when May Department Stores acquired ADG, it sold off nine of the chain's twelve stores and renamed the others. The flagship store in downtown Denver was converted into apartments in 1994.

7662. Denver Dry Goods Co. Building
400 Feet Long—7 Acres Floor Area
Sixteenth and California and Fifteenth Streets
Denver, Colorado

An early-twentieth-century postcard shows The Denver building. Public domain.

FAMOUS-BARR

Founded: 1911

Closed: 2006 (converted to Macy's)

Headquarters: St. Louis, Missouri

Locations: 12

Slogan: "You're Never Far From Famous-Barr"

Famous-Barr was formed out of a merger between the Famous Clothing Company and William Barr Dry Goods in 1911.

According to legend, the "Famous" half of the business earned its name when the farmers who frequented the store remarked that it was growing famous in the region. As for the other half of the business, William Barr founded St. Louis's first department store as a dry-goods shop in 1849; by 1880, it had grown into what he called the "largest and most complete extensive retail house in America." The four-story building was hailed in the press as a "mammoth iron palace" that was "to St. Louis what A.T. Stewart's establishment was to New York some years ago." It expanded to cover the entire block.

Still, it faced competition from Stix, Baer & Fuller, the self-proclaimed "Grand Leader," which built an eight-story headquarters in 1906.

Barr, meanwhile, had sold the business to a company led by Thomas McKittrick, who began laying the groundwork for a new building to compete with the Grand Leader. It would house the store on its lower floors and railroad offices above. McKittrick couldn't do it alone, though, and he found an ally in David May, who had purchased the Famous Clothing Company in 1885. Now, he brought McKittrick's business into the fold of what would become his May Department Stores empire.

The merger was finalized in 1911, and the new combined company had the wherewithal to open the first air-conditioned store in the country in the new Railway Exchange Building three years later. That cube-shaped building would rise from the dust of the old Barr block, which was entirely razed to make way for it. With thirty-three acres of floor space, it would be the largest office building in the world, even larger than the Woolworth building (then under construction and destined to be the world's tallest).

Thirty-eight elevators would travel 800 miles a day in the Railway Exchange Building, which would be be twenty-one stories high. Two more penthouse levels were above it and two basement levels were below. It would have 4,142 windows and a central court "into which a 10-story skyscraper of average size could be contained without touching the walls," the St. Louis Post-Dispatch reported. The Famous-Barr store itself would occupy the first seven floors; May's company was also headquartered in the building.

Houston-based Foley's touted itself as "tops in Texas." Public domain.

It looked solid, and it was. "I do not believe that anything could wreck this building when it is finished," McKittrick crowed. "Dynamite? Well, that might twist it."

Famous-Barr opened its first suburban store in 1948, by which time it was making twice as much profit as any other company in St. Louis. The new Clayton store (which would close in 1991) was just eight miles from downtown. It had a distinctly curved exterior that looked a bit like an undulating wave as you turned the corner in front of the building.

Famous-Barr would cease to exist in 2006 after May Department Stores was acquired by Macy's.

FOLEY'S

Founded: 1900
Closed: 2006 (converted to Macy's)
Headquarters: Houston, Texas
Locations: 16
Slogan: "Tops in Texas"

Two young Irish brothers, James and Pat Foley, founded Houston's most recognizable department store in 1900 as a dry-goods store on Main Street, offering fabrics, needles, and men's fashions. By 1922, it was the city's largest department store.

The business changed hands in 1917 and again in 1947 when it became part of Federated Department Stores. That was only a year after it opened its "store

of tomorrow"—a ten-story, fully air-conditioned brick building that cost $13 million to build. It was the first new department store to be built in nearly two decades, since before the Great Depression in 1928.

Foley's didn't just modernize downtown. It expanded in 1961 by opening its first branch store in Sharpstown, a Houston suburb thirteen miles from the city center. The chain eventually grew to include sixteen branches, not only in Texas but also in Arizona, Colorado, Louisiana, New Mexico, and Oklahoma.

Federated sold Foley's to May Department Stores in 1988, then reacquired it in 2005 when it bought the May group. Within a year, Foley's was no more, having been converted to Macy's. Its store of tomorrow became the store of yesterday when it was demolished in the fall of 2013, the brick structure collapsing in a mere ten seconds.

GARFINCKEL'S

Founded: 1905
Closed: 1990
Headquarters: Washington, DC
Locations: 13
Slogan: "Only the Best Goods"

Folk aficionados might be forgiven for thinking this high-end department store had something to do with a prominent musical duo from the sixties. But shoppers in the nation's capital were familiar with the store long before Simon and Garfunkel hit the scene.

Garfinckel's was named for Julius Garfinckel, who got his feet wet as a stockroom boy for the Denver Dry Goods Company in the 1890s before moving to the nation's capital, where he founded the business in 1905.

Garfinckel was the polar opposite of the discounters that would come to dominate retailing decades later. When one clerk suggested offering a lower rate to a customer making a large purchase, Garfinckel replied: "If your customer should purchase as much as a thousand dollars' worth of goods from you and offer to pay you in cash and should then ask the question, 'Could there be a discount?' you are instructed to tell the customer that the one thing the personnel in Garfinckel & Co. is instructed NOT to do is to approach the head of the firm with the suggestion for discounts. This store will have but one price for every customer."

"For decades," the *New York Times* reported, Garfinckel's "was the department store of choice for wealthy shoppers in the nation's capital . . . selling classical styles of day and evening wear and serving them up with sterling service." The core business didn't expand as far or as fast as other department stores, operating a dozen branches at one time or another in addition to its downtown flagship store. But it did form a conglomerate thanks to a couple of strategic acquisitions: Brooks Brothers menswear in 1946 and the Richmond-based Miller & Rhoads department stores in 1967.

At one point, those three businesses and four others that Garfinckel's had acquired had a total of 190 stores.

Garfinckel's filed for bankruptcy in 1990, by which time it was losing nearly $2.5 million a month, having experienced a 40 percent decline in sales over just three years. Like many stores, it was unable to navigate the gap between upscale prices and the demand for convenience. "A store like Nordstrom's offers wonderful service," one woman said, "so I'm willing to pay higher prices. [Washington-area rivals] Hecht's and Woodie's offer lots of variety at good prices, but you do more self-shopping. I didn't want to go to Garfinckel's, pay higher prices and still have to do self-shopping."

Garfinckel's was out of business by the end of the year. Woodward & Lothrop, aka Woodie's, lasted only five more years, while Hecht's lasted long enough to be swallowed up by Macy's in 2006. One piece of the Garfinckel's empire did survive: Garfinckel's had sold off its Brooks

Brothers division in 1988. Three decades later, it was the oldest men's clothier in the United States, having been in business since 1818.

GOLDWATER'S

Founded: 1860

Closed: 1989 (converted to Robinson's, May Co.)

Headquarters: Phoenix, Arizona

Locations: 10

Slogan: "The Best Always"

Under most circumstances, the former company chairman's nomination to be president of the United States would be the best story in a department store's history. And, indeed, Senator Barry Goldwater *was* serving as chairman of the family business when he accepted the Republican nomination in 1964. But so many other wild and wacky things happened long before that, it's hard to view a political campaign—even for the presidency—as anything but tame by comparison.

The story of Goldwater's starts the same way so many other department store histories do—as the story of a Jewish immigrant who came to the United States and founded a successful business. The immigrant in this case was Michael Goldwasser, who changed his name to Goldwater after moving to London, where he married Sarah Nathan in 1850. London was nice enough, but Goldwater's brother Joe persuaded him to head to California in search of gold.

Instead, he ended up starting a saloon in the mining town of Sonora on the western slopes of the Sierra Nevada. His wife, who'd stayed behind in London, wasn't too happy when she arrived to find her husband running such a business, especially when a brothel was renting space on the second floor. It wasn't long before she left for San Francisco to set up the family home, while he went on the road in search of opportunity. That road took him to a mining camp north of Yuma where his brother gave him enough money to buy merchandise to sell, a peddler's wagon, and four mules to pull the wagon.

Joe got into debt, and the sheriff took Michael's merchandise in order to satisfy it, but Michael found a new opportunity when a friend named Roy Cohn hired him to work at Cohn's general store on the Colorado

River. Cohn was an absentee owner, so Goldwater ran the store and, ultimately, bought him out. But it wasn't like running a dry-goods shop in Chicago or Pittsburgh. Robbers held Michael up at gunpoint. Brother Joe was ambushed and shot by tribesmen on a dusty road in Arizona, leaving him with a souvenir for his watch fob in the form of a bullet that was extracted from his body.

A few years later, he was running the Goldwater-Castaneda store in Bisbee—which doubled as the town bank—when five armed outlaws rode into town with guns drawn and ordered Joe to open the safe. They thought they'd find a big payroll for miners working in the area, but they'd gotten there too soon. The stagecoach bringing the haul into town hadn't arrived yet, so they had to make do with $800 and a couple of gold watches. As they made their escape, they started shooting, killing four people, including an eight-months-pregnant woman and a sheriff's deputy. Joe escaped with his life, but the incident went down in history as the Bisbee Massacre.

Barry Goldwater later said that early Goldwater's general stores stocked everything from stock hats to horseshoes to herrings from Holland. Bisbee was one of several locations for Goldwater's general stores in those frontier days. Michael Goldwater tried to open a store in Phoenix when it was a town of a few hundred people back in 1872, but the enterprise didn't take, so four years later he moved to Prescott, which at the time was a bit larger. By 1885, he'd had enough of Arizona, so he left the business in the hands of sons Morris and Baron while he went back to join his wife in San Francisco.

Under Morris, the business thrived in Prescott, and he was even elected mayor, but when Phoenix started to boom, Baron wanted to shift operations there in 1896 against Morris's better judgment. The issue was decided when Baron challenged Morris to a card came called Casino and won, resulting in Goldwater's move to Phoenix that year.

Goldwater's would evolve into a department store and returned to Prescott with a branch store in 1937, later adding three more locations in Phoenix malls, along with stores in Scottsdale, Tucson, Mesa, and two out-of-state locations in Albuquerque and Las Vegas (the last store to open, in 1981). It became part of Associated Dry Goods in 1963, just a year before Barry Goldwater lost his presidential bid. May Department Stores bought that company in 1986 and, three years later, Goldwater's was rebranded as J.W. Robinson and May Co.

HECHT'S

Founded: 1857

Closed: 2006 (converted to Macy's)

Headquarters: Baltimore, Maryland

Locations: 61

Slogan: "50 Feet from Broadway Market"

Hecht's, which competed with Woodward & Lothrop and Garfinckel's for customers in the nation's capital, was named for founder Samuel Hecht, a Bavarian Jewish immigrant who got his start as a traveling peddler before opening his Broadway Furniture Store in Baltimore in 1857. The store was rechristened Hecht's Reliable in 1870 and added clothing to its stock nine years later. Another store opened not long afterward selling carpeting.

Hecht's kept its various stores distinct until 1951, with the separate but affiliated Hecht's Reliable carving out a niche that targeted a different kind of customer than the high-end shoppers served by, say, Garfinckel's. Hecht's Reliable offered its patrons a rent-to-own option. An ad in the *Baltimore Sun* from 1893 offered payment plans for ladies' coats on a "small weekly payment plan . . . and at prices that are particularly low." In 1920, you could pay $3.50 a week for a player piano or 50 cents a week for a Victrola phonograph.

Hecht's Reliable carried "everything to wear for men, women, boys and girls, also radios, electric washing machines and tires."

The company made a splash when it moved into the nation's capital in 1925, debuting in a seven-story building with 550,000 square feet of space. Large stand-alone branch stores—each more than 250,000 square feet—opened in Silver Spring, Maryland, and Arlington, Virginia, in 1947 and '51, respectively. Later stores opened in a number of shopping malls around the area. Among them: the Landmark Mall in 1965, the first in the area to feature three department stores (Sears and Woodward & Lothrop were the others), and Tysons Corners Center three years later.

May Department Stores acquired Hecht's in 1958 and consolidated a number of later acquisitions under the Hecht's name over the years. Among them: Miller & Rhoads and Thalhimers, two former rivals based in Richmond, Virginia; Wanamaker's; ten Allentown-based Hess's stores and seventeen Woodward & Lothrop's. Hecht's itself was subsumed by the Macy's nameplate in 2006.

HIGBEE'S

Founded: 1860
Closed: 1992 (converted to Dillard's)
Headquarters: Cleveland, Ohio
Locations: 14

Higbee's in Cleveland, to the left of Terminal Tower, hosted filming for *A Christmas Story* in 1983. These days, the building houses a casino. Stephen H. Provost, 2019.

Higbee's was one of the Midwest's oldest department stores, tracing its origins to 1860, when Edwin Higbee and John Hower founded it as Higbee & Hower Dry Goods (Hower's name was removed following his death in 1902). The Higbee's building was hard to miss. In 1929, it moved into the Terminal Tower complex on Cleveland's Public Square, which was then the tallest building west of New York City.

Higbee's became a small chain, with fourteen stores in northeast Ohio, and was the area's sales leader for high-end fashion goods. In addition to six stores in the Cleveland suburbs, it had locations in Canton and Akron.

Dillard's purchased Higbee's in 1992 and operated it under the Dillard's nameplate until 2002, when it closed the iconic downtown store. It has since been transformed into a casino.

The final scene of the 1983 holiday film *A Christmas Story* was filmed inside Higbee's, which offered to feed the crew, build sets, and provide employees as extras. It was good publicity. But the store's vice president had one condition: that profanity in the original script be edited out to preserve Higbee's family-friendly image. Unintelligible grumbling by one of the characters was originally supposed to have been cursing.

HUDSON'S

Founded: 1881
Closed: 2001
Headquarters: Detroit, Michigan
Locations: 22
Slogan: "Detroit's World-Famous Department Store"

Hudson's fit hand-in-glove with Detroit's automotive industry. In fact, the founding family also started the Hudson Motor Car Company, which eventually became part of Chrysler.

The chain expanded by establishing branches in Buffalo, Cleveland, New York, Pittsburgh, St. Louis, Toledo, and St. Paul, where it competed with Dayton's. But Hudson's was known above all else for its massive downtown Detroit department store, which was not only tall but massive, rising like a modern-day castle that covered an entire city block.

Brightly lit HUDSON'S signs on each of the building's four sides beckoned customers to flock from all directions. Unlike some other big department stores that remained standing, however, Hudson's gigantic monument to retailing is gone. It closed in 1983 and fell to demolition crews in 1998 as a crowd of 20,000 watched. The resulting debris pile was an average of 35 feet high and rose as high as 60 feet where the tower itself had been.

The demolition set three records: The 439-foot tower was the tallest building ever imploded, erasing a record that had stood for twenty-three years. It was also the tallest structural steel building ever imploded and the largest single building ever imploded, by square footage.

Dayton's of Minnesota purchased Hudson's in 1969 to form Dayton-Hudson, but despite the success of both those chains, the company prospered even more thanks to its discount retailer, Target. It eventually rebranded itself as Target Corp. in 2000 and jettisoned the last of its department stores four years after that.

HUTZLER'S

Founded: 1858

Closed: 1990

Headquarters: Baltimore, Maryland

Locations: 10

Slogan: "A Maryland Institution"

A regional concern, Hutzler's consisted of a single store in downtown Baltimore for most of its existence and never operated outside Maryland. A Bavarian Jewish immigrant named Moses Hutzler founded the business in 1858 as M. Hutzler & Son, leaving his son Abram in charge of the day-to-day operations (two other sons, Charles and David, came on board in 1867).

During the Civil War, when Baltimore was under martial law, Hutzler's established a bargain counter to boost sales—an early forerunner of the "bargain basement." It also had Maryland's first fleet of delivery trucks.

The business' hallmark was stability. It operated as a "One-Price House," where customers could be sure they'd pay the marked price instead of having to haggle for a better deal. An anomaly in an age when city department

stores routinely sold out to larger, regional chains, the business remained in the Hutzler family throughout its existence. When it celebrated its fiftieth anniversary in 1908, brothers Abram and David Hutzler made it a point not only to attend the festivities but to shake each customer's hand.

The flagship emporium remained on Howard Street for its entire 132 years, believed to be a record for American department store in a single location. It was, according to a slogan adopted in 1931, "a Maryland institution."

Of course, changes were made along the way as the business grew. The store added three other storefronts on Howard Street between 1874 and 1887, then tore everything down and started from scratch with the five-story Hutzler Brothers Palace Building (later expanded to ten stories), featuring a Romanesque façade that was redesigned in Art Deco style in 1931. The Colonial Restaurant, which had opened in 1917 on the fourth floor, moved to the sixth floor of the new building, serving more than 1,000 people on the day it reopened.

The main store took up a mammoth 325,000 square feet in the fifties, the decade when Hutzler's finally opened its first of ten branch stores. In 1984, the business moved next door into a new Atrium building on the same block and shrank to 70,000 square feet.

Six years later, the company closed its doors and liquidated all its assets. It did not go through bankruptcy.

IVEY'S

Founded: 1900

Closed: 1990 (sold to Dillard's)

Headquarters: Charlotte, North Carolina

Ivey's was named for Joseph Benjamin Ivey, the son of a Methodist minister who started his business in a rented storeroom at the turn of the twentieth century. The store began in Charlotte, North Carolina, but expanded to other locations, including Jacksonville, Florida. Ivey's Methodist background led him to insist on drawing the curtains over the store windows on Sundays to guard pedestrians from the temptation of looking at his "worldly goods." Dillard's purchased Ivey's in 1990.

The Ivey's building in Jacksonville, Florida. Stephen H. Provost, 2019.

KAUFMANN'S

Founded: 1871

Closed: 2006 (converted to Macy's)

Headquarters: Pittsburgh, Pennsylvania

Locations: 59 in five states

Slogan: "Meet me under the Kaufmann's clock"

Other stores came and went, but Kaufmann's *was* downtown Pittsburgh for nearly a century and a half. Jacob Kaufmann, like other pioneers, started off as a traveling peddler selling cloth, buttons, ribbon, and thread from a knapsack he carried as he traveled the roads that connected towns and farms southeast of Pittsburgh. He and brother Isaac opened a tailor shop in 1871 and were joined by younger brothers Morris and Henry in opening J. Kaufmann & Brothers six years later. They advertised it as "Kaufmann's, Cheapest Corner Reliable One Price Clothing House Men's & Boys Clothing."

They quickly expanded into a twelve-story building with 700,000 square feet. They enticed customers by offers of free "bonus" gifts with major purchases. If you bought a suit, they'd throw in a pair of suspenders, or you might get a free photo album if you paid for a boy's overcoat.

Some members of the family broke away in 1913 and established a rival store called Kaufmann Baer, which was purchased by Gimbels twelve years later. But Kaufmann's outlasted Gimbels and a host of other stores (Lord & Taylor, Saks, Horne's, Frank & Seder, Rosenbaum's, and others) in downtown Pittsburgh, and its iconic clock became a symbol of the city. "Meet me under the Kaufmann's clock" became a company slogan and a good piece of advice for anyone who got lost downtown. The ornate timepiece was a distinctive landmark that jutted out from the corner of the store at Fifth Avenue and Smithfield Street. At 2,000 pounds, the Victorian-style brass timepiece was hard to miss.

The store closed in 2002, but the clock, installed in 1913, is still there.

Kaufmann's was an early merger target, but it retained its own identity after being swallowed up by May Department Stores in 1946. It eventually grew to include fifty-nine stores in five states before Macy's purchased the chain in 2006 and converted the more-than-century-old Kaufmann's nameplate to its own.

LEONARD'S

Founded: 1918

Closed: 1967

Headquarters: Fort Worth, Texas

Slogan: "Fort Worth's Only Complete One-Stop Shopping Center"

Leonard's grew from a 1,500-square-foot grocery store in 1918 to six city blocks by 1948. Its "Greater Leonard's" empire encompassed four stores: The Greater Leonard's Food Store, adjacent Department Store, Playground Store, and Farm Store, with two more blocks set aside for free parking.

When even that wasn't enough, it built a new parking lot a mile away and a "subway" rail system to shuttle customers to and from the department store. Leonard's had its own brands of coffee, bread, bicycles, cigars, and motor oil. Whenever a new family arrived in town, the store sent out a welcome box that included a city map, a pound of coffee, a loaf of bread, and an egg separator.

In 1967, the family sold the store to Tandy Corp., the parent company of Radio Shack, for $8.5 million. The business was sold again seven years later to Dillard's, although Tandy kept the land and demolished the store, replacing it with its own corporate headquarters. The subway kept running until 2002. A subway driver and Radio Shack bookkeeper exchanged wedding vows aboard the train in 1978, and the parking lot (with embedded train tracks) remained in place, along with an old maintenance shed and a blocked-off passenger underpass beneath the place where the tracks used to run.

Lit Brothers

Founded: 1891

Closed: 1977

Headquarters: Philadelphia, Pennsylvania

Locations: 11

Slogan: "A Great Store in a Great City"

Despite its masculine name, Lit Brothers was one of the few department stores that got its start thanks to a woman—Rachel Lit Weddel, who opened a women's millinery and apparel shop at Market and 8 in Philadelphia back in 1891. Her brothers joined her in the business the following year, and the store grew over the years as it absorbed various buildings on Market Street, eventually taking up a full city block.

The combined structure, cobbled together from pieces built between 1859 and 1918, was remodeled to create a common interior and became known as the "cast-iron building," even though only two of the original building's fronts were cast iron. Its ornate arched windows and octagonal tower at the corner gave it a

distinctive presence in downtown Philadelphia, and the 720,000-square-foot building earned a place on the National Register of Historic Places.

The store closed in 1977.

Maas Brothers

Founded: 1886

Closed: 1991

Headquarters: Tampa, Florida

Locations: 39

Slogan: "Greater Tampa's Greatest Store"

Abe and Isaac Mass founded their first store in 1880 in Dublin, Georgia, before moving to Tampa six years later. There, they established what they first dubbed "the Dry Goods Palace," in 1886—the first in what would grow to a chain of thirty-nine department stores on Florida's Gulf Coast.

Maas Brothers opened what was, at the time, Florida's second-largest department store in 1921, featuring the state's first escalator.

Eight years later, the company was acquired by Hahn's Department Stores, a holding company that later became known as Allied Stores. Canadian entrepreneur Robert Campeau purchased the entire Allied chain in 1986, consolidating it with Jordan Marsh; five years later, he combined it with Miami-based Burdines, eliminating the Maas Brothers name altogether.

Burdines stores were converted into Macy's in 2005.

J.M. McDonald

Founded: 1934

Closed: 1983

Headquarters: Hastings, Nebraska.

Locations: 96

Slogan: "Your Finer, Friendlier Department Store"

The eponymous founder of the J.M. McDonald chain grew up with retailing in his blood—and just down the block. His father, Daniel, ran a store in Hamilton, Missouri, where the McDonalds lived a block away from the Penney family. McDonald got in on the ground floor of one of the biggest retailing successes of the twentieth

DISCOVER McDonald's

YOUR FINER, FRIENDLIER DEPARTMENT STORE

"A Little Off the Beaten Path, But Well Worth the Trip"

McDonald's stores were "a little off the beaten path," but this 1968 ad in the *San Mateo Times* declared them "well worth the trip." Public domain.

century when he helped his former neighbor, James Cash Penney, open his first store in Kemmerer, Wyoming, in 1905.

McDonald later became manager of the Penney's store in Moscow, Idaho, before rising to a seat on the board of directors and then, in 1921, to company vice president. He retired in 1929, but got back into the business five years later when he purchased controlling interest in a retailer that became known as Brown-McDonald. By 1947, the chain had forty stores, and it added thirty-three more six years later with the purchase of W.W. Virtue.

J.M. McDonald, as it became known, added ten more locations two years later with the acquisition of J.P. Croff.

McDonald's version of the bargain basement was The Loft, "an end-of-season clearing point" that offered surplus (not irregular) stock at 40 percent or more off the original price.

McDonald's had stores in places such as Yuma, Arizona; Helena, Montana; Hastings, Nebraska; and Fresno, San Mateo, and Roseville, California. Locations were "a little off the beaten path, but well worth the trip." There were ninety-six of them in the chain by the time the family sold it in 1968 to Gamble-Skogmo, which owned an array of businesses ranging from hardware and furniture outlets to Alden's mail-order house and Mode O'Day women's clothing stores.

Wickes, a furniture company, bought the whole lot of them in 1980 but found itself overextended and declared bankruptcy just two years after the sale. It closed the last ten J.M. McDonald stores in 1983.

MERVYN'S

Founded: 1949
Closed: 2009
Headquarters: Hayward, California
Locations: 189 in ten states
Slogan: "Big Brands. Small Prices"

Mervyn's occupied a niche similar to that of Kohl's, somewhere between discounters like Kmart and middle-tier stores like Sears and Penney's. Mervin Morris opened the first store in the Bay Area suburb of San Lorenzo in 1949, using a variant spelling of his name because an architect thought it looked catchier. It remained the only Mervyn's location until 1962, when a second store opened in Fremont.

Rapid expansion followed. Stores opened in some two dozen Northern California locations and branched out into Southern California in Fullerton and Huntington Beach. In 1977, Morris sold the chain to Dayton-Hudson, the forerunner of Target Corporation, which took it national by opening stores in Florida, Georgia, Arizona, Texas, Michigan, and elsewhere.

Morris made a cool $300 million on the deal, but he wasn't pleased with the results after Target, in turn, sold it to a group of equity investors in 2004. The new owners—in Morris's words—"raped" the company, immediately closing sixty-two stores in the Midwest and South, and sent it on the road to ruin. All stores were closed and assets liquidated in 2008 under Chapter 7 bankruptcy.

The Morris family was not pleased, to say the least. "My dad built a fabulous chain of stores which was unfortunately mismanaged in the last few years," son Jeff Morris said in announcing the family had bought back the rights to the Mervyn's name. They planned to restart the business online, but those plans never materialized.

RICH'S

Founded: 1867

Closed: 2005 (converted to Macy's)

Headquarters: Atlanta, Georgia

Locations: 13

Slogan: "Atlanta Born, Atlanta Owned, Atlanta Managed"

Rich's put a premium on customer service. According to one legend, founder Morris Rich would carry goods out of the store to streetside for women who preferred to stay in their horse-drawn carriages while they shopped.

The store went out of its way to make customers feel as though they'd gotten a fair shake, even if it meant taking a short-term financial hit. The long-term reward of customer loyalty was worth it. To this end, the store established a policy in the early 1920s allowing any item to be exchanged for full refunds or store credit, no questions asked. That included noticeably used items and even some goods Rich's didn't have in stock—they'd obviously been bought elsewhere.

Rich, a Hungarian Jew, started his dry-goods business in 1867 with $500 he borrowed from his brother, and it grew steadily into a six-story behemoth encompassing 1.2 million square feet divided among a Store for Homes, a Store for Men, and a Store for (women's) Fashion. Among its notable features was a four-story "crystal bridge" over Forsythe Street, connecting the Store for Homes to the rest of the complex.

Rich's flagship store in downtown Atlanta was among the biggest in the South. Library of Congress.

Although Rich's became a chain, its growth outside Atlanta was modest, and its focus remained the downtown store. An initial attempt to expand outside the state took Rich's into Knoxville in 1955, but the store pulled back after a few years and remained content to open satellite stores in Georgia during the sixties. It ventured beyond the state line by opening two branches in Birmingham and another in Columbia, South Carolina, between 1974 and '77, but that was as far afield as the chain ever went.

The company was sold to Federated Department Stores in 1976 after more than a century as a family-owned business, and Rich's stores were rebranded as Macy's in 2005.

The former Rhodes store at Manchester Center in Fresno, California, became Liberty House and, later, a home store before being transformed into offices for the California Department of Transportation. Stephen H. Provost, 2013.

RHODES

Founded: 1903
Closed: 1974
Headquarters: Tacoma, Washington
Locations: 13
Slogan: "All Roads Lead to Rhodes"

Rhodes was the name of two separate department stores in the Pacific Northwest, both founded by the same family. The first was founded in Tacoma by the four siblings (Albert, William, Henry, and Charles Rhodes) and thus became known as Rhodes Brothers. It started off as a coffee shop in 1892 but became a department store in 1903. Albert Rhodes left the company four years later and moved to Seattle, where he founded Rhodes of Seattle.

The family name had vanished from the retail world by the early seventies. One group bought Rhodes of Seattle and rebranded it as Lamonts in 1968, and Liberty House of Hawaii expanded to the mainland when it purchased Rhodes Brothers the following year. By 1974, all Rhodes Brothers stores had been renamed Liberty House, but

the expansion proved ill-fated, and the chain sold the last of its mainland stores a decade later.

Eventually, the chain went bankrupt, and Macy's acquired the remaining stores in 2001.

ROBINSON'S

Founded: 1883
Closed: 2006 (converted to Macy's from Robinsons-May)
Headquarters: Los Angeles, California
Locations: 29

Boston carried a certain cachet, especially in the West, as a gateway to European tastes and fashion during the late nineteenth and early twentieth centuries. It was therefore no accident that J. W. Robinson christened his new store the Boston Dry Goods Store, touting its "fine stocks and refined 'Boston' service."

Robinson was in a position to know. He had operated a dry-goods business in Waltham, Massachusetts, before leaving for Southern California in 1882 with the intent of developing orange groves. But he noticed the poor quality of the merchandise available on the West Coast and decided he could do better. He had contacts back in Boston and New York whom he could call upon to send him quality goods via ship that would enable him to establish a top-flight carriage trade in Los Angeles.

Shifting his focus back to retailing, he opened a shop on Spring Street in downtown Los Angeles, advertising all-new stock that had been "brought from New York and Boston within the past thirty days."

Robinson's store was unrelated to another Boston store, which would open in Milwaukee fifteen years later, also trading on the prestige of the Massachusetts city. Indeed, Robinson's business would be renamed in his honor after he died in 1891, and the Boston Dry Goods Store was no more.

The store earned a reputation for "catering to the most exclusive trade" and outgrew its original building, so

Robinson's was one of the anchors at Fashion Island in Newport Beach, California. Courtesy Orange County Archives.

the company bought a lot on Seventh Street, outside the established business district, where it built a seven-story emporium of nearly 400,000 square feet that opened in 1915. A seven-story addition followed just eight years later, giving the store a total selling space of more than nine acres.

Amid the Depression, Robinson's hired Edward Mayberry to undertake the task of "completely modernizing the structure and binding the two buildings together as a solid unit." Hundreds of men worked on the project, and the result was what the *Los Angeles Times* called "one of the outstanding beautiful structures of America," featuring a Persian tile exterior in an Art Deco style.

Beverly Hills was chosen for the site of the second J.W. Robinson store in 1952, and other suburban branches followed in places like Palm Springs and Pasadena before the chain began focusing on mall stores, affirming

its presence alongside Bullock's and Buffums' as a store catering to the more well-to-do set. In 1957, it was acquired by Associated Dry Goods, which used the Robinson's name to spin off a related chain of ten stores in Florida starting in 1974.

The Florida stores were sold to Maison Blanche of New Orleans when May Department Stores bought the chain in 1986. Three years later, it converted the Goldwater's chain of Arizona to the J.W. Robinson nameplate, and Robinson's itself was combined with May Co. to form Robinsons-May in 1992. Both those names disappeared in 2006 when Macy's purchased the chain.

SCHUSTER'S

Founded: 1883
Closed: 1969
Headquarters: Milwaukee, Wisconsin

Locations: 6

Slogan: "Let's go by Schuster's, where the streetcar bends the corner round"

The birthplace of the trading stamp was the second department store to open in Milwaukee, later adding two other stores in the city as well as shops in Madison and Cudahy.

Schuster's also offered an early charge plate called the Budga-Plate and sponsored an annual Christmas parade that was such a hit it drew 100,000 people in 1927—more than turned out to see Charles Lindbergh the same year.

Goldie Mabowehz, a Jewish immigrant who arrived in Milwaukee from Russia in 1906 at the age of of eight, remembered being enchanted by the "pretty new clothes, by the soda pop, and ice cream and by the excitement of being in (Schuster's)." She was so taken with the store that she began later began working there as a sales clerk. Mabowehz married Morris Myerson in 1917, and the couple moved to Palestine four years later. After his death, she Hebraized her surname in 1956, becoming Golda Meir—the future prime minister of Israel.

Schuster's sales peaked at $50 million in 1958, and Gimbels purchased the chain four years later, rebranding it as Gimbels-Schusters.

It became simply Gimbels in 1969, and all the stores were closed by 1984.

STRAWBRIDGE & CLOTHIER

Founded: 1868

Closed: 2006 (converted to Macy's)

Headquarters: Philadelphia, Pennsylvania

Locations: 21

Slogan: "Seal of Confidence" depicting William Penn shaking hands with a Lenape tribal leader

Isaac Clothier was running a wholesale cloth business, and Justus Strawbridge already had a small store when the two Quakers rented a house together in New Jersey during the 1860s. By 1868, they had decided to join forces in the business that would bear their two names for more than a century.

Strawbridge & Clothier opened one of the first suburban stores in the nation—this branch at Suburban Square in Ardmore, Pennsylvania—in 1930. Library of Congress.

They already had plenty of history behind them on the day they opened their first store, which was located in a three-story brick building that had served as Thomas Jefferson's office during his tenure as secretary of state in the 1790s. From there, the business made more history by becoming the first major department store to anchor a suburban shopping center (Suburban Square in Ardmore) in 1931.

At the center of its downtown flagship store stood a bronze boar that, according to legend, would bring good luck to anyone who rubbed its (consequently very shiny) nose.

The chain expanded to thirteen stores at its zenith, never expanding beyond its core area of eastern Pennsylvania, Delaware, and southern New Jersey. Stockton Strawbridge, who became president of the company in 1955, helped develop the first enclosed shopping center east of Chicago: Cherry Hill Mall, designed by Victor Gruen of Southdale Center fame. Strawbridge & Clothier opened as one of two main anchors—Bamberger's was the other—when the mall was complete in 1961. Strawbridge also started a chain of discount stores, most of them in strip malls, in a largely failed effort to compete with Target and other discounters in 1969. The chain did grow to a maximum of twenty-six stores, five more than were in the parent Strawbridge & Clothier chain, before going out of business in the late nineties.

In 1996, S&C was acquired by May Department Stores, which in turn was acquired by Macy's in 2005. A year later, S&C locations became Macy's.

THALHIMERS

Founded: 1842

Closed: 1992 (converted to Hecht's)

Headquarters: Richmond, Virginia

Locations: 26

Slogan: "The complete store for all seasons"

William Thalhimer, a German Jewish immigrant, followed in the footsteps of Adam Gimbel but ended up in Virginia instead of the Midwest. Like Gimbel, he arrived from Europe in New Orleans and got there just five years later, in 1840. Thalhimer was one of four friends who sailed from France, each of whom, interestingly enough, wound up starting department stores.

Again like Gimbel, the four traveling companions began making their way up the Mississippi River, earning a living as traveling peddlers. They had their eye on Pittsburgh but got sidetracked thanks to their poor understanding of English and wound up in Petersburg, Virginia, instead.

One of the four, Anthony Rosenstock, stayed there, where he opened Rosenstock's "Temple of Fancy," a dry-goods emporium. The store would merge with rival Rucker Dry Goods in 1930 to form Rucker-Rosenstock, the premier department store in the town of some 30,000 people. Louis Stern, meanwhile, headed farther north and wound up opening Stern's in New York City, which lasted 134 years before being taken over by Macy's in 2001. The only one of the four to actually make it as

far as Pittsburgh was Edgar Kaufmann, who founded Kaufmann's there.

As for Thalhimer, he wound up in Richmond, Virginia, where he founded Thalhimers in 1842. His grandson and namesake, William B. Thalhimer, guided the store through its years of greatest success.

That success came to a screeching halt during the Depression. Unable to pay its employees or buy any more stock, William B. Thalhimer asked a family friend for a $100,000 loan—a loan that was eventually repaid as the company managed to survive. Things improved after the Depression and following World War II. Thalhimers store opened its first branch in Winston-Salem, North Carolina, in 1949, and soon became a dominant force across Virginia and North Carolina.

In Virginia, Thalhimers planted branches in Danville, Hampton Roads, Lynchburg, Norfolk, Petersburg, Roanoke, and Virginia Beach. In North Carolina, Durham, Fayetteville, Greensboro, High Point, and Raleigh joined the Winston-Salem location. It also added a store in Memphis and two in Charleston, South Carolina.

Thalhimers had been in the family for more than 130 years when it was acquired in 1978 by Carter Hawley Hale, owner of The Broadway in Southern California. It had acquired Wanamaker's a year earlier, but declining fortunes forced it to sell Thalhimers to May Department Stores in 1990, and it was merged into Hecht's two years later.

WOODWARD & LOTHROP

Founded: 1887

Closed: 1995

Headquarters: Washington, DC

Locations: 13

Slogan: "They profit most who serve best"

Woodward & Lothrop started out in Boston in 1873 as a partnership between Samuel Woodward and Alvin Lothrop, but they moved their business to the nation's capital seven years later in partnership with Charles Cochrane. An ad in the *National Republican* announced the opening of the "One-price Boston Dry Goods House" with a full line of goods ranging from black silks

Woodward & Lothrop in Washington, DC, seen in the early twentieth century. Library of Congress.

and French novelties to linens, hosiery, gloves, and men's goods. It promised patrons to refrain from high-pressure sales tactics: "No one importuned to buy."

Woodward and Lothrop bought out Cochrane's share in 1886, and it was Woodward & Lothrop from then on.

The chain opened branch stores in Chevy Chase, Maryland, in 1950 and Alexandria, Virginia, in 1952, later expanding into various shopping centers—all in the Virginia-Maryland area—beginning with the Seven Corners mall in 1956. It was even the only store to have a shop inside the Pentagon: an 8,000-square-foot shop that opened in 1943 and closed in 1994.

But "Woodies" would go out of business a year later, a casualty of changes in the retail environment in the eighties and early nineties. After it filed for bankruptcy in 1995, its assets were liquidated. Seven locations were sold to J.C. Penney; the Washington National Opera purchased the flagship location but couldn't afford the cost of converting it into an opera house. Eventually, it became a mixed-use site for retail stores and offices.

REFERENCES

"A&P History," groceteria.com, April 6, 2009.

"About Curtain & Bath," curtainandbathoutlet.com.

"About Us," costco.com.

Abrams, Jeanne. "David May (1848–1927)," Immigrant Entrepreneurship: German-American Business Biographies, immigrantentrepreneurship.org, May 31, 2016.

Ackerman, Marsha. Cool Comfort: America's Romance with Air-Conditioning, Smithsonian Books, Washington, DC, 2002, 2010.

Adamson, Tola. "Piedmont Mall in Danville Undergoes Major Changes," WSET-TV, wset.com, Feb. 27, 2013.

Addison, Brian. "Long Beach Lost: The Buffums' Department Store in DTLB," Long Beach Post, lbpost.com.

"Ads from The Akron," The Mystery of the Hawaiian Fern Wood Tiki, tikiroom.com.

"Advertising Urged on Super-markets," New York Times, timesmachine.nytimes.com, Sept. 30, 1938.

Aguilera, Diana. "Diversity in Fresno: How Racial Covenants Once Ruled Prestigious Neighborhoods," kvpr.org, Dec. 8, 2015.

Alexander, Jessica. "New Owner Revives Local Mall," News & Advance, newsadvance.com, Feb. 2, 2014.

Allen, David. "When Reagan Went to Buffums," David Allen Blog, Inland Valley Daily Bulletin, insidesocal.com, Jan. 24, 2008.

Amerian, Stephanie. "Fifth Avenue's First Lady," Travel Grant Report, escholarship.org, 2009.

American Marketing Association. "Science, Technology & Marketing," fall conference proceedings, p. 228, 1966.

"America's Shrinking Middle Class: A Close Look at Changes Within Metropolitan Areas," Pew Research Center, pewsocialtrends.org, May 11, 2016.

"Ames Department Stores, Inc. History," fundinguniverse.com.

Andrews, Edmund L. "First Altman's, Now Garfinckel's," New York Times, nytimes.com, June 28, 1990.

Andrews, Evan. "The 'Black Friday' Gold Scandal," history.com, Sept. 24, 2014.

Ash, Agnes. "Woolco Stores Ready For Debut," Miami News, p. 14, Jan. 14, 1962.

Auerbach, Alexander. "America Discovers Columbus: It's a More Expensive Akron," Los Angeles Times, pt. 3, p. 8, Sept. 3, 1974.

Baca, Maria Elena. "Desperate Shoppers Not Laughing at Tickle Me Elmo," Minneapolis Star Tribune, p. 24, Dec. 10, 1996.

Bailey, Matthew. "Rich's Department Store," New Georgia Encyclopedia, georgiaencyclopedia.org, Nov. 17, 2005.

Baker, George L., and Steele, Ray. "$5 Million Blaze Guts Gemco Discount Store; Fireman Dies," Fresno Bee, p. 1, Oct. 26, 1970.

Baker, Henry G. Rich's of Atlanta: The Story of a Store Since 1867, University of Georgia, 1953.

"Bargain Town Is Now Toys 'R' Us!," Pleasant Valley Shopping, pleasantvalleyshopping.blogspot.com, June 15, 2008.

Barksdale, David C., and Sekula, Robyn Davis, New Albany in Vintage Postcards, Arcadia Publishing, Charleston, SC, 2005.

Barmash, Isadore. "Interstate Stores Tries Surgery for Survival," New York Times, nytimes.com, Aug. 3, 1974.

Barmash, Isadore. "Sears Net Rises 47.4% in Quarter," New York Times, nytimes.com, April 22, 1987.

Barnhouse, Mark A. Lost Department Stores of Denver, History Press, Charleston, SC, 2018.

Bass, Scott. "Mall Mystery," Style Weekly, styleweekly.com, July 21, 2004.

Battaglia, Danielle. "Tenant Loses 6-year Fight with Eden Landlord," Greensboro News & Record, godanriver.com, Nov. 23, 2016.

Bauder, Donald C. "Expanded Fedco Store to Open," San Diego Union-Tribune, nlnewsbank.com, April 4, 1984.

Beckerman, Jim. "With Sears in Bankruptcy, a Look through a 110-year-old Catalog from a Headier Era," New Jersey Record, northjersey.com, Oct. 17, 2018.

"Bertha L. Wilbur Used Charge Coin in Theft," Boston Globe, p. 32, Jan. 15, 1931.

Beutner, Jeff. "Schuster's Delivery Wagon, 1908," urbanmilwaukee.com, May 4, 2016.

Biddle, Frederic M. "Jordan's Brings Back Sweet Taste of Victorian Past," Boston Globe, p. 62, Nov. 23, 1990.

"Big Bear Stores Co. History," fundinguniverse.com.

"Big Bear: 386 W. Lane Ave.," columbusneighborhoods.org.

"Big Lots, Inc.," fundinguniverse.com.

"Big Retail Shopping Center in Framingham Previewed," Boston Globe, p. 15, June 6, 1951.

"Black Friday," Investopedia, investopedia.com.

Blackwell, John. "1951: American Dream Houses, All in a Row," Trentonian, capitalcentury.com.

"The Bon Marché, Inc. History," fundinguniverse.com.

"Borders Now Down to Its Last Few Days," Visalia Times-Delta, p. 1, July 20, 2011.

"Bored by Her Social Life; Mrs. Belmont Enters Trade," New York Daily News, p. 3, Aug. 14, 1924.

Boyle, Hal. "How to Get a $1,000,000 Idea," Lewiston (Maine) Evening Journal, p. 4, Dec. 15, 1951.

Bradbury, Ray. "The Aesthetics of Lostness" in Yestermorrow, Ray Bradbury Enterprises, 1991.

Bradbury, Ray. "The Pomegranate Architect," Paris Review, theparisreview.org, Jan. 29, 2015.

"Breathtaking Santa's Village Opens Monday at Jordan's," Boston Globe, p. 1, Nov. 4, 1959.

Brott, Tamar. "The Price Is Right, p. 42, Los Angeles Magazine, August 2000.

"Brownsville Store Shut Down," Valley Morning Star (Harlingen, Texas), p. 3, March 19, 1975.

Buckner, Lori D. "Play's the Thing at Indoor Escapes," Baltimore Sun, p. 107, Nov. 28, 1996.

"Buffums' Is Forced to Open Sundays by Competition" (ad), Long Beach Independent Press-Telegram, p. 3, Dec. 13, 1969.

"Buildings Then and Now: Think Strawbridge & Clothier First," pillyliving.com, Jan. 12, 2013.

"Bullock's Wilshire/Southwestern Law School," laconservancy.org.

"Burdines, Inc. History," fundinguniverse.com.

"Burlington: It's Not Called 'Coat Factory' Anymore for a Reason," youtube.com.

Burnes, Brian. "Katz Drug Co. of Kansas City: The Kings of Cut-Rate" (video), Oct. 24, 2011, youtube.com.

"Business Units Will Be Opened," Los Angeles Times, pt. V, p. 5, Nov. 17, 1929.

"Butler Bros.," Encyclopedia of Chicago, encyclopedia. chicagohistory.org.

"A Call Is Issued by the Ladies of the Red Cross to the Citizens of Atlanta," Atlanta Constitution, p. 14, May 23, 1917.

Cano, Debra. "Buena Park to Weigh Backing Fedco Move," Los Angeles Times, articles.latimes.com, Jan. 4, 1993.

"C.A. Penn and the Lucky Strike Brand," ncdcr.gov.

Caron, Christina. "The Mishaps and Milestones of the Macy's Thanksgiving Day Parade Balloons," New York Times, nytimes.com, Nov. 22, 2017.

Carroll, Gerald, and Hernandez, Luis. "Mervyns Closing All 149 of Its Stores," Visalia Times-Delta, p. 1, Oct. 18, 2008.

"Carson's History: Thru Its Builders' Eyes," Chicago Tribune, pt. 2, p. 48, Jan. 1, 1954.

Carter, Wilf. "Punkinhead (The Little Bear)," youtube.com.

"Changes Made after Shopping Death," Waterloo (Iowa) Courier, p. 21, Nov. 26, 2009.

"Chapter 4: The Fulton Mall," www.fresno.gov/mayor.

"Charleston Sit-Down Goes On Despite Threat," Greenville News, p. 10, April 2, 1960.

Chase, Al. "Chicago to Have World's First Windowless Department Store," Chicago Tribune, p. 26, May 20, 1934.

Childress, Tammy. "Bristol's Pickin' Porch and Mountain Music Museum Moving to Kingsport," Bristol Herald Courier, heraldcourier.com, Nov. 1, 2017.

"A Christmas Story House & Museum," christmasstoryhouse. com.

Clapp, Newell A. "Trading Stamps," Ohio State Law Journal 23, 1962.

Clemmons, Jeff. Rich's: A Southern Institution, History Press, Charleston, SC, 2012.

"The Clock Market, a Good Time to Buy a Porsche," beverlyhillsporsche.blogspot.com, Oct. 30, 2009.

Clough, Bethany. "Retail Therapy: Forever 21 Downsizes in Valley, Teen Stores Struggle," Fresno Bee, fresnobee.com, Feb. 20, 2016.

Clough, Bethany, and Sheehan, Tim. "Former Gottschalks CEO Joe Levy Dies at 82," Fresno Bee, fresnobee.com, Feb. 11, 2014.

"Cloverleaf Mall; Richmond Virginia," Labelscar, labelscar.com, Nov. 26, 2007.

Collins, Michael. "In 1960s, Knoxville Mayor John Duncan Sought to Defuse Racial Tensions," Knoxville News Sentinel, archive. knoxnews.com, June 17, 2013.

"Colonial Village," Philadelphia Inquirer Magazine, p. 29, Dec. 2, 1962.

Cooper, Patricia. "The Limits of Persuasion: Race Reformers and the Department Store Campaign in Philadelphia, 1945–1948," journals.psu.edu.

Coughlan, Anne T., and Soberman, David A. "A Survey of Outlet Mall Retailing: Past, Present, and Future," flora.insead.edu, 2004.

"Cowtown Underground (Part 1): 'All Aboard' the M&O Subway," Hometown by Handlebar, hometownbyhandlebar.com, Feb. 15, 2018.

Crawford, Margaret. "The World in a Shopping Mall," essay in Variations on a Theme Park, edited by Michael Sorkin, p. 14, Noonday Press, 1992.

Crockett, Zachary. "How a Basket on Wheels Revolutionized Grocery Shopping," Ben's Shares, tumblr.benjamintseng.com, Feb. 21, 2016.

Crum, John Burdine. "Burdine & Son—'The Bartow Store,'" Polk County Historical Quarterly, pp. 1–3, June 1996.

"CSS Industries, Inc. History," fundinguniverse.com.

"The Customer Is Always Right," Phrase Finder, phrases.org.uk.

Davis, Ennis. "May-Cohens: Jacksonville's Big Store," Metro Jacksonville, metrojacksonville.com, Nov. 21, 2011.

Davis, Melissa G., Lundman, Richard J., and Martinez, Ramiro Jr. "Private Corporate Justice: Store, Police, Shoplifters, and Civil Recovery," Social Problems, 38, no. 3, citeseerx.ist.psu.edu, Aug. 1991.

Davison, Benjamin. "Why the Supermarket Was Born in Los Angeles," zocalopublicsquare.org, Nov. 17, 2015.

"Dayton Hudson Corporation History," fundinguniverse.com.

"Dead Mall—Eden Mall—Carolina's Secret" (video), Ace's Adventures, youtube.com, Sept. 20, 2018.

"Dead Mall Stories," deadmalls.com.

"Death of a Sales Floor," Los Angeles Times letter to the editor from Barry J. Stone, p. C8, Aug. 8, 1999.

"Department Store Price War Spreads," Austin American-Statesman, p. 3, June 5, 1951.

"Department Store Profits Drop 21 Percent in 1947," Atlanta Constitution, p. 19, March 23, 1948.

"Department Stores Seek to Match Discounters," Atlanta Constitution, p. 7F, Aug. 18, 2002.

Dinneen, Joseph F. "25,000 at Ceremony Opening Shoppers' World," Boston Globe, p. 1, Oct. 4, 1951.

D'innocenzio, Anne. "Bargain Shoppers Fill Stores," Bismarck Tribune, p. 1, Nov. 27, 2004.

D'innocenzio, Anne. "Shoppers Out in Force, but Cautious," Sunbury (Pennsylvania) Daily Item, p. A2, Nov. 29, 2008.

Directory, shermanoaksgalleria.com.

"Discount Stores of the '60s," wtv-zone.com.

"Discount Store Will Be Built in Crystal," Minneapolis Star, p. 12, March 8, 1962.

"Discover McDonalds's" (ad), San Mateo (California) Times, p. 80, Jan. 20, 1968.

Doctorow, Cory. "Ray Bradbury's Original Concept Script for Epcot's Spaceship Earth," boingboing.net, June 7, 2012.

Dumay, Jan. "The Enduring Legacy of Katz Drug Stores," 435 Magazine, 435mag.com, Aug. 2014.

Dunn, Charles. "Tarrytown Mall," oldrockymount.pbworks.com, June 18, 2009.

"Economic Leaders Dedicate New Mall," Rocky Mount (North Carolina) Telegram, p. 13, Aug. 16, 1995.

"Eden Mall: Eden, NC," Sky City Retail History, skycity2blogspot.com, May 22, 2011.

Ellis, Donna. "Hutzler Brothers Company, 1784–1977," Maryland Historical Society, mdhs.org, July 1987.

Elsner, David M. "Startup Problems Vex May Discount Stores," Chicago Tribune, pt. 5, p. 6, Dec. 3, 1978.

Emond, Mark. "Trading Stamps Boosting Prices, Hearing Is Told," Casper Tribune-Herald, p. 2, Feb. 8, 1955.

"Enchanted Village Back at Jordan's on Monday," Boston Globe, p. 60, Nov. 17, 1963.

Ephross, Peter. "How Jews Both Segregated and Integrated Levittown," Baltimore Jewish Times, jewishtimes.com, Feb. 9, 2009.

"Erecting the World's Biggest Office Building," St. Louis Post-Dispatch Magazine, p. 5, Nov. 3, 1912.

Eschner, Kat. "The Bizarre Story of Piggly Wiggly, the First Self-Service Grocery Store," Esri and Geiling, Natasha. "The Death and Rebirth of the American Mall," smithsonianmag.com, Nov. 25, 2014.

Estes, Andrea. "A Farewell to the Muffin Man," Boston Globe, p. 17, Dec. 27, 2004.

Evans, Stephen. "The Death of the Department Store," news.bbc.co.uk, March 1, 2005.

"The Evolution of Retail Over the Last Century," mi9retail.com.

"Facts about Barr's," St. Louis Public School Library Bulletin, no. 12, Nov.–Dec., 1880.

"Fascinating Facts about Sylvan Goldman Inventor of the Shopping Cart," Great Idea Finder, ideafinder.com.

"Fedco Lives!," youtube.com.

"Fedco—SoCal's Store for Everything," L.A.'s Forgotten Treasures, furrywawordpress.com, May 27, 2013.

"Fedco Superstores," csulibrarywhatsnew.blogspot.com.

"Fedco to Have Grand Opening of Its New San Diego Store at 54th and Euclid Soon," Chula Vista (California) Star-News, p. 18, Oct. 24, 1957.

Ferguson, Don K. "Blue Laws Kept Local Stores Closed on Sundays," Knoxville News Sentinel, archive.knoxnews.com, Dec. 18, 2011.

FirstCarbon Solutions. "Initial Study of Fulton Mall Reconstruction Project," fresno.gov.

"First Service of Its Kind in the World!," Charga-Plate ad, Boston Globe, p. 18, March 10, 1934.

Flanagan, Neil. "When the Future Was Cleveland Park," tsarchitect.nsflanagan.net, Feb. 8, 2014.

"Fliers Hit Balloon, Plunge 5,000 Feet," New York Times, timesmachine.nytimes.com, Nov. 25, 1932.

Foran, Chris. "Schuster's Brings Parade to Town—in 1950," Milwaukee Journal Sentinel, archive.jsonline.com, Nov. 17, 2015.

Forgosh, Linda B. Louis Bamberger: Department Store Innovator and Philanthropist, pp. 93–96, Brandeis University Press, Waltham, Mass., 2016

"4 Million Stores Are Okayed by Planners," Fresno Bee, p. 1, Jan. 16, 1970.

"4th Target Store Opens Monday," Minneapolis Star, p. 10B, Oct. 25, 1962.

Francis, Patt. "Rockville Closing Like Losing Old Friend," Greenfield (Massachusetts) Recorder, Sept. 12, 1972.

"Fresno Area," groceteria.com, Feb. 2, 2009.

"Fresno, California . . . A 1968 Documentary and How Fulton Mall Came to Be," www.youtube.com/watch?v=eR_ZGop3UFw.

"Gas Bomb Tossed in B'ham Store," Alabama Journal, p. 1, Aug. 15, 1963.

Gatch, Loren. "Local Money in the United States During the Great Depression," ebhsoc.org.

"Gemco Building New Store in San Leandro," Oakland Tribune, p. 17, July 24, 1966.

"Gemco Buys Site for Store," Los Angeles Times, p. J19, Nov. 10, 1963.

"Gemco Goal Is New Store by Easter," Fresno Bee, p. 37, Oct. 30, 1970.

Gellene, Denise. "Lucky to Close Gemco, Sell Most Stores to Dayton Hudson," Los Angeles Times, articles.latimes.com, Oct. 10, 1986.

Geneen, Paul. Schuster's and Gimbels: Milwaukee's Beloved Department Stores, History Press, Charleston, SC, 2012.

Gilmore, Paul. "Building Markets, Inside and Out: Supermarket Foundations in Urban America, 1916–1941" (unpublished dissertation).

Gilmore, Paul. "Remodeling Markets: Independent Grocers and the Anti-Chain Store Movement in the 1930s" (unpublished dissertation).

Gilpin, Kenneth N. "G. Stockton Strawbridge, 83, Dies; Retail Industry Executive," New York Times, nytimes.com, Feb. 11, 1997.

Gilpin, Kenneth N. "TJX Will Buy Marshalls Chain from Melville," New York Times, nytimes.com, Oct. 17, 1995.

Gladwell, Malcolm. "The Terrazzo Jungle," New Yorker, newyorker.com, March 15, 2004.

"Globman's," mhchistoricalsociety.org, Oct. 6, 2009.

Gnerre, Sam. "Old Towne Mall," South Bay Daily Breeze, blogs.dailybreeze.com, May 25, 2011.

Gnerre, Sam. "Piggly Wiggly Grocery Chain Had South Bay Locations," South Bay Daily Breeze, dailybreeze.com, May 31, 2014.

Goldberger, Paul. "In Downtown San Diego, a Freewheeling Fantasy," New York Times, nytimes.com, March 19, 1986.

"Goldie Mabowehz (Golda Meir), from the Milwaukee Public Library to Prime Minister of Israel," Milwaukee Public Library, mpl.org, March 15, 2017.

Goldman, Abigail. "Hundreds of Stores to Get Different Name—Macy's," Los Angeles Times, articles.latimes.com, Sept. 8, 2006.

"Goldwaters," Department Store Museum, thedepartmentstoremuseum.org, Feb. 2012.

Goodman, David. The European Cities and Technology Reader, Routledge, London, 1999.

Gordon, Andrea. "77-year-old Yuletide Tradition Victim of Economic Hard Times," Edmonton Journal, p. C7, Aug. 10, 1982.

"The Gorin Building," Bouseblog: Local History from Somerville, Mass., bouseblog.wordpress.com.

"Gottschalks Chain Files Chapter 11," Palm Springs Desert Sun, p. B1, Jan. 31, 2009.

"Gottschalks, Inc. History," fundinguniverse.com.

"Gottschalk's Names New Store Aides," Fresno Bee, p. 24, Sept. 8, 1970.

"Gottshalks Will Make November Debut in Clovis," sandiegouniontribune.com, April 27, 2010.

Green, David B. "The Man Who Figured Out What You Really Want Dies," Haaretz, haaretz.com, June 5, 2015.

Greenpoints.com.

Griswold, Alison. "You Could Buy Anything from the Sears Catalog—Even a House," Quartz, qz.com, Oct. 20, 2018.

"Grocery and Supermarket," Ad Age, Sept. 15, 2003.

Groves, Martha. "The Broadway: Bright History, Uncertain Future," Los Angeles Times, articles.latimes.com, Feb. 12, 1991.

Grunt, Doomie. "A Visit to Eden Mall" (video), youtube.com, June 18, 2017.

Gutierrez, Lisa. "Attention, Kmart Shoppers, Code Blue Returns to the Aisles," Des Moines Register, p. 2E, April 9, 2001.

Halberstam, David. The Fifties, Random House, New York, 1993.

Hall, Beverly Y. "Sears to Try Out 'Discover' Credit Card Here," Atlanta Constitution, p. C1, April 25, 1985.

Handy, Shannon. "Once a Downtown San Diego Star, Horton Plaza Is Fading Fast," cbs8.com, May 2, 2018.

"Haves Battle the Have Nots," Rocky Mount (North Carolina) Telegram, p. 5, Oct. 30, 1981.

Hawley, Chris. "You Need a Bulletproof Vest," Anniston (Alabama) Star, p. 2, Nov. 27, 2011.

Hesser, Fran. "3 Warehouse Outlets Set for Atlanta," Atlanta Constitution, p. B1, May 16, 1984.

"Historical Perspective: Downtown Fresno Gottschalks store," Fresno Bee, March 26, 2012.

Hix, Lisa. "From Retail Palace to Zombie Mall: How Efficiency Killed the Department Store," Collectors Weekly, collectorsweekly.com, May 5, 2014.

Hogan, Bill. "Washington's Merchant Prince," billhogan.com, Sept. 1981.

Holecek, Andrea. "Carson's Fate Shocks State Street," p. D1, Munster (Indiana) Times, Aug. 26, 2006.

Hoover, Will. "Attention, Hawaii: Your First 'Blue-Light' Specials," Honolulu Advertiser, p. 1B, Oct. 14, 1992.

Howard, Vicki. From Main Street to Mall, University of Pennsylvania Press, 2015.

Howard, Vicki. "The Rise and Fall of Sears," smithsonianmag.org, July 25, 2017.

Huard, Ray. "Horton Plaza Sold," San Diego Business Journal, sdbj.com, Aug. 26, 2018.

"Hudson's," Department Store Museum, thedepartmentstoremuseum.org.

Huffman, E.S. "How 'Tickle Me Elmo' Caused Holiday Hysteria Back in 1996," Uproxx, uproxx.com, Dec. 16, 2015.

Hyman, Louis. "Consumption and Undermining White Supremacy" (video), youtube.com.

"In the Matter of the Sperry and Hutchison Company," court decision, June 26, 1968, ftc.gov.

"Introducing the Modern Credit Card," about.bankofamerica.com.

"ITG Brands Moving Tobacco Production from Reidsville to Greensboro," News & Observer, greensboro.com, Nov. 1, 2018.

"Ivey's Department Store," Brumley.com/tour/history/iveys.htm.

"'Jail Instead of Bail' Says Rev. M.L. King," Gettysburg (Pennsylvania) Times, p. 11, Oct. 21, 1960.

"Jews and Department Stores," citycongregation.org, April 26, 2015.

"JG Industries, Inc. History," findinguniverse.com.

"Jitney-Jungle Stores of America, Inc. History," fundinguniverse. com.

"J.L. Hudson Department Store," Controlled Demolition, Inc., controlled-demolition.com.

"J.M. McDonald Foundation History," jmmcdonaldfoundation. org.

Johnson, Steven. "The Strange, Surprisingly Radical Roots of the Shopping Mall," ideas.ted.com, Nov. 29, 2016.

"Jordan Marsh Blueberry Muffins," Yankee Magazine, newengland.com, Sept. 6, 2018.

"Jordan's to Keep Enchanted Village Open Extra Week," Boston Globe, p. 19, Dec. 11, 1959.

"Joseph Horne Co.," ad, Pittsburgh Press, p. 11, Oct. 29, 1935.

"Just Tickled," People Magazine, people.com, Jan. 13, 1997.

Kappler, Olivia. "Kaufmann's Clock: The History of Downtown's Iconic Timepiece," pittsburghmagazine.com, Sept. 20, 2017.

"Katz Discount City Presents Flapper the Million Dollar Dolphin" (ad), Springfield Leader and Press, p. 5, Sept. 26, 1970.

"Katz Firm Opens Largest Store Here," Springfield News-Leader, p. 19, Dec. 7, 1961.

"Katz in the Cradle," KC History, kchistory.org.

"Katz Store Opening Thursday," Des Moines Register, p. 15, March 17, 1957.

Kelly, Brian J. "8,000 Pieces of Furniture Needed," Edmonton Journal, p. C5, Dec. 22, 1983.

Kelly, Jacques. "Shopping in Fells Point at Hecht's Reliable Store," Baltimore Sun, articles.baltimoresun.com, Aug. 27, 2010.

Kelly, Kate. "Who Invented the Shopping Cart?," America Comes Alive!, americacomesalive.com.

Khouri, Andrew. "Westfield Proposes $1.5-billion Mixed-use Complex at Site of Aging Warner Center Mall," Oct. 17, 2016, latimes.com.

Kiester, Ed. "Is This the City of Tomorrow?," St. Louis Post-Dispatch, p. 198, Aug. 12, 1956.

Kindervater, David. "The Romantic Story Behind Kaufmann's Clock in Pittsburgh, PA," theculturetrip.com, Feb. 12, 2018.

"King Kullen Grocery Co., Inc. History," fundinguniverse.com.

Kinney, Jim. "Murray Candib Invented the Discount Department Store with King's in Springfield," Mass Live, masslive.com, June 24, 2013.

Kleiner, Richard. "Country Tycoon Claims Largest Food Market under One Roof," Jackson Sun, p. 7, July 30, 1951.

Kleinfield, N.R. "Woolworth Calls It Quits on Woolco," New York Times, nytimes.com, Sept. 25, 1982.

Kmart ad, Port Huron (Michigan) Times Herald, p. 10, July 11, 1969.

"Kmart Chef Restaurants," Retroist, retroist.com, June 23, 2011.

"Kmart Corporation," encyclopedia.com.

"Kmart to Buy Membership Stores," Lincoln Star, p. 25, Oct. 19, 1989.

"Knox Sit-Ins to Continue Say Negroes," Kingsport (Tennessee) Times, p. 1, June 28, 1960.

"Korvette's Closes Its Last 17 Stores," New York Times, p. D3, Dec. 30, 1980.

Krieg, Katherine. Sam Walton: Founder of the Walmart Empire, ABDO Publishing, North Mankato, MN, 2014.

Kropo, M.R. "FBI: Heist Linked to Black Friday Loot," Springfield (Ohio) News-Sun, p. 16, Dec. 4, 2007.

"Kuhn's Big K Stores Plans Wal-Mart Tie," New York Times, nytimes.com, June 23, 1981.

Kurutz, Steven. "An Ode to Shopping Malls," New York Times, nytimes.com, July 26, 2017.

Lambert, Bruce. "At 50, Levittown Contends with Its Legacy of Bias," New York Times, nytimes.com, Dec. 28, 1997.

Lambert, Cynthia, and Wilson, Nick. "Forever 21 in San Luis Obispo to Close after Holidays," San Luis Obispo Tribune, sanluisobispo.com, Nov. 16, 2015.

LaSalle, Mick. "The True Titanic Love Story," San Francisco Chronicle, sfgate.com, July 23, 2000.

Last Dime Store Shutting Down," Albuquerque Journal, p. D4, Nov. 30, 2001.

"Leasks, the Department Store," leask.co.uk.

Leeright, Bob. "Legislature Puts Okay on 254 Bills," Casper Star-Tribune, p. 1, Feb. 21, 1955.

Lefler, Jack. "Big Department Store Chains to Enter Discount Field," Hagerstown (Maryland) Daily Mail, p. 5, June 6, 1961.

"Le Gran Corp., L.B., Continues Growth," Long Beach Press-Telegram, p. B-4, Nov. 8, 1969.

"Leonard's Department Store: A Buy-Gone Era," Hometown by Handlebar, hometownbyhandlebar.com, Aug. 26, 2018.

"Let's Go Fedco!" (ad), Chula Vista (California) Star-News, p. 5, Oct. 24, 1957.

Levine, Alexandra S. "New York Today: Welcome Back, Felix," New York Times, nytimes.com, Nov. 22, 2016.

"Levitt Communities," levittownbeyond.com.

"L'Histoire du Bon Marché," 24sevres.com.

Lindt, John. "Visalia Sears to Be Cut in Half, Empty Sport Chalet Will Be Filled Soon," Visalia Times-Delta, Aug. 22, 2018.

Lisicky, Michael J. Filene's: Boston's Great Specialty Store, Arcadia Publishing, Charleston, SC, 2012.

Lisicky, Michael J. Hutzler's: Where Baltimore Shops, History Press, Charleston, SC, 2009.

Lisicky, Michael J. Remembering Maas Brothers, Arcadia Publishing, Charleston, SC, 2005.

Lisicky, Michael J. Woodward & Lothrop: A Store Worthy of the Nation's Capital, History Press, Charleston, SC, 2005.

Livingston, Mike. "Past Is Present D.C. Buildings with a History," Washington Business Journal, bizjournals.com, April 13, 1998.

Lloyd, Paula. "Ask Me: Coffee's Store Was an 82-Year Fresno Landmark," fresnobee.com, Jan. 8, 2016.

Long, Tom. "Max Coffman, 95; Delivery Boy Became Store Tycoon," Boston Globe, July 1, 2005.

"A Look Back at the Salem Mall," daytondailynews.com."Lord & Taylor Historical Timeline," Hudson's Bay Company History Foundation, hbcheritage.ca.

Lucas, Laurie. "Forever 21 Opens in old Borders Location," Riverside Press-Enterprise, pe.com, Aug. 12, 2013.

"Lucky Stores Buys Gemco in Anaheim," Long Beach Press-Telegram, p. 7, Jan. 1, 1961.

Lugibihl, Jaime. "Rebuilding of Former TG&Y Store Underway," houmatoday.com, Jan. 7, 2001.

MacDonald, Jay. "Layaway Makes a Comeback," Smart Money, bankrate.com, Nov. 9, 2009.

"Macy Christmas Parade Big Thanksgiving Day Feature," Central New Jersey Home News, p. 9, Nov. 26, 1924.

"Made a Holiday," Boston Globe, p. 6, Sept. 4, 1912.

"Manchester Center," Mall Hall of Fame, mall-hall-of-fame.blogspot.com.

Maney, R.D. "Round Town with the Tribune," Tipton (Indiana) Daily Tribune, p. 2, May 13, 1950.

"Man Jumps to Death from Horton Plaza," Los Angeles Times, articles.latimes.com, Nov. 2, 1985.

"Marchitecture: Architecture Past and Present at the Merchandise Mart," merchandisemart.com/marchitecture.

Martin, Danielle A. "Boom Goes Business in Tulare County," Visalia Times-Delta, April 21, 2017.

Martin, Douglas. "Eugene Ferkauf, 91, Dies; Restyled Retail," New York Times, nytimes.com, June 6, 2012.

Martin, Edward. "Eden's Tough Transition as MillerCoors Departs," Business North Carolina, businessnc.com.

"Martin Luther King, 35 Others Jailed," Louisville Courier-Journal, p. 8, Oct. 20, 1960.

Masters, Nathan. "When Hollywood Boulevard Became Santa Claus Lane," Lost LA, kcet.org, Dec. 20, 2012.

Mastrangelo, Joseph P. "Green Stampede: The Redeeming History of Trading Stamps," Washington Post, washingtonpost.com, Jan. 22, 1980.

"Matchless Memories of Mammoth Mart," Pleasant Valley Shopping, pleasantfamilyshopping.blogspot.com, March 13, 2009.

"Max Coffman, Discount Chain Owner" (obituary), Washington Post, washingtonpost.com.

"Max Kohl," nndb.com.

"The May Department Stores Company," Lehmann Brothers Collection, library.hbs.edu.

McCarthy, Erin. "16 Fun Facts About the Macy's Thanksgiving Day Parade," mentalfloss.com, Nov. 21, 2017.

McClellan, Lila. "A Viral Twitter Thread Revealed Sears's History as Disruptor of Jim Crow-era Racism," Quartz at Work, qz.com, Oct. 16, 2018.

"Melton, Mary. "A Brief History of the Mini-Mall," Los Angeles Times Magazine, pp. 26-28, Nov. 16, 1997.

"Men! A Shirt Sensation!" (Bloomingdale's ad), New York Daily News, p. 7, Dec. 1, 1935.

"Men Join Rush to Bargains As Price War Spreads West," Tampa Tribune, p. 6, June 3, 1951.

"Mervyn's," amesfanclub.com.Michel, Claire. "Wanamaker's Department Store: Wanamaker's—Philadelphia's Largest Department Store," philaplace.org.

Mikolay, Anne. "The Pink Christmas Piggy," ahherald.com, Dec. 14, 2013.

Milford, Maureen. "Upper Floors of Philadelphia Store to Become Offices," New York Times, nywtimes.com, April 7, 2002.

Millville (New Jersey) Daily, p. 4, Aug. 8, 1947.

Mimes, Cynthia. "Nichols' Folly," Retail Traffic, retailtrafficmag.com, Feb. 13, 2012.

Moffatt, Susan. "Bullock's Wilshire Closes Doors Today," Los Angeles Times, articles.latimes.com, April 13, 1993.

Moore, Joe, and Balch, Elliott. "The (Broken) Heart of Our City: A Fulton Mall Timeline," fresno.gov/mayor.

Morales, Melinda. "Crafts Store Set for Former Mervyn's Spot," Visalia Times-Delta, p. 1, Aug. 14, 2018.

Morales, Melinda. "Kohl's, Ross Coming in Spring," Visalia Times-Delta, p. C1, Jan. 7, 2004.

"M. Rich Brothers and Company Complete Great Department Store," Atlanta Constitution, p. 8B, April 28, 1907.

"Mr Isidor Straus," Encyclopedia Titanica, encyclopedia-titanica.org.

"Mrs Leila Meyer," Encyclopedia Titanica, encyclopedia-titanica.org.

"Mrs. Straus Refused to Board a Lifeboat, Instead Choosing to Die by Her Husband's Side," titanicstory.wordpress.com.

Muir, Frederick M. "Price Co. Ties Its Success to Low Prices: 9-Year-Old Retailing Giant Nearly Doubled Earnings Each Year," Los Angeles Times, articles.latimes.com, March 11, 1985.Mullen, Perry. "Negro Sit-ins Spread Quickly Through South," Alton (Illinois) Evening Telegraph, p. 2. April 28, 1960.

Mullen, Perry. "Sit-ins May Be Result of White Boys' Trick," Alton (Illinois) Evening Telegraph, p. 2, April 26, 1960.

"Negro Students Are Returning to College Classes," Greeley (Colorado) Daily Tribune, p. 10, April 2, 1960.

Nevarez, Joe R. "Paramount Profits in Sharp Turnaround," Los Angeles Times, pt. II, p, 8, Nov. 16, 1963.

"New Gemco Unit," Los Angeles Times, pt. III, p. 13, Jan. 9, 1963.

"New Gorin's to Feature Low Prices," Boston Globe, p. 28A, Sept. 30, 1951.

"New Gourmet Center a Place to Give Taste Buds a Treat," Boston Globe, p. 25, Dec. 30, 1962.

"New Katz Store to Open Friday," Des Moines Register, p. 3-A, Nov. 23, 1952.

Newman, Bill. "Two Guys from Harrison," Old Newark Memories, oldnewark.com.

"New Self-Service-Plan Groceries Open," Atlanta Constitution, p. 4, Sept. 4, 1924.

"New Sharaf's Restaurant Serves Area," Boston Globe, p. A32, Sept. 30, 1951.

Nilsson, Jeff. "Woolworth: A Five and Dime Story," saturdayeveningpost.com, Feb. 22, 1879.

"No Trading Stamp Prices Here" (J.N. Adam & Co. ad), Buffalo Evening News, p. 12, Jan. 20, 1915.

"Norfolk Stores End Lunch Bias," Bridgeport (Connecticut) Telegram, July 26, 1960.

"Northland Center," Mall Hall of Fame, mall-hall-of-fame. blogspot.com.

Nutt, Amy Ellis. "Elizabeth Fire Claims a Storied Building," Star-Ledger (Newark), nj.com, Dec. 25, 2011.

O'Connell, Rebecca. "Remembering Keedoozle, America's First Fully Automated Grocery Store," mentalfloss.com.

"Off the Ticker," Billboard Magazine, p. 7, Jan. 11, 1975.

O'Loughlin, Kathy. "History: Leading the Way in Architecture and Retail; Strawbridge & Clothier," Main Line Media News, mainlinemedianews.com, Jan. 25, 2013.

"Old Towne Mall Will Make Shopping Fun," Los Angeles Times, p. L1, June 11, 1972.

"Opening!!," Woodward, Lothrop & Cochrane ad, National Republic (Washington, DC), p. 4, Feb. 26, 1880.

"Our Departments," tuesdaymorning.com.

Overall, Michael. "40 Years Later, Tulsa Remembers Worse Tornado in City's History," Tulsa World, tulsaworld.com, June 1, 2014.

Owen, Ryan W. "Remembering Downtown Lowell's Bon Marché Through the Years, 1878–1976," forgottennteengland.com.

"Pace Membership Warehouse," pacemembershipwarehouse.com.

Page, Ronald D. "Uptown Hackensack Giants Teamed In Two Sales," Bergen (New Jersey) Evening Record, p. 32, April 29, 1959.

"Parcel Post," United States Postal Service, about.usps.com.

Parmley, Suzette. "Macy's Prepares to Close a Store," Philadelphia Inquirer, p. A5, Jan. 9, 2016.

Patches, Matt. "Inside Walt Disney's Ambitious, Failed Plan to Build the City of Tomorrow," Esquire, esquire.com, May 20, 2015.

"Patrick-Henry Mall: Martinsville, VA," Sky City Retail History, skycity2.blogspot.com, Nov. 4, 2012.

Peirce, Neal R. "The Shopping Center and One Man's Shame," Los Angeles Times, pt. IV, p. 5, Oct. 22, 1978.

Penfold, Steve. "The Eaton's Santa Claus Parade and the Making of a Metropolitan Spectacle, 1905–1982," Social History 44, no. 87, May 2011.

"Penney Store Opens Today at Martinsville," Danville (Virginia) Bee, p. 3, Jan. 6, 1966.

"Pennrose Mall," lexingtonco.com.

"Pennrose Mall: Reidsville, NC," Sky City Retail History, skycity2. blogspot.com, Aug. 11, 2011.

Peters, Bill, and Prager, Mike. "Window Displays Bring Historic Holiday Spirit of the Crescent Store to Downtown Spokane," Spokesman- Review, spokesman.com, Dec. 14, 2017.

"Petersburg, Virginia," Encyclopedia of Southern Jewish Communities, isjl.org.

Peterson, Hayley. "Wal-Mart Founder: 'Most Everything I've Done I've Copied from Someone Else," Business Insider, businessinsider.com, Dec. 16, 2014.

Pitz, Marilyn. "The Kaufmann Legacy," newsinteractive.post-gazette.com.

Plainfield (New Jersey) Courier-News, ads, p. 4, April 7, 1905.

"Plan $1,000,000 pile," Chicago Tribune, p. 13, May 28, 1898.

Polunsky, Ann. "Goldwater's Fine Department Store," Arizona Jewish Life, azjewishlife.com.

Popular Mechanics, classifieds, p. 65, December 1948.

"Price Club Offers Discounts for 'Middle' Businessmen," Chula Vista (California) Star-News, p. 16, Oct. 7, 1976.

Price, Robert E. "Sol Price: Retail Revolutionary the FedMart Years—1954 to 1975," sandiegohistory.org.

Provost, Stephen H. Fresno Growing Up: A City Comes of Age, 1945–1985, pp. 26, 43, Craven Street Books, Fresno, Calif., 2015.

"Public Is Invited to Dedication of TG&Y Complex," Shreveport Times, p. 2-F, Oct. 13, 1968.

"Punkinhead—Santa's Very Special Little Bear," Ontario Ministry of Government and Consumer Services, archives.gov.on.ca.

"The Queerest Grocery in the World May Be the Memphis 'Piggly Wiggly,'" Topeka Merchants Journal, p. 6, Oct. 7, 1916.

"Railway Exchange Building," National Register of Historic Places, dnr.mo.gov, Oct. 1990.

"Ralphs Grocery Company History," fundinguniverse.com.

"Ralphs' Pasadena Store Plans Ready," Los Angeles Times, pt. V, p. 8, April 28, 1929.

Rappoport, John. "Criminal Justice, Inc.," Chicago Unbound, University of Chicago Law School, chicagounbound.uchicago.edu, 2017.

Rasmussen, Cecilia. "Hollywood Christmas Tradition Still on Parade," Los Angeles Times, articles.latimes.com, Nov. 26, 2006.

Rasmussen, Cecilia. "Much Was in Store for 2 Family Enterprises," Los Angeles Times, articles.latimes.com, Oct. 19, 2003.

Raucher, Alan R. "Dime Store Chains: The Making of Organization Men," Business History Review 65, no. 1, Small Business and Its Rivals, pp. 130–163, Spring 1991, Harvard College.

"Retailer Bought Its Own Plant to Satisfy L.A. Craving for Ice Cream," Los Angeles Times, pt. 1-A, p. 4, June 7, 1989.

"Retail History: Mammoth Mart, One of the First Discount Stores," retailhellunderground.com.

"Retailing Legend Born with Blue-Light Special," El Paso Times, p. 2E, March 1, 1992.

"Retail Price War Spreads Over U.S.," Great Falls Tribune, p. 1, June 6, 1951.

"Return Trip: Does Anyone Remember the Akron Store?," mymarthasandme.blogspot.com, Aug. 18, 2010.

"Rex Trailer at the Enchanted Village," youtube.com.

"Rich Delivery Wagons to Collect Clothing," Atlanta Constitution, p. 10, May 24, 1917.

Rich, Stuart U., and Portis, Bernard D. "The 'Imageries' of Department Stores," Journal of Marketing 28, no. 2, pp. 10–15, April 1964.

Riddell, Mary. "Spend! Spend! Spend!" New Statesman, Dec. 20, 1996, questia.com.

"Riot Aftermath," Los Angeles Times, articles.latimes.com, May 7, 1992.

"Riot for Trading Stamps," Chicago Tribune, p. 3, April 21, 1905.

Rivera, Nancy. "Firm Bets on 'Superstores' in Southland: Circuit City to Push Electronics Products at 15 New Outlets," Los Angeles Times, articles.latimes.com, Oct. 21, 1985.

Robb, Inez. "Price War Grows in New York," Minneapolis Star Tribune, p. 1, June 1, 1951.

"Robert Diggs Gorham Jr. Obituary," Rocky Mount Telegram, legacy.com, April 1, 2009.

"Robinson's California," Department Store Museum, thedepartmentstoremuseum.com, Feb. 2012.

"Rocky Mount Residents Ready to Say Good-Bye to Tarrytown Mall," wral.com, March 2, 2006.

Rose, Lisa. "Gone but Not Forgotten, a Time When Thanksgiving Day Parades Graced Newark," nj.com, Nov. 23, 2011.

"Ross Stores, Inc. History," fundinguniverse.com.

Rothbardt, Helen. "Lits Is a Youngsters' Delight," Philadelphia Inquirer, p. 39, Dec. 16, 1966.

Rowe, Peter. "Horton Plaza: From Remarkable Vision to Troubled Reality," sandiegouniontribune.com, Jan. 20, 2017.

Ruch, John. "Macy's Pink Pig Ride Returns to Lenox Square Mall Nov. 3," Reporter Newspapers, reporternewspapers.net, Oct. 25, 2018.

"Rudolph the Red-Nosed Reindeer," Snopes, webcitation.org.

Russell, John. "Kent Man Basks in Blue Light of Fame," Akron Beacon Journal, p. 1, April 14, 2001.

Ruth, Brooke. "Taco Trucks Told to Hit the Road or Pay a Fine," Daily Bruin, dailybruin.com, May 5, 2008.

Rylah, Juliet Bennett. "Once a Luxury Department Store, The Bullocks Wilshire Opens for a Public Tour This Month," laist.com, July 12, 2016.

"Safeway History," groceteria.com, Jan. 13, 2009.

Sansone, Gina. "Stores of Yesteryear—TG&Y," Gtownma's Genealogy, gtownma.wordpress.com, Aug. 19, 2008.

"Santa Claus Comes to Eaton's Saturday," Winnipeg Evening Tribune, p. 36, Nov. 15, 1929.

"Santa Claus Comes to Eaton's Saturday," Edmonton Journal, p. 34, Nov. 22, 1929.

"Santa Claus Lane Parade," Bruce Torrence Hollywood Photograph Collection, hollywoodphotographs.com.

Satterthwaite, Ann. "Going Shopping: Consumer Choices and Community Consequences," Yale University, 2001.

Saulny, Susan. "Woman Hurt in '97 Macy's Parade Settles Suit," New York Times, nytimes.com, March 7, 2001.

Scharoun. Lisa. "America at the Mall," p. 39, McFarland & Company, Inc., Jefferson, NC, 2012.

Schoen, John W., Thomas, Lauren, and Hirsch, Lauren. "This Map Shows All the Locations Sears Once Operated and What It Has Left Today," cnbc.com, Oct. 15, 2018.

Scovil, Lindsay. "The Story of Houston: Foley's Department Stores," localhoustonmagazine.com.

Sears 1918 catalog, University of Illinois at Urbana-Champaign, babel.hathitrust.org.

Sederberg, Arelo. "BankAmericard Service to Be Offered Other California Banks," Los Angeles Times, pt. III, p. 9, June 27, 1967.

Shanahan, Eileen. "'Fair Trade' Laws Coming to an End," New York Times, nytimes.com, Dec. 13, 1975.

Shaneen, Salem K. "Supermarkets" (thesis), Massachusetts Institute of Technology, dspace.mit.edu, Aug. 18, 1952.

Sheehan, Tim. "Chinese Firm Drops Gottschalks," Fresno Bee, Dec. 19, 2008.

Shiver, Jube. "A Short in Electronics Market: Federated Is the Latest to Trip Up, as Retailers Are Finding They Have No Hot Gadgets to Lure Consumers into Stores," Los Angeles Times, articles.latimes.com, March 13, 1989.

"Shoppers Fair Discount House Doors Open Tomorrow," Battle Creek (Michigan) Enquirer and News, pt. 3, p. 6, May 22, 1962.

"Shoppers Tend to Drop Off as Names Disappear," Chicago Tribune, pt. 5, p. 4, Aug. 13, 2006.

"Shoppers' World Facts and Figures," Boston Globe, p. 34, Oct. 3, 1951.

"Shopping Trips to Factory Outlet Stores Prove Popular," Shamokin (Pennsylvania) News-Item, p. 18, April 10, 1974.

"A Short History of the G.C. Murphy Co," gcmurphy.org, Sept. 10, 2014.

Smartt, Elizabeth Thalhimer. "Thalhimers Department Store: Story, History, and Theory," Virginia Commonwealth University thesis, scholarscompass.vcu.edu, 2005.

Smith, Eric. "Friday: Enchanted Colonial Village Opens @ the Please Touch Museum," uwishunu.com, Nov. 16, 2009.

Snyder, Jesse. "No New Cars, but That Didn't Stop U.S. Automakers, Dealers during WWII," Automotive News, autonews.com, Oct. 31, 2011.

"Sol Price: Founder of Costco," anbhf.org.

Sorkin, Ross, and Rozhon, Tracie. "2 Big Retailers Agree to Merge for About $11 Billion," New York Times, nytimes.com, Feb. 28, 2005.

Sosin, Milt. "Police Bar Burdine's Sitdown," Miami News, p. 1, March 4, 1960.

"Sprouse-Reitz Seeks Buyer, Focuses on Market Niche," upi.com, June 15, 1990.

Srivastava, Jyoti. "Tiffany Dome at Marshall Field's," chicago-architecture-jyoti.blogspot.com, Jan. 2, 2009.

"Stars Cement Friendship with White Front at Gala Opening," San Francisco Examiner, p. W-2, Oct. 17, 1968.

Stein, Alan J. "Bellevue Square Opens on August 20, 1946," historylink.org, Feb. 15, 2003.

Sterling, Charles. "Ground Broken for Akron Store in Pasadena," Pasadena Independent Star-News, p. 3, Feb. 18, 1967.

"Store Redesign, Space Increase to Cost $70,000," Los Angeles Times, pt. V, p. 7, Aug. 9, 1953.

"Store Repeats Past History," Los Angeles Times, p. 28, Sept. 3, 1934.

Strauss, Robert. "$2 Billion Later," New York Times, nytimes.com, Feb. 5, 2006.

Street, John G. "Price Maintenance as Affected by the Schwegmann Decision," 6 Sw L.J. 117, 1952.

Stuart, Mark A. "Frank Packard," Hackensack Record, p. C-18, April 22, 1981.

"A Surprise Visit to Katz City," Pleasant Family Shopping, pleasantfamilyshopping.blogspot.com, Jan. 23, 2011.

Sylvia R., fieldsfanschicago.org, Dec. 12, 2008.

Tabler, Dave. "First RFD Mail Delivery in America," appalachianhistory.net, Oct. 1, 2018.

"Target through the Years," corporate.target.com.

"Target to Open at 6 p.m. on Thanksgiving Day," Chippewa (Wisconsin) Herald-Telegram, p. 5, Nov. 10, 2015.

Taylor-Blake, Bonnie. "'Black Friday' (Day after Thanksgiving), 1951," listserv.linguistlist.org.

Thebault, Reis. "Fresno's Mason-Dixon Line," Atlantic, theatlantic.com, Aug. 20, 2018.

"3rd Largest Drug Chain Formed by Katz, Skaggs," Springfield News-Leader, p. 36, Dec. 31, 1970.

"The 300 Block of Gay Street, West Side—The Gaps of Gay Street Part 5," Knoxville Lost and Found, knoxvillelostandfound.com, Oct. 5, 2017.

"Thrifty Buys Ice Cream Plant for Own Production," Los Angeles Times, pt. V, p. 3, Sept. 22, 1940.

Tinsley, Jesse. "Then and Now: Bernards and Zukor's," Spokesman-Review, spokesman.com, Jan. 1, 2018.

Tomkins-Walsh, Teresa. "Remembering Foley's," houstonhistorymagazine.org, March 21-Sept. 21, 2011.

Toone, Stephanie. "Five Reasons Atlantans Love Macy's Pink Pig," Atlanta Journal-Constitution, ajc.com, Nov. 1, 2017.

"Topeka Grocer Visits Piggly Wiggly but Is Not Allowed to Take a Snap Shot," Topeka Merchants Journal, p. 6, Oct. 21, 1916.

"Torched, Looted Fedco Store Reopens," Los Angeles Times, articles.latimes.com, May 22, 1992.

"Tornadoes Strike Houma," Shreveport Times, p. 5B, March 16, 2000.

"Toy Cat Expires in Blaze," New York Times, timesmachine.nytimes.com, Dec. 3, 1931.

Trimble, Marshall. "The Bisbee Massacre," True West, truewestmagazine.com, July 11, 2016.

"2 Producers Send Ultimatums to Macy's in Price-War Battle," Baltimore Sun, p. 1, June 2, 1951.

Uchalid, Michael J. "Throwback Thursday: Do You Remember Mammoth Mart?," mynewsroundup.com, Oct. 23, 2014.

"Under New Management," Eden Mall Business Center, shoprockinghamcounty.com/edenmall (cached), Sept. 29, 2018.

Usdansky, Margaret L. "Kmart Gives Green Light to Inventor of 'Blue Light Special' Game," Atlanta Constitution, p. 2E, Dec. 27, 1988.

Velez, Alexis. "Do You Remember Zayres," "The Walmart Digital Museum," walmartmuseum.auth.cap-hosting.com.

Vestergaard, Frank, and Pett, Gina. "Frank Packard, Pioneer Retailer of Hackensack," Hackensack Record, p. A-10, April 14, 1981.

"The Village of Oak Lawn 100 Year Anniversary 1909–2009," olpl.org/documents/OakLawn100thBooklet2009.pdf.

"Virginia's Seven Corners Center," Mall Hall of Fame, mall-hall-of-fame.blogspot.com.

"Vornado Realty Trust History," fundinguniverse.com.

Vraspir, Will. "End of an Era," Hastings Tribune, p. 1, March 21, 2014.

"Wal-Mart Stores, Inc.," encyclopedia.com.

"Walt Disney's Original E.P.C.O.T Film (1966)," youtube.com/watch?v=r9d2FEAR2t4.

Wanamaker, John. "Annual Report of the Postmaster General, 1891," pp. 84–85.

Wang, Yang. "Macy's Building Comes Down with a Bang," chron.com, Sept. 23, 2013.

Warner, Susan. "Going the Way of Yesterday's Hats," Philadelphia Inquirer, p. 12B, Nov. 30, 1990.

Watts, Elizabeth. "'Shoppers' World' Opens Thursday," Boston Globe, p. A25, Sept. 30, 1951.

Wayne, Leslie. "Ardmore Mall to Mark Its 50th," Philadelphia Inquirer, p. B1, Sept. 10, 1978.

"The Wednesday Inquirer," St. Louis Post-Dispatch Seen Magazine, p. 14, July 17, 1991.

"We Guarantee 5 to 1 She'll Be Happier with Hamilton Beach" (ad), Long Beach Press-Telegram, p. 180, Dec. 1, 1957.

"What Is the Truth about Trading Stamps?" (ad), Paducah (Kentucky) Sun, p. 11, Dec. 4, 1955.

Wheatley, Thomas. "Flashback: The Pink Pig at Rich's, 1990," Atlanta Magazine, atlantamagazine.com, Dec. 8, 2017.

Whitaker, Jan. "Lunching in the Bird Cage," restaurant-ingthroughhistory.com, Aug. 7, 2008.

Whitaker, Jan. Service and Style, St. Martin's Press, New York, 2006.

"White Front Plans Large Valley Store," Valley News (Van Nuys), p. 3B, March 3, 1957.

"White Front Revolutionizes Concepts in Retail Business," Valley News (Van Nuys), p. 46, Aug. 29, 1961.

"White Front to Build Stores in San Diego," Desert Sun, Aug. 13, 1965.

Whitney, David C. "Subway Shoppers Have Field Day As New York Declares Price War," Columbus (Indiana) Republic, p. 5, May 29, 1951.

"William J. Levitt," *Time*, content.time.com, July 3, 1950.

"William Levitt, Co-Founder of Levitt & Sons, Founded 1929," entrepreneur.com, Oct. 10, 2008.

"Who Invented the Shopping Cart?," Today I Found Out, todayifoundout.com, Dec. 29, 2015.

"Why 'Off-price' Shops Are Trouncing Department Stores," Economist, economist.com, Jan. 7, 2016.

Wolfson, Lisa. "Mini-malls: A Boom Going Bust," White Plains (New York) Journal News, p. F1, Dec. 18, 1987.

"Woolco Goal," Poughkeepsie (New York) Journal, p. 12A, Oct. 22, 1961.

"'Woolco' New Store Name," San Francisco Examiner, p. 56, June 5, 1961.

"Woolco's Quit-Business Sale Drawing Crowds in 40 States," newsok.com, Nov. 23, 1982.

Worden, Amy. "When the Doors Closed at the Last S.S. Kresge . . . ," upi.com, July 28, 1994.

"World's Largest Underground Aquarium," sharky.tv, https://bit.ly/2CNqQpY.

Wright, Barnett. "1963 in Birmingham, Alabama: A Timeline of Events," blog.al.com, Jan. 1, 2013.

"Wyoming Bans Trading Stamps," Vernal (Utah) Express, p. 2, Dec. 8, 1969.

Yanul, Thomas. "The Untold Story of Schlesinger & Mayer," thomasyanul.com.

Yurong, Dale. "First Look Inside Manchester Center's Makeover," abc30.com, July 13, 2018.

Yurong, Dale. "Piece of Downtown Fresno History Being Revitalized and Made a Big Part of Its Future," abc30.com, July 26, 2016.

"Zayre's Fabulous Department Stores," Pleasant Family Shopping, pleasantfamilyshopping.blogspot.com, Sept. 14, 2008.

Zimmer, Ben. "The Origins of 'Black Friday,'" Word Routes, visualthesaurus.com, Nov. 25, 2011.

"Zody's to Open in Garden Grove," Los Angeles Times, pt. III, p. 6, June 14, 1960.

"Zukor's Women's Apparel Store Will Open Saturday," Fresno Bee, p. 5, Aug. 20, 1936.

INDEX

ABOUT THE AUTHOR

Stephen H. Provost is an author and journalist who has worked as an editor, columnist, and reporter at newspapers throughout California. His previous books include the *California Historic Highways* series, comprising *Highway 99: The History of California's Main Street* and *Highway 101: The History of El Camino Real*; the civic history *Fresno Growing Up: A City Comes of Age 1945–1985*; and the fantasy novels *Memortality* and *Paralucidity*. Provost frequently blogs on writing and current events at his website, **stephenhprovost.com**.

ALSO BY STEPHEN H. PROVOST

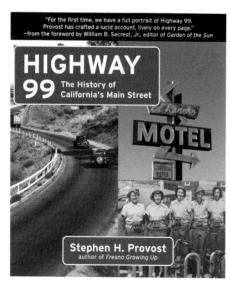

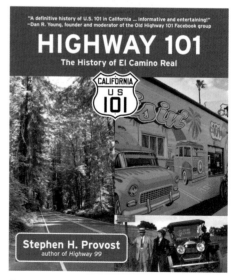

Highway 99: The History of California's Main Street
8½" × 10" trade paperback • 270 pages • $20.95 US
978-1-61035-296-3

Highway 101: The History of El Camino Real
8½" × 10" trade paperback • 233 pages • $20.95 US
978-1-61035-352-6

**Available from bookstores, online bookstores, and CravenStreetBooks.com,
or by calling toll-free 1-800-345-4447.**